Handbook of Digital Multimedia

Handbook of Digital Multimedia

Aubrey Thomas

CLANRYE
INTERNATIONAL
www.clanryeinternational.com

Clanrye International,
750 Third Avenue, 9ᵗʰ Floor,
New York, NY 10017, USA

ISBN: 978-1-64726-100-9

Cataloging-in-Publication Data

Handbook of digital multimedia / Aubrey Thomas.
    p. cm.
Includes bibliographical references and index.
ISBN: 978-1-64726-100-9
1. Multimedia systems. 2. Digital media. I. Thomas, Aubrey.
QA76.575 .H36 2022
006.7--dc23

For information on all Clanrye International publications
visit our website at www.clanryeinternational.com

Table of Contents

Preface

This book is a culmination of my many years of practice in this field. I attribute the success of this book to my support group. I would like to thank my parents who have showered me with unconditional love and support and my peers and professors for their constant guidance.

The content which uses a combination of various content forms is known as multimedia. It can be in the form of digital audio, digital video and digital images. Electronic devices can be used to record, play, interact with or access multimedia. The varied types of multimedia can be broadly categorized as linear multimedia and non-linear multimedia. Linear multimedia, such as cinema, progresses without any navigational control for the viewer. Non-linear multimedia uses interactivity to allow the user to control the progress such as in video games and self-paced training. Multimedia is applied in various industries such as creative industries, education, journalism and in language communication. This book contains some path-breaking studies in the field of digital multimedia. It elucidates new techniques and their applications in a multidisciplinary manner. This book will prove to be immensely beneficial to students and researchers in this field.

The details of chapters are provided below for a progressive learning:

Chapter – Introduction

Multimedia is the combination of five major components namely texts, images, animations, audios and videos. One of the major applications of multimedia is the use of digital textbooks for the purpose of education. This is an introductory chapter which will briefly introduce about multimedia and its significance.

Chapter – Types of Digital Multimedia

There are many types of digital multimedia which include audio, video, digital publishing, information, photos, holograms, social media, advertising, etc. Audio coding format, digital recording, reconstruction of 3D modeling, etc. also fall under its domain. This chapter closely examines these types of digital multimedia to provide an extensive understanding of the subject.

Chapter – Multimedia Compression Technologies

Image compression, audio compression and video compression fall within the compression technologies of multimedia. It also involves transform coding, discrete cosine and wavelet transform, run length encoding, Huffman coding, etc. All these compression technologies used in multimedia have been carefully analyzed in this chapter.

Chapter – Multimedia Software

Multimedia software is used to edit digital data such as images, audios and videos. Audio and video software perform operations such as cut, copy, paste, play, record, etc. on media files. Some of the multimedia software includes DAZ3D, MakeHuman, RawTherapee, Baudline, Djay, Final Scratch, Astra, etc. These diverse multimedia software have been thoroughly analyzed in this chapter.

Chapter – Applications

There are a wide-range of applications of multimedia in the fields of teaching and language learning, digital libraries, video conferencing, webcasting, interactive gaming, etc. This chapter delves into these varied applications of multimedia to provide an in-depth understanding of the subject.

Aubrey Thomas

1
Introduction

Multimedia is the combination of five major components namely texts, images, animations, audios and videos. One of the major applications of multimedia is the use of digital textbooks for the purpose of education. This is an introductory chapter which will briefly introduce about multimedia and its significance.

Multimedia

Multimedia is the term used to describe two or more types of media combined into a single package—usually denoting a combination of some or all of the following: Video, sound, animation, text, and pictures. Multimedia gives the user the opportunity to influence the presentation of material. The selection and manipulation of various aspects of the presentation material is the interactive aspect of a multimedia presentation. Interactive features could range from a question-and-answer function to choosing from a menu of particular subjects or aspects of a presentation. One application of multimedia, for example, involves presenting the user with a "what if" scenario, in which the choices the user makes affect the outcome of the presentation. This affords the user a degree of control, not unlike directing a motion picture and having the opportunity to make changes to the plot at various junctures.

Analog and Digital Media

Analog media saves sounds, pictures, and text in non-electronic forms. This can include more traditional types of media, such as cassette tapes, records, and videocassettes, which use waves to transmit information. Analog equipment is generally more specialized than digital. Analog devices rely on tape recorders, video cameras, and older playback equipment to edit their contents.

Digital media transmits the information recorded in the waves into a more flexible format, namely, digitized code that can be transferred across a variety of devices, such as computers, internet systems, digital cameras, and more. Scanners, sound cards, and video compression are all used to record these types of media. Businesses currently use digital media most often in their multimedia applications, such as:

- Accounting and employee records management.

- CDs for catalogs, records and presentations.

- Interactive training sessions for employees.

- Internet tools such as company Web sites.

- Product refinement and development using various computer-assisted design programs.

- Sales presentations, and other communication to a wide audience.

- Self-running media presentations that can be used for commercial purposes.

The Mechanics of Digital Multimedia

The CD-ROM and its successor, the DVD-ROM, store data in the form of a binary code. The binary code is placed onto the discs by a stamping process that impresses lands (flat areas that represent the zero in binary code) and hollows (pits that represent the one in binary code) onto the surface of the disc. When the discs are placed into a player or computer drive, the playing mechanism spins the disc and flashes a laser beam over the surface of the disc. The reflected light patterns caused by the embossed data contained on the surface of the disc are then decoded by the reader/player and translated back into audio and video. The storage capacity of a CDROM disc is 635 megabytes, while the storage capacity of a DVD-ROM disc can be as great as 5.2 gigabytes. Since sound, graphics, and other visuals take up considerably more data space than text alone, the increased storage capacities of the CD-ROM and DVD-ROM discs have played an integral part in making the use of multimedia more commonplace. The durability, portability, and relatively low manufacturing cost of the discs also play a critical role in their proliferation. While the Read Only Memory (ROM) format is still the most common for both CDs and DVDs, today recordable disc drives are widely available to enable users to "burn" data (write, erase, and/or rewrite data) to a disc on their own.

Rich Media

Rich media is a term referring to digital, interactive multimedia programs, the newest type of multimedia, most often found online via company Web sites or social networks. Rich media involves a combination of sound, pictures, animations, and video with integrated interactivity so that users, by pointing and clicking, can access online information as they desire. Rich media, because of its use of video and animation, can be built in two different formats. The first type is downloadable, which means Internet users can download the presentation and view it with a media player of their own, such as Apple's Quick-Time, Microsoft's Media Player, or Real Network's Real-Player. The second type of rich media is embedded into a Web site, meaning that it does not need to be downloaded, only accessed by the online user. This involves more cost on the producer's part, but makes it easier for users to have a seamless, interactive experience.

As the use of rich media increases, so do the benefits and complications. More and more companies are making use of rich media as marketing tools and training programs. However, downloadable media is dependent on its format, and problems can arise when transmitting rich media from one player to another. Animations and audio files may play differently from one media player to another. A successful rich media presentation will be interesting, informative, and easily accessed by any user.

Hypermedia

Hypermedia, used in online multimedia presentations such as rich media, refers to the hyperlinks embedded in visual media. When a customer or employee clicks on a Web site link to learn more about a subject or choose a certain option, this is an example of hypermedia. It is ideal as a tool for allocating information on appropriate levels, giving users knowledge in pertinent pieces.

These types of nonlinear interaction are becoming increasingly common in the business world. As more people internationally gain access to hypermedia, companies are beginning to develop multimedia presentations to communicate their visions, opportunities, outsource training, and updates.

Uses of Multimedia

Multimedia devices have an almost innumerable variety of applications. They are used in home-entertainment systems and can be extremely powerful educational tools. Educators, for example, have been exceptionally creative in combining some of the exciting elements of video-game applications with select features of educational material. By doing this, the concept of "edutainment" was created. The goal of using the multimedia edutainment approach is to entertain the user so effectively that the user remains unaware that he or she is actually learning in the process.

Multimedia can also offer critical services in the business world. While information can certainly be conveyed adequately by the singular use of still pictures, video, film, audio, or text, multimedia potentially multiplies the degree of effectiveness, in no small part due to the added entertainment value and the extent to which the viewers feel a part of the action. Such benefits cannot easily be matched by the application of a singular medium. The effectiveness of teaching, selling, informing, entertaining, promoting, and presenting are all dependent upon one factor: The ability of the presented material to hold the attention of the desired audience. A dynamic multimedia presentation can usually be more effective than earlier methods at accomplishing this task with an audience that was raised on television and motion pictures. The computerized multimedia presentation offers the added benefit of cost-effective flexibility, allowing easy editing of the basic materials in order to tailor them to specific target audiences.

Training, informational and promotional materials, sales presentations, and point-of-sale displays that allow for customer interaction and communication both within and outside the organization are all common applications of multimedia in the business world. Multimedia presentations for many such applications can be highly portable, particularly in the cases of the CD-ROM, DVD-ROM, and videotape. The equipment required to produce these presentations is relatively commonplace or otherwise easy to access.

Perhaps the vanguard application of multimedia is virtual reality, a combination of video, stereo, and computer graphics that attempts to create an interactive three-dimensional environment that immerses the user within the simulation. Virtual reality has been employed in a wide range of practical applications: To train military troops, to streamline manufacturing and architectural design processes, to create simulated test environments for industry, and as a form of public entertainment.

One should still keep in mind, however, that even if rendered in a highly advanced multimedia format, an ineffectual presentation is still an ineffectual presentation. One should remain focused on the message being conveyed while shaping the choice and use of materials in accordance with that message.

Components of Multimedia

There are five components of multimedia i.e., text, sound, images, animation and video. These are explained in detail as under:

Text

Text or written language is the most common way of communicating information. It is one of the basic components of multimedia. It was originally defined by printed media such as books and newspapers that used various typefaces to display the alphabet, numbers, and special characters. Although multimedia products include pictures, audio and video, text may be the most common data type found in multimedia applications. Besides this, text also provides opportunities to extend the traditional power of text by linking it to other media, thus making it an interactive medium.

Static Text

In static text, the words are laid out to fit in well with the graphical surroundings. The words are built into the graphics just like the graphics and explanation given in the pages of the book, the information is well laid out and easy to read. The learners are able to look at the pictures and read the textual information, as they are available on the similar screen.

Hypertext

A hypertext system consists of nodes. It contains the text and links between the nodes, which define the paths the user can follow to access the text in non-sequential ways. The links represent associations of meaning and can be thought of as cross-references. This structure is created by the author of the system, although in more sophisticated hypertext systems the user is able to define their own paths. The hypertext provides the user with the flexibility and choice to navigate through the material. Text should be used to convey imperative information and should be positioned at appropriate place in a multimedia product. Well-formatted sentences and paragraphs are vital factors, spacing and punctuation also affects the readability of the text. Fonts and styles should be used to improve the communication of the message more appropriately.

Image

Images are an important component of multimedia. These are generated by the computer in two ways, as bitmap or raster images and as vector images.

Raster or Bitmap Images

The most common and comprehensive form of storage for images on a computer is a raster or bitmap image. Bitmap is a simple matrix of the tiny dots called pixel that forms a raster or bitmap image. Each pixel consists of two or more colours. The colour depth is determined by how much data, in bits is used to determine the number of colours e.g., one bit is two colours, four bits means sixteen colours, eight bits indicates 256 colours, 16 bits yields 65,536 colours and so on. Depending on the hardware capabilities, each point can display from two to millions of colours. Comprehensive image means that an image looks as much as possible like the real word or original product. This means that the proportion, size, colour, and texture must be as accurate as possible. Bitmap formats are Windows Bitmap (BMP), Device Independent Bitmap (DIB), and Windows Run Length Encoded (RLE).

Vector Images

Vector images base on drawing elements or objects such as lines, rectangles, circles and so forth to create an image. The advantage of vector image is the relatively small amount of data required to represent the image and therefore, it does not requires a lot of memory to store. The image consists of a set of commands that are drawn when needed. A bitmap image requires the number of pixels to produce appropriate height, width and colour depth, the vector image is based on a relatively limited number of drawing commands. The falls drop of vector images is the limited level of detail that can be presented in an image. Mostly used vector format is Windows metfile in windows operating system.

Compression techniques are used to reduce the file size of images that is useful for storing large number of images and speeding transmission for networked application. Compression formats used for this purpose are GIF, TIFF and JPEG.

Animation

Animation consists of still images displayed so quickly that they give the impression of continuous movement. The screen object is a vector image in animation. The movement of that image along paths is calculated using numerical transformations applied to their defining coordinates. To give the impression of smoothness the frame rate has to be at least 16 frames per second, and for natural looking motion it should be at least 25 frames per second. Animations may be two or three dimensional. In two dimensional animation the visual changes that bring an image alive occur on the flat X and Y axis of the screen, while in three dimensional animation it occurs along the entire three axis X, Y and Z showing the image from all the angles. Such animations are typically rendered frame by high-end three dimensional animation softwares. Animation tools are very powerful and effective. There are two basic types of animations, path animation and frame animation.

Path Animation

Path animations involve moving an object on a screen that has a constant background e.g., a cartoon character may move across the screen regardless any change in the background or the character.

Frame Animation

In frame animations, several objects are allowed to move simultaneously and the objects or the background can also change.

The moving objects are one of the most appropriate tools to enhance understanding, as they allow the learner to see the demonstration of changes, processes and procedures. Animation uses very little memory in comparison to digital video as it consists of drawing and moving instructions. Animation is very useful for such multimedia applications where moving visuals are required, but where digital video may be unsuitable, unnecessary, or too expensive in terms of disc space or memory.

Sound

Sound is probably the most sensuous element of multimedia. It is meaningful speech in any language, from a whisper to a scream. It can provide the listening pleasure of music, the startling accent of special effects, or the ambience of a mood setting background. It can promote an artist, add interest to a text site by humanizing the author, or to teach pronouncing words in another language. Sound pressure level (volume) is measured in decibels, which is actually the ratio between a chosen reference point on a logarithmic scale and the level that is actually experienced.

Musical Instrument Digital Identifier (MIDI)

Musical Instrument Digital Identifier (MIDI) is a communication standard developed in the early 1980s for electronic musical instruments and computers. It is the short hand representation of music stored in numeric form. MIDI is the quickest, easiest and most flexible tool for composing original score in a multimedia project. To make MIDI scores sequencer, software and sound synthesizer is needed. A MIDI keyboard is also useful for simplifying the creation of musical scores. Its quality depends upon the quality of musical instruments and the capabilities of sound system. It is device dependent.

Digital Audio

Digitised sound is sampled sound. The every nth fraction of a second, a sample of sound is taken and stored as digital information in bits and bytes. The quality of this digital recording depends upon how often the samples are taken (sampling rate) and how many numbers are used to represent the value of each sample (bit depth, sample size, resolution). The more often the sample is taken and the more data is stored about that sample, the finer the resolution and quality of the captured sound when it is played back. The quality of digital audio also relies on the quality of the original audio source, capture devices, supporting software and the capability of playback environment.

The main benefit of audio is that it provides a channel that is separate from that of the display. Sound plays a major role in multimedia applications, but there is a very fine balance between getting it right and overdoing it. Multimedia products benefit from digital audio as informational content such as a speech or voice-over and as special effects to indicate that a program is executing various actions such as jumping to new screens. The three sampling frequencies used in multimedia are CD-quality 44.1 kHz, 22.05 kHz and 11.025 kHz. Digital audio plays a key role in digital video.

Video

Video is defined as the display of recorded real events on a television type screen. The embedding of video in multimedia applications is a powerful way to convey information. It can incorporate a personal element, which other media lack. The personality of the presenter can be displayed in a video. The video may be categorised in two types, analog video and digital video.

Analog Video

Analog video is the video data that is stored in any non-computer media like videotape, laserdisc, film etc. It is further divided in two types, composite and component analogue video.

Composite Analog Video has all the video components including brightness, colour, and synchronization, combined into one signal. Due to the composition or combining of the video components, the quality of the composite video is resulted as colour bleeding, low clarity and high generational loss. Generational loss means the loss of quality when the master is copied to edit or for other purpose. This recording format was used for customer analog video recording tape formats (such as Betamax and VHS) and was never adequate for most multimedia presentations. Composite video is also susceptible to quality loss from one generation to other.

Component analog video is considered more advanced than composite video. It takes different components of video such as colour, brightness and synchronization and breaks them into separate signals. S-VHS and Hi-8 are examples of this type of analog video in which colour and brightness, information are stored on two separate tracks. In early 1980s, Sony has launched a new portable, professional video format, 'Betacam' in which signals are stored on three separate tracks.

There are certain analogue broadcast video standards commonly used round the globe. These are National Television Standard Committee (NTSC), Phase Alternate Line (PAL), Sequential Colour with Memory (SECAM) and HDTV. In the United States, Canada, Japan NTSC standard is used, while in United Kingdom, China, South Africa PAL is used. SECAM is used in France. A new standard has been developed known as High Definition Television (HDTV) which bears better image and colour quality in comparison to other standards.

Digital Video

It is the most engaging of multimedia venues, and it is a powerful tool for bringing computer users closer to the real world. Digital video is storage intensive. A high quality colour still image on a computer screen requires one megabyte or more of storage memory. To provide the appearance of motion, picture should be replaced by at least thirty times per second and the storage memory required is at least thirty megabyte for one second of video. The more times the picture is replaced, the better is the quality of video.

Video requires high bandwidth to deliver data in networked environment. This overwhelming technological bottleneck is overcome using digital video compression schemes. There are video compression standards as MPEG, JPEG, Cinepak and Sorenson. In addition to compressing video data, streaming technologies such as Adobe Flash, Microsoft Windows Media, QuickTime and Real Player are being implemented to provide reasonable quality low bandwidth video on the web. QuickTime and Real Video are the most commonly used for wide spread distribution.

Digital video formats can be divided into two categories, composite video and component video. Composite digital recording formats encode the information in binary (0"s and 1"s) digital code. It retains some of weakness of analogue composite video like colour and image resolution and the generation loss when copies are made.

Component digital is the uncompressed format having very high image quality. It is highly expensive. Some popular formats in this category are, 'Digital Bitacam' and D-5 developed in 1994 and DVCAM developed in 1996.

There are certain standards for digital display of video i.e., Advanced Television System Committee (ATSC), Digital Video Broadcasting (DVB), and Integrated Services Digital Broadcasting (ISBD). ATSC is the digital television standard for the United States, Canada and South Korea, DVB is used commonly in Europe and ISBD is used in Japan to allow the radio and television stations to convert into digital format.

Video can be used in many applications. Motion pictures enhance comprehension only if they match the explanation. For example, if we want to show the dance steps used in different cultures, video is easier and more effective than to use any graphics or animation.

Significance of Multimedia Technologies Learning

Rationale for a Computer-based Multimedia Learning Platform

A multimedia learning platform has the following strengths:

- Personalized education: Learning and teaching with the assistance of technologies benefit both students who are able to process information easily and students who need more time to learn and digest study content. In addition, students can complete the instructional goal through self-learning in instances where teachers are not able to provide individual consultation.

- Flexibility of time and space: The multimedia learning platform allows students to suspend and revisit study material at their convenience and within a flexible time frame.

- Comfortable for a variety of personality types: A multimedia learning platform environment is impartial. The introverted student, for example, has the opportunity to function in a comfortable learning environment that provides privacy and independent operation, without pressure from classmates or a professor. In addition, the features of the multimedia learning platform include courses or question repetitions so that students have more opportunities for self-learning. A well-developed instructional multimedia platform is a collective effort by educators, teachers, students, and programmers, and can be used by most teachers to reduce time and effort. A multimedia platform can also be applied for practice of potentially dangerous practical experiments or the use of difficult-to-obtain teaching materials.

- More concrete learning experiences: Dale introduced the famous Cone of Experience to explain that the human learning experience is based on three aspects: practice, observation, and thought. Multimedia learning platforms combine concrete ideas and abstractions, with teaching conducted through image presentation texts, numbers, and audio presentations in sequence. This is a representative model and is a theoretical method in addition to practical instruction methods.

- Diversified teaching materials: The multimedia platform provides diversified teaching materials thorough text, music, pictures, and animation, which can provide assistance to student's cognitive development.

- Effective motivation: The attractive live designs and audio and flash effects included in a multimedia platform can attract interest and encourage student edification.

- A hyperlinked learning method: The multimedia platform provides dynamic learning patterns through hyperlinks instead of a non-linear learning method, which aides in the acquisition of additional and related information.

- Dedicated teaching materials: Due to the high cost of instructional multimedia platforms, the designers apply effort and resources toward designing and planning the content of the platform as opposed to individuals teaching without specific goals.

- Enhancement for traditional learning methods: The instructional multimedia platform incorporates the interactivity of the traditional learning platform as well as personalized learning, mass production, immediate test feedback, and flexibility of time and space, allowing improvement upon learning speed. Based on the above, it is possible to summarize the rationale of applying a multimedia learning platform to skills learning as follows:

  ○ Personalized teaching: The features of a personalized teaching platform include immediate feedback and self-controlled learning schedules. The multimedia learning platform allows students to learn at any time, without emotional factors affecting the learning schedule. The multimedia resources can also be used as preparation material for study. Students may be able to learn skills at their own pace, having their individual learning demands satisfied.

  ○ Effective teaching materials: Presentations using multimedia applications can encourage student learning and effectively integrate a variety of media elements. The multimedia learning platform can also simulate situational applications, allowing students to understand the subject more easily and observe its relevance. With respect to preparation of teaching resources, the high cost of production and widespread service area of a multimedia learning platform provides assurance that more time and effort will be spent on evaluating the selection and arrangement of teaching materials. The hyperlinks included in teaching material increase overall effectiveness and range of subject comprehension.

○ High quality teaching and broadened education for students: The multimedia platform eradicates the human factors present in traditional teaching activities, so the teaching scenario and process provides a more stable environment. Negative factors caused by a teachers psychological status or other aspects are decreased, and a certain level of instructional quality is assured. In addition, a multimedia platform allows students to learn during convenient times and under optimal conditions.

○ Simulated learning scenarios: In technical and vocational fields, the acquisition and practice of many skills may be dangerous or risky, or the cost of training and practice may be too high. In these cases, the multimedia platform can simulate the actual scenario without the risks or damages economically.

○ Reduced psychological obstacles: Some students may be afraid of asking questions in real time due to psychological factors, such as embarrassment or shyness, leading to ineffective learning. The multimedia platform can reduce these factors by providing a neutral response, private space, and reduced pressures from teachers and classmates. In this sense, the multimedia platform creates a more comfortable learning environment.

○ Repetitive learning and immediate feedback: The multimedia platform may enhance learning effectiveness through immediate feedback. In a traditional teaching setting, the learning effectiveness of students is related to the teaching attitude and methods of individual teachers. The multimedia learning platform provides opportunities to learn and practice repetitively.

The Design and Development of a Multimedia Skill-learning Platform

The design and development of a multimedia skill-learning platform, such as computer-aided courses, focus on a curriculum and the learning of the concepts necessary for a particular field of study. The developers of a computer aided teaching program should have knowledge of the field, the computer technology necessary to teach the field and a comprehensive understanding and respect for different cultural and social environments. The concepts that should be applied in computer-aided teaching design include:

• Constructive learning.

- Scenario learning.

- Case study experience.

- Apprentice learning.

- Cooperative learning.

- Subject learning.

- Story learning.

Because these seven concepts are independent of each other, an effective approach would be to integrate these concepts into the process learning for any particular subject.

Many studies have suggested that an instructional multimedia platform should include tutorials, drill and practice, simulation, instructional games, problem solving, dialog inquiry, and tests.

In this study a multimedia skill-learning platform was designed and applied, creating instruction for architectural design. The platform integrated case studies and architectural concepts that taught students to create architectural drawings and designs.

Flash is icon-based software. Icons are the basic elements of the system. Each icon serves a certain function, for example, showing pictures, playing audio, initiating interactive talking, or making decisions. The icons are interlinked to each other to constitute an interactive, multimedia system. Based on this and following the goals of teachers and the level and demands of students, the system was arranged into six main sections.

The main objective here is to teach skills and commands, focusing on the designs and skill applications in the service core of architecture. Each unit will integrate with detailed descriptions of commands and steps to operate the case graphs. Through the dedicated arrangement of each learning unit, students will understand the meaning of each command. Also, different drawing cases will be presented for student's reference. This is a teaching system integrated with related learning units and complete service core designs and skills. The system uses module-based tutorial design pattern to discuss and solve the problems that may be encountered during architectural design and construction drawings. Students can understand the principles and methods of service core design through problem solving, or working on projects. During the teaching process, the designed and final results will be shown to motivate students to inquire further into the subject. From the design point of view, the system has the features of both the tutorial-based multimedia learning platform and simulation-based multimedia learning platform and the dialog inquiry function. The main functions on the interface include:

- Previous Page: Move back to the browsed previous page, with the hyperlinks to other units.

- Next Page: Move the browsed next page, with the hyperlinks to other units.

- Home Page: Return to the first page of this unit.

- Last Page: Jump to the last page of this unit.

- Process: Review a page that has been browsed before.

- Search: Find some contents in this unit.

- Quick View: Move to the first page of other units.

- Related Knowledge: Move to the related knowledge.

- Skills Guidance: Move to the contents of service core designs.

- Exit: Bring up a dialog box with the option to exit, restart, or cancel.

- Other: Show hyperlinks in the contents of this unit in order to link to other knowledge descriptions when the mouse icon becomes a finger.

The "return to teaching" icon is added to allow students to switch between the Teaching Section and Related Knowledge. When the user wishes to switch between the Teaching Section and Related Knowledge areas, it is possible to track the page he or she has visited before, in order to avoid starting all over again. Thus, this study designs the system from the user's point of view to evaluate the overall arrangement of courses and to eliminate the waste of time and repeated reading.

During teaching, teachers often use some tests education, which would also be used as a base of teaching schedule and teaching improvement. The tests and questions can be modified from time to time. The test system integrated in multimedia skill learning platform can achieve the above mentioned goals. Tests are the easiest and simplest medium to evaluate the effectiveness of teaching techniques. However, considering that the level of test difficulty should be consistent among classes, the questions must be modified, and the question numbers must be changed, it is necessary to evaluate and change the questions when designing a test-based multimedia skill-learning platform. On the selection of questions, it is possible to integrate drawings or command operations into the tests in the form of animations to stress the application of skills and professional cognitions.

Regarding test feedback, proper encouragement or incentives shall be provided by animations and points for questions answered correctly. For incorrect answers, the correct answers shall be given. Moreover, it is necessary to use random numbers in program design to make the same questions with different answer orders, to prevent students from memorizing test answers.

From the above, in this study, the design and development includes case study and project learning concepts, and encouragement to students for self-construction. In the teaching arrangement, the practical commands exercises and constructive service core elements design skills are used to guide the students to apply the knowledge they have acquired within the tutorial design pattern, which is included in the system. In addition, on the test design, random numbers are used on questions to prevent students from memorizing the orders of questions and answers, and provide a reliable test result. The ultimate purpose for acquisition of skills is to allow the students to draw and design by themselves and have a chance for actual practice and application in order to master their skills. As a result, the drill and practicing design pattern is required to reach this target. In other words, the multimedia skill learning platform designed and developed in this study includes more than one learning concept and design patterns. The criteria used in this system are most common and accepted for both teachers and students in teaching activities.

2
Types of Digital Multimedia

There are many types of digital multimedia which include audio, video, digital publishing, information, photos, holograms, social media, advertising, etc. Audio coding format, digital recording, reconstruction of 3D modeling, etc. also fall under its domain. This chapter closely examines these types of digital multimedia to provide an extensive understanding of the subject.

Multimedia comes in many different formats. It can be almost anything you can hear or see like text, pictures, music, sound, videos, records, films, animations, and more.

On the Internet you can often find multimedia elements embedded in web pages, and modern web browsers have support for a number of multimedia formats.

Audio and video are used for enhancing the experience with Web pages (e.g. audio background) to serving music, family videos, presentations, etc. The Web content accessibility guidelines recommend to always provide alternatives for time-based media, such as captions, descriptions, or sign language.

Digital Image

A digital image is a representation of a real image as a set of numbers that can be stored and handled by a digital computer. In order to translate the image into numbers, it is divided into small areas called pixels (picture elements). For each pixel, the imaging device records a number, or a small set of numbers, that describe some property of this pixel, such as its brightness (the intensity of the light) or its color. The numbers are arranged in an array of rows and columns that correspond to the vertical and horizontal positions of the pixels in the image.

Digital images have several basic characteristics. One is the type of the image. For example, a black and white image records only the intensity of the light falling on the pixels. A color image can have three colors, normally RGB (Red, Green, Blue) or four colors, CMYK (Cyan, Magenta, Yellow, blacK). RGB images are usually used in computer monitors and scanners, while CMYK images are used in color printers. There are also non-optical images such as ultrasound or X-ray in which the intensity of sound or X-rays is recorded. In range images, the distance of the pixel from the observer is recorded. Resolution is expressed in the number of pixels per inch (ppi). A higher resolution gives a more detailed image. A computer monitor typically has a resolution of 100 ppi, while a printer has a resolution ranging from 300 ppi to more than 1440 ppi. This is why an image looks much better in print than on a monitor.

The color depth (of a color image) or "bits per pixel" is the number of bits in the numbers that describe the brightness or the color. More bits make it possible to record more shades of gray or more colors. For example, an RGB image with 8 bits per color has a total of 24 bits per pixel ("true color"). Each bit can represent two possible colors so we get a total of 16,777,216 possible colors. A typical GIF image on a web page has 8 bits for all colors combined for a total of 256 colors. However, it is a much smaller image than a 24 bit one so it downloads more quickly. A fax image has only one bit or two "colors," black and white. The format of the image gives more details about how the numbers are arranged in the image file, including what kind of compression is used, if any. Among the most popular of the dozens of formats available are TIFF, GIF, JPEG, PNG, and Post-script.

Digital images tend to produce big files and are often compressed to make the files smaller. Compression takes advantage of the fact that many nearby pixels in the image have similar colors or brightness. Instead of recording each pixel separately, one can record that, for example, "the 100 pixels around a certain position are all white." Compression methods vary in their efficiency and speed. The GIF method has good compression for 8 bit pictures, while the JPEG is lossy, i.e. it causes some image degradation. JPEG's advantage is speed, so it is suitable for motion pictures.

One of the advantages of digital images over traditional ones is the ability to transfer them electronically almost instantaneously and convert them easily from one medium to another such as from a web page to a computer screen to a printer. A bigger advantage is the ability to change them according to one's needs. There are several programs available now which give a user the ability to do that, including Photoshop, Photopaint, and the Gimp. With such a program, a user can change the colors and brightness of an image, delete unwanted visible objects, move others, and merge objects from several images, among many other operations. In this way a user can retouch family photos or even create new images. Other software, such as word processors and desktop publishing programs, can easily combine digital images with text to produce books or magazines much more efficiently than with traditional methods.

A very promising use of digital images is automatic object recognition. In this application, a computer can automatically recognize an object shown in the image and identify it by name. One of the most important uses of this is in robotics. A robot can be equipped with digital cameras that can serve as its "eyes" and produce images. If the robot could recognize an object in these images, then it could make use of it. For instance, in a factory environment, the robot could use a screwdriver in the assembly of products. For this task, it has to recognize both the screwdriver and the various parts of the product. At home a robot could recognize objects to be cleaned. Other promising applications are in medicine, for example, in finding tumors in X-ray images. Security equipment could recognize the faces of people ap proaching a building. Automated drivers could drive a car without human intervention or drive a vehicle in inhospitable environments such as on the planet Mars or in a battlefield.

To recognize an object, the computer has to compare the image to a database of objects in its memory. This is a simple task for humans but it has proven to be very difficult to do automatically. One reason is that an object rarely produces the same image of itself. An object can be seen from many different viewpoints and under different lighting conditions, and each such variation will produce an image that looks different to the computer. The object itself can also change; for instance, a smiling face looks different from a serious face of the same person. Because of these difficulties, research in this field has been rather slow, but there are already successes in limited areas such as inspection of products on assembly lines, fingerprint identification by the FBI, and optical character recognition (OCR).

Digital Imaging

Digital imaging or digital image acquisition is the creation of a digitally encoded representation of the visual characteristics of an object, such as a physical scene or the interior structure of an object. The term is often assumed to imply or include the processing, compression, storage, printing, and display of such images. A key advantage of a digital image, versus an analog image such as a film photograph, is the ability make copies and copies of copies digitally indefinitely without any loss of image quality.

Digital imaging can be classified by the type of electromagnetic radiation or other waves whose variable attenuation, as they pass through or reflect off objects, conveys the information that constitutes the image. In all classes of digital imaging, the information is converted by image sensors into digital signals that are processed by a computer and made output as a visible-light image. For example, the medium of visible light allows digital photography (including digital videography) with various kinds of digital cameras (including digital video cameras). X-rays allow digital X-ray imaging (digital radiography, fluoroscopy, and CT), and gamma rays allow digital gamma ray imaging (digital scintigraphy, SPECT, and PET). Sound allows ultrasonography (such as medical ultrasonography) and sonar, and radio waves allow radar. Digital imaging lends itself well to image analysis by software, as well as to image editing (including image manipulation).

Changing Environment

Great strides have been made in the field of digital imaging. Negatives and exposure are foreign concepts to many, and the first digital image in 1920 led eventually to cheaper equipment, increasingly powerful yet simple software, and the growth of the Internet.

The constant advancement and production of physical equipment and hardware related to digital imaging has affected the environment surrounding the field. From cameras and webcams to printers and scanners, the hardware is becoming sleeker, thinner, faster, and cheaper. As the cost of equipment decreases, the market for new enthusiasts widens, allowing more consumers to experience the thrill of creating their own images.

Everyday personal laptops, family desktops, and company computers are able to handle photographic software. Our computers are more powerful machines with increasing capacities for running programs of any kind—especially digital imaging software. And that software is quickly becoming both smarter and simpler. Although functions on today's programs reach the level of precise editing and even rendering 3-D images, user interfaces are designed to be friendly to advanced users as well as first-time fans.

The Internet allows editing, viewing, and sharing digital photos and graphics. A quick browse around the web can easily turn up graphic artwork from budding artists, news photos from around the world, corporate images of new products and services, and much more. The Internet has clearly proven itself a catalyst in fostering the growth of digital imaging.

Online photo sharing of images changes the way we understand photography and photographers. Online sites such as Flickr, Shutterfly, and Instagram give billions the capability to share their photography, whether they are amateurs or professionals. Photography has gone from being a luxury medium of communication and sharing to more of a fleeting moment in time. Subjects have also changed. Pictures used to be primarily taken of people and family. Now, we take them of anything. We can document our day and share it with everyone with the touch of our fingers.

In 1826 Niepce was the first to develop a photo which used lights to reproduce images, the advancement of photography has drastically increased over the years. Everyone is now a photographer in their own way, whereas during the early 1800s and 1900s the expense of lasting photos was highly valued and appreciated by consumers and producers. According to the magazine article on five ways digital camera changed us states the following: "The impact on professional photographers has been dramatic. Once upon a time a photographer wouldn't dare waste a shot unless they were virtually certain it would work." The use of digital imaging (photography) has changed the way we interacted with our environment over the years. Part of the world is experienced differently through visual imagining of lasting memories, it has become a new form of communication with friends, family and love ones around the world without face to face interactions. Through photography it is easy to see those that you have never seen before and feel their presence without them being around, for example, Instagram is a form of social media where anyone is allowed to shoot, edit, and share photos of whatever they want with friends and family. Facebook, snapshot, vine and twitter are also ways people express themselves with little or no words and are able to capture every moment that is important. Lasting memories that were hard to capture, is now easy because everyone is now able to take pictures and edit it on their phones or laptops. Photography has become a new way to communicate and it is rapidly increasing as time goes by, which has affected the world around us.

Field Advancements of Multimedia

Medical Imaging

Medical imaging is the technique and process of creating visual representations of the interior of a body for clinical analysis and medical intervention, as well as visual representation of the function of some organs or tissues (physiology). Medical imaging seeks to reveal internal structures hidden by the skin and bones, as well as to diagnose and treat disease. Medical imaging also establishes a database of normal anatomy and physiology to make it possible to identify abnormalities. Although imaging of removed organs and tissues can be performed for medical reasons, such procedures are usually considered part of pathology instead of medical imaging.

As a discipline and in its widest sense, it is part of biological imaging and incorporates radiology, which uses the imaging technologies of X-ray radiography, magnetic resonance imaging, medical ultrasonography or ultrasound, endoscopy, elastography, tactile imaging, thermography, medical photography, and nuclear medicine functional imaging techniques as positron emission tomography (PET) and single-photon emission computed tomography (SPECT).

Measurement and recording techniques that are not primarily designed to produce images, such as electroencephalography (EEG), magnetoencephalography (MEG), electrocardiography (ECG), and others, represent other technologies that produce data susceptible to representation as a parameter graph vs. time or maps that contain data about the measurement locations. In a limited comparison, these technologies can be considered forms of medical imaging in another discipline.

As of 2010, 5 billion medical imaging studies had been conducted worldwide. Radiation exposure from medical imaging in 2006 made up about 50% of total ionizing radiation exposure in the United States. Medical imaging equipment are manufactured using technology from the semiconductor industry, including CMOS integrated circuit chips, power semiconductor devices, sensors such as image sensors (particularly CMOS sensors) and biosensors, and processors such as microcontrollers, microprocessors, digital signal processors, media processors and system-on-chip devices. As of 2015, annual shipments of medical imaging chips amount to 46 million units and $1.1 billion.

Medical imaging is often perceived to designate the set of techniques that noninvasively produce images of the internal aspect of the body. In this restricted sense, medical imaging can be seen as the solution of mathematical inverse problems. This means that cause (the properties of living tissue) is inferred from effect (the observed signal). In the case of medical ultrasonography, the probe consists of ultrasonic pressure waves and echoes that go inside the tissue to show the internal structure. In the case of projectional radiography, the probe uses X-ray radiation, which is absorbed at different rates by different tissue types such as bone, muscle, and fat.

The term "noninvasive" is used to denote a procedure where no instrument is introduced into a patient's body, which is the case for most imaging techniques used.

Types

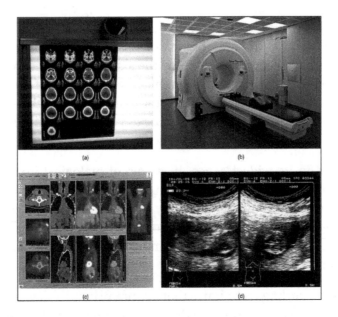

(a) The results of a CT scan of the head are shown as successive transverse sections. (b) An MRI machine generates a magnetic field around a patient. (c) PET scans use radiopharmaceuticals to create images of active blood flow and physiologic activity of the organ or organs being targeted. (d) Ultrasound technology is used to monitor pregnancies because it is the least invasive of imaging techniques and uses no electromagnetic radiation.

In the clinical context, "invisible light" medical imaging is generally equated to radiology or "clinical imaging" and the medical practitioner responsible for interpreting (and sometimes acquiring) the images is a radiologist. "Visible light" medical imaging involves digital video or still pictures that can be seen without special equipment. Dermatology and wound care are two modalities that use visible light imagery. Diagnostic radiography designates the technical aspects of medical imaging and in particular the acquisition of medical images. The radiographer or radiologic technologist is usually responsible for acquiring medical images of diagnostic quality, although some radiological interventions are performed by radiologists.

As a field of scientific investigation, medical imaging constitutes a sub-discipline of biomedical engineering, medical physics or medicine depending on the context: Research and development in the area of instrumentation, image acquisition (e.g., radiography), modeling and quantification are usually the preserve of biomedical engineering, medical physics, and computer science; Research into the application and interpretation of medical images is usually the preserve of radiology and the medical sub-discipline relevant to medical condition or area of medical science (neuroscience, cardiology, psychiatry, psychology, etc.) under investigation. Many of the techniques developed for medical imaging also have scientific and industrial applications.

Radiography

Two forms of radiographic images are in use in medical imaging. Projection radiography and fluoroscopy, with the latter being useful for catheter guidance. These 2D techniques are still in wide use despite the advance of 3D tomography due to the low cost, high resolution, and depending on the application, lower radiation dosages with 2D technique. This imaging modality utilizes a wide beam of x rays for image acquisition and is the first imaging technique available in modern medicine.

- Fluoroscopy produces real-time images of internal structures of the body in a similar fashion to radiography, but employs a constant input of x-rays, at a lower dose rate. Contrast media, such as barium, iodine, and air are used to visualize internal organs as they work. Fluoroscopy is also used in image-guided procedures when constant feedback during a procedure is required. An image receptor is required to convert the radiation into an image after it has passed through the area of interest. Early on this was a fluorescing screen, which gave way to an Image Amplifier (IA) which was a large vacuum tube that had the receiving end coated with cesium iodide, and a mirror at the opposite end. Eventually the mirror was replaced with a TV camera.

- Projectional radiographs, more commonly known as x-rays, are often used to determine the type and extent of a fracture as well as for detecting pathological changes in the lungs. With the use of radio-opaque contrast media, such as barium, they can also be used to visualize the structure of the stomach and intestines – this can help diagnose ulcers or certain types of colon cancer.

Magnetic Resonance Imaging

A magnetic resonance imaging instrument (MRI scanner), or "nuclear magnetic resonance (NMR) imaging" scanner as it was originally known, uses powerful magnets to polarize and excite hydrogen nuclei (i.e., single protons) of water molecules in human tissue, producing a detectable signal which is spatially encoded, resulting in images of the body. The MRI machine emits a radio frequency (RF) pulse at the resonant frequency of the hydrogen atoms on water molecules. Radio frequency antennas ("RF coils") send the pulse to the area of the body to be examined. The RF pulse is absorbed by protons, causing their direction with respect to the primary magnetic field to change. When the RF pulse is turned off, the protons "relax" back to alignment with the primary magnet and emit radio-waves in the process. This radio-frequency emission from the hydrogen-atoms on water is what is detected and reconstructed into an image. The resonant frequency of a spinning magnetic dipole (of which protons are one example) is called the Larmor frequency and is determined by the strength of the main magnetic field and the chemical environment of the nuclei of interest. MRI uses three electromagnetic fields: a very strong (typically 1.5 to 3 teslas) static magnetic field to polarize the hydrogen nuclei, called the primary field; gradient fields that can be modified to vary in space and time (on the order of 1 kHz) for spatial encoding, often simply called gradients; and a spatially homogeneous radio-frequency (RF) field for manipulation of the hydrogen nuclei to produce measurable signals, collected through an RF antenna.

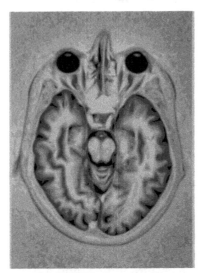

A brain MRI representation.

Like CT, MRI traditionally creates a two-dimensional image of a thin "slice" of the body and is therefore considered a tomographic imaging technique. Modern MRI instruments are capable of producing images in the form of 3D blocks, which may be considered a generalization of the single-slice, tomographic, concept. Unlike CT, MRI does not involve the use of ionizing radiation and is therefore not associated with the same health hazards. For example, because MRI has only been in use since the early 1980s, there are no known long-term effects of exposure to strong static fields and therefore there is no limit to the number of scans to which an individual can be subjected, in contrast with X-ray and CT. However, there are well-identified health risks associated with tissue heating from exposure to the RF field and the presence of implanted devices in the body, such as pacemakers. These risks are strictly controlled as part of the design of the instrument and the scanning protocols used.

Because CT and MRI are sensitive to different tissue properties, the appearances of the images obtained with the two techniques differ markedly. In CT, X-rays must be blocked by some form of dense tissue to create an image, so the image quality when looking at soft tissues will be poor. In MRI, while any nucleus with a net nuclear spin can be used, the proton of the hydrogen atom remains the most widely used, especially in the clinical setting, because it is so ubiquitous and returns a large signal. This nucleus, present in water molecules, allows the excellent soft-tissue contrast achievable with MRI.

A number of different pulse sequences can be used for specific MRI diagnostic imaging (multiparametric MRI or mpMRI). It is possible to differentiate tissue characteristics by combining two or more of the following imaging sequences, depending on the information being sought: T1-weighted (T1-MRI), T2-weighted (T2-MRI), diffusion weighted imaging (DWI-MRI), dynamic contrast enhancement (DCE-MRI), and spectroscopy (MRI-S). For example, imaging of prostate tumors is better accomplished using T2-MRI and DWI-MRI than T2-weighted imaging alone. The number of applications of mpMRI for detecting disease in various organs continues to expand, including liver studies, breast tumors, pancreatic tumors, and assessing the effects of vascular disruption agents on cancer tumors.

Nuclear Medicine

Nuclear medicine encompasses both diagnostic imaging and treatment of disease, and may also be referred to as molecular medicine or molecular imaging and therapeutics. Nuclear medicine uses certain properties of isotopes and the energetic particles emitted from radioactive material to diagnose or treat various pathology. Different from the typical concept of anatomic radiology, nuclear medicine enables assessment of physiology. This function-based approach to medical evaluation has useful applications in most subspecialties, notably oncology, neurology, and cardiology. Gamma cameras and PET scanners are used in e.g., scintigraphy, SPECT and PET to detect regions of biologic activity that may be associated with a disease. Relatively short-lived isotope, such as ^{99m}Tc is administered to the patient. Isotopes are often preferentially absorbed by biologically active tissue in the body, and can be used to identify tumors or fracture points in bone. Images are acquired after collimated photons are detected by a crystal that gives off a light signal, which is in turn amplified and converted into count data.

- Scintigraphy ("scint") is a form of diagnostic test wherein radioisotopes are taken internally, for example intravenously or orally. Then, gamma cameras capture and form two-dimensional images from the radiation emitted by the radiopharmaceuticals.

- SPECT is a 3D tomographic technique that uses gamma camera data from many projections and can be reconstructed in different planes. A dual detector head gamma camera combined with a CT scanner, which provides localization of functional SPECT data, is termed a SPECT-CT camera, and has shown utility in advancing the field of molecular imaging. In most other medical imaging modalities, energy is passed through the body and the reaction or result is read by detectors. In SPECT imaging, the patient is injected with a radioisotope, most commonly Thallium 201TI, Technetium ^{99m}Tc, Iodine 123I, and Gallium 67Ga. The radioactive gamma rays are emitted through the body as the natural decaying process of these isotopes takes place. The emissions of the gamma rays are captured by detectors that surround the body. This essentially means that the human is now the source of the radioactivity, rather than the medical imaging devices such as X-ray or CT.

- Positron emission tomography (PET) uses coincidence detection to image functional processes. Short-lived positron emitting isotope, such as ^{18}F, is incorporated with an organic substance such as glucose, creating F18-fluorodeoxyglucose, which can be used as a marker of metabolic utilization. Images of activity distribution throughout the body can show rapidly growing tissue, like tumor, metastasis, or infection. PET images can be viewed in comparison to computed tomography scans to determine an anatomic correlate. Modern scanners may integrate PET, allowing PET-CT, or PET-MRI to optimize the image reconstruction involved with positron imaging. This is performed on the same equipment without physically moving the patient off of the gantry. The resultant hybrid of functional and anatomic imaging information is a useful tool in non-invasive diagnosis and patient management.

Fiduciary markers are used in a wide range of medical imaging applications. Images of the same subject produced with two different imaging systems may be correlated (called image registration) by placing a fiduciary marker in the area imaged by both systems. In this case, a marker which is visible in the images produced by both imaging modalities must be used. By this method, functional information from SPECT or positron emission tomography can be related to anatomical information provided by magnetic resonance imaging (MRI). Similarly, fiducial points established during MRI can be correlated with brain images generated by magnetoencephalography to localize the source of brain activity.

Ultrasound

Medical ultrasonography uses high frequency broadband sound waves in the megahertz range that are reflected by tissue to varying degrees to produce (up to 3D) images. This is commonly associated with imaging the fetus in pregnant women. Uses of ultrasound are much broader, however. Other important uses include imaging the abdominal organs, heart, breast, muscles, tendons, arteries and veins. While it may provide less anatomical detail than techniques such as CT or MRI, it has several advantages which make it ideal in numerous situations, in particular that it studies the function of moving structures in real-time, emits no ionizing radiation, and contains speckle that can be used in elastography. Ultrasound is also used as a popular research tool for capturing raw data, that can be made available through an ultrasound research interface, for the purpose of tissue characterization and implementation of new image processing techniques. The concepts of ultrasound differ from other medical imaging modalities in the fact that it is operated by the transmission and receipt of sound waves. The high frequency sound waves are sent into the tissue and depending on the composition of the different tissues; the signal will be attenuated and returned at separate intervals. A path of reflected sound waves in a multilayered structure can be defined by an input acoustic impedance (ultrasound sound wave) and the Reflection and transmission coefficients of the relative structures. It is very safe to use and does not appear to cause any adverse effects. It is also relatively inexpensive and quick to perform. Ultrasound scanners can be taken to critically ill patients in intensive care units, avoiding the danger caused while moving the patient to the radiology department. The real-time moving image obtained can be used to guide drainage and biopsy procedures. Doppler capabilities on modern scanners allow the blood flow in arteries and veins to be assessed.

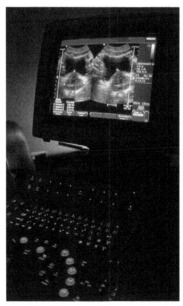

Ultrasound representation of Urinary bladder (black butterfly-like shape) and hyperplastic prostate.

Elastography

Elastography is a relatively new imaging modality that maps the elastic properties of soft tissue. This modality emerged in the last two decades. Elastography is useful in medical diagnoses, as elasticity can discern healthy from unhealthy tissue for specific organs/growths. For example, cancerous tumours will often be harder than the surrounding tissue, and diseased livers are stiffer than healthy ones. There are several elastographic techniques based on the use of ultrasound, magnetic resonance imaging and tactile imaging. The wide clinical use of ultrasound elastography is a result of the implementation of technology in clinical ultrasound machines. Main branches of ultrasound elastography include Quasistatic Elastography/Strain Imaging, Shear Wave Elasticity Imaging (SWEI), Acoustic Radiation Force Impulse imaging (ARFI), Supersonic Shear Imaging (SSI), and Transient Elastography. In the last decade a steady increase of activities in the field of elastography is observed demonstrating successful application of the technology in various areas of medical diagnostics and treatment monitoring.

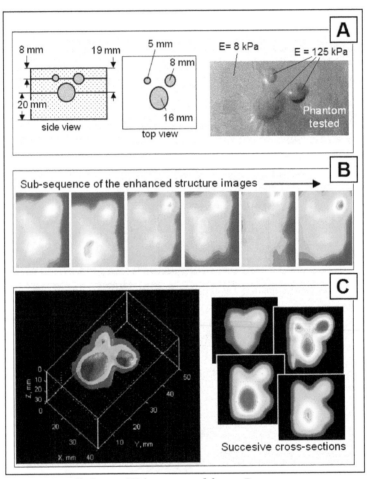

3D tactile image (C) is composed from 2D pressure maps
(B) recorded in the process of tissue phantom examination (A).

Photoacoustic Imaging

Photoacoustic imaging is a recently developed hybrid biomedical imaging modality based on the photoacoustic effect. It combines the advantages of optical absorption contrast with an ultrasonic spatial resolution for deep imaging in (optical) diffusive or quasi-diffusive regime. Recent studies have shown that photoacoustic imaging can be used in vivo for tumor angiogenesis monitoring, blood oxygenation mapping, functional brain imaging, and skin melanoma detection, etc.

Tomography

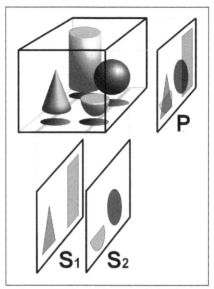

Basic principle of tomography: superposition free tomographic cross
sections S_1 and S_2 compared with the (not tomographic) projected image P.

Tomography is the imaging by sections or sectioning. The main such methods in medical imaging are:

- X-ray computed tomography (CT), or Computed Axial Tomography (CAT) scan, is a helical tomography technique (latest generation), which traditionally produces a 2D image of the structures in a thin section of the body. In CT, a beam of X-rays spins around an object being examined and is picked up by sensitive radiation detectors after having penetrated the object from multiple angles. A computer then analyses the information received from the scanner's detectors and constructs a detailed image of the object and its contents using the mathematical principles laid out in the Radon transform. It has a greater ionizing radiation dose burden than projection radiography; repeated scans must be limited to avoid health effects. CT is based on the same principles as X-Ray projections but in this case, the patient is enclosed in a surrounding ring of detectors assigned with 500–1000 scintillation detectors (fourth-generation X-Ray CT scanner geometry). Previously in older generation scanners, the X-Ray beam was paired by a translating source and detector. Computed tomography has almost completely replaced focal plane tomography in X-ray tomography imaging.

- Positron emission tomography (PET) also used in conjunction with computed tomography, PET-CT, and magnetic resonance imaging PET-MRI.

- Magnetic resonance imaging (MRI) commonly produces tomographic images of cross-sections of the body.

Echocardiography

When ultrasound is used to image the heart it is referred to as an echocardiogram. Echocardiography allows detailed structures of the heart, including chamber size, heart function, the valves of the heart, as well as the pericardium (the sac around the heart) to be seen. Echocardiography uses 2D, 3D, and Doppler imaging to create pictures of the heart and visualize the blood flowing through each of the four heart valves. Echocardiography is widely used in an array of patients ranging from those experiencing symptoms, such as shortness of breath or chest pain, to those undergoing cancer treatments. Transthoracic ultrasound has been proven to be safe for patients of all ages, from infants to the elderly, without risk of harmful side effects or radiation, differentiating it from other imaging modalities. Echocardiography is one of the most commonly used imaging modalities in the world due to its portability and use in a variety of applications. In emergency situations, echocardiography is quick, easily accessible, and able to be performed at the bedside, making it the modality of choice for many physicians.

Functional Near-infrared Spectroscopy

FNIR Is a relatively new non-invasive imaging technique. NIRS (near infrared spectroscopy) is used for the purpose of functional neuroimaging and has been widely accepted as a brain imaging technique.

Magnetic Particle Imaging

Using superparamagnetic iron oxide nanoparticles, magnetic particle imaging (MPI) is a developing diagnostic imaging technique used for tracking superparamagnetic iron oxide nanoparticles. The primary advantage is the high sensitivity and specificity, along with the lack of signal decrease with tissue depth. MPI has been used in medical research to image cardiovascular performance, neuroperfusion, and cell tracking.

In Pregnancy

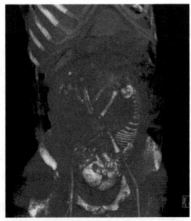

CT scanning (volume rendered in this case) confers a radiation dose to the developing fetus.

Medical imaging may be indicated in pregnancy because of pregnancy complications, intercurrent diseases or routine prenatal care. Magnetic resonance imaging (MRI) without MRI contrast agents as well as obstetric ultrasonography are not associated with any risk for the mother or the fetus, and are the imaging techniques of choice for pregnant women. Projectional radiography, X-ray computed tomography and nuclear medicine imaging result some degree of ionizing radiation exposure, but have with a few exceptions much lower absorbed doses than what are associated with fetal harm. At higher dosages, effects can include miscarriage, birth defects and intellectual disability.

Maximizing Imaging Procedure Use

The amount of data obtained in a single MR or CT scan is very extensive. Some of the data that radiologists discard could save patients time and money, while reducing their exposure to radiation and risk of complications from invasive procedures. Another approach for making the procedures more efficient is based on utilizing additional constraints, e.g., in some medical imaging modalities one can improve the efficiency of the data acquisition by taking into account the fact the reconstructed density is positive.

Creation of Three-dimensional Images

Volume rendering techniques have been developed to enable CT, MRI and ultrasound scanning software to produce 3D images for the physician. Traditionally CT and MRI scans produced 2D static output on film. To produce 3D images, many scans are made and then combined by computers to produce a 3D model, which can then be manipulated by the physician. 3D ultrasounds are produced using a somewhat similar technique. In diagnosing disease of the viscera of the abdomen, ultrasound is particularly sensitive on imaging of biliary tract, urinary tract and female reproductive organs (ovary, fallopian tubes). As for example, diagnosis of gallstone by dilatation of common bile duct and stone in the common bile duct. With the ability to visualize important structures in great detail, 3D visualization methods are a valuable resource for the diagnosis and surgical treatment of many pathologies. It was a key resource for the famous, but ultimately unsuccessful attempt by Singaporean surgeons to separate Iranian twins Ladan and Laleh Bijani in 2003. The 3D equipment was used previously for similar operations with great success.

Other proposed or developed techniques include:

- Diffuse optical tomography.

- Elastography.

- Electrical impedance tomography.

- Optoacoustic imaging.

- Ophthalmology.

  - A-scan.

  - B-scan.

  - Corneal topography.

  - Optical coherence tomography.

  - Scanning laser ophthalmoscopy.

Some of these techniques are still at a research stage and not yet used in clinical routines.

The latest development and research in the field of Artificial Intelligence and neural science has shown the possibilities of converting 2D images into 3D images using deep learning. A group of scientist, worked on a machine learning model called Deep-z. They tested this model on feeding images that were tilted and turned and the result, the model provided the exact match of the 3D structures.

It's not only 2D models, but researchers are able to recover lost data from images and videos. These AI and neural science models can optimize blurry pictures and videos to increase its resolution, which can be helpful in working with medical imaging.

Non-diagnostic Imaging

Neuroimaging has also been used in experimental circumstances to allow people (especially disabled persons) to control outside devices, acting as a brain computer interface.

Many medical imaging software applications are used for non-diagnostic imaging, specifically because they do not have an FDA approval and not allowed to use in clinical research for patient diagnosis. Note that many clinical research studies are not designed for patient diagnosis anyway.

Archiving and Recording

Used primarily in ultrasound imaging, capturing the image produced by a medical imaging device is required for archiving and telemedicine applications. In most scenarios, a frame grabber is used in order to capture the video signal from the medical device and relay it to a computer for further processing and operations.

DICOM

The Digital Imaging and Communication in Medicine (DICOM) Standard is used globally to store, exchange, and transmit medical images. The DICOM Standard incorporates protocols for imaging techniques such as radiography, computed tomography (CT), magnetic resonance imaging (MRI), ultrasonography, and radiation therapy.

Compression of Medical Images

Medical imaging techniques produce very large amounts of data, especially from CT, MRI and PET modalities. As a result, storage and communications of electronic image data are prohibitive without the use of compression. JPEG 2000 is the state-of-the-art image compression DICOM standard for storage and transmission of medical images. The cost and feasibility of accessing large image data sets over low or various bandwidths are further addressed by use of another DICOM standard, called JPIP, to enable efficient streaming of the JPEG 2000 compressed image data.

Medical Imaging in the Cloud

There has been growing trend to migrate from on-premise PACS to a Cloud Based PACS. A recent article by Applied Radiology said, "As the digital-imaging realm is embraced across the healthcare enterprise, the swift transition from terabytes to petabytes of data has put radiology on the brink of information overload. Cloud computing offers the imaging department of the future the tools to manage data much more intelligently."

Use in Pharmaceutical Clinical Trials

Medical imaging has become a major tool in clinical trials since it enables rapid diagnosis with visualization and quantitative assessment.

A typical clinical trial goes through multiple phases and can take up to eight years. Clinical endpoints or outcomes are used to determine whether the therapy is safe and effective. Once a patient reaches the endpoint, he or she is generally excluded from further experimental interaction. Trials that rely solely on clinical endpoints are very costly as they have long durations and tend to need large numbers of patients.

In contrast to clinical endpoints, surrogate endpoints have been shown to cut down the time required to confirm whether a drug has clinical benefits. Imaging biomarkers (a characteristic that is objectively measured by an imaging technique, which is used as an indicator of pharmacological response to a therapy) and surrogate endpoints have shown to facilitate the use of small group sizes, obtaining quick results with good statistical power.

Imaging is able to reveal subtle change that is indicative of the progression of therapy that may be missed out by more subjective, traditional approaches. Statistical bias is reduced as the findings are evaluated without any direct patient contact.

Imaging techniques such as positron emission tomography (PET) and magnetic resonance imaging (MRI) are routinely used in oncology and neuroscience areas,. For example, measurement of tumour shrinkage is a commonly used surrogate endpoint in solid tumour response evaluation. This allows for faster and more objective assessment of the effects of anticancer drugs. In Alzheimer's disease, MRI scans of the entire brain can accurately assess the rate of hippocampal atrophy, while PET scans can measure the brain's metabolic activity by measuring regional glucose metabolism, and beta-amyloid plaques using tracers such as Pittsburgh compound B (PiB). Historically less use has been made of quantitative medical imaging in other areas of drug development although interest is growing.

An imaging-based trial will usually be made up of three components:

- A realistic imaging protocol. The protocol is an outline that standardizes (as far as practically possible) the way in which the images are acquired using the various modalities (PET, SPECT, CT, MRI). It covers the specifics in which images are to be stored, processed and evaluated.

- An imaging centre that is responsible for collecting the images, perform quality control and provide tools for data storage, distribution and analysis. It is important for images acquired at different time points are displayed in a standardised format to maintain the reliability of the evaluation. Certain specialised imaging contract research organizations provide end to end medical imaging services, from protocol design and site management through to data quality assurance and image analysis.

- Clinical sites that recruit patients to generate the images to send back to the imaging centre.

Shielding

Lead is the main material used for radiographic shielding against scattered X-rays.

In magnetic resonance imaging, there is MRI RF shielding as well as magnetic shielding to prevent external disturbance of image quality.

Privacy Protection

Medical imaging are generally covered by laws of medical privacy. For example, in the United States the Health Insurance Portability and Accountability Act (HIPAA) sets restrictions for health care providers on utilizing protected health information, which is any individually identifiable information relating to the past, present, or future physical or mental health of any individual. While there has not been any definitive legal decision in the matter, at least one study has indicated that medical imaging may contain biometric information that can uniquely identify a person, and so may qualify as PHI.

The UK General Medical Council's ethical guidelines indicate that the Council does not require consent prior to secondary uses of X-ray images.

Industry

Organizations in the medical imaging industry include manufacturers of imaging equipment, freestanding radiology facilities, and hospitals.

The global market for manufactured devices was estimated at $5 billion in 2018. Notable manufacturers as of 2012 included Fujifilm, GE, Siemens Healthineers, Philips, Shimadzu, Toshiba, Carestream Health, Hitachi, Hologic, and Esaote. In 2016, the manufacturing industry was characterized as oligopolistic and mature; new entrants included in Samsung and Neusoft Medical.

In the United States, as estimate as of 2015 places the US market for imaging scans at about $100b, with 60% occurring in hospitals and 40% occurring in freestanding clinics, such as the RadNet chain.

In Technology

Image Editing

| A colorized version of originally black and white photo, colorized using GIMP. | Original black and white photo: Migrant Mother, showing Florence Owens Thompson, taken by Dorothea Lange in 1936. |

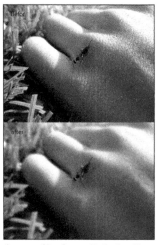

This is a photo that has been edited as a Bokeh effect, using a Gaussian blur.

Image editing encompasses the processes of altering images, whether they are digital photographs, traditional photo-chemical photographs, or illustrations. Traditional analog image editing is known as photo retouching, using tools such as an airbrush to modify photographs or editing illustrations with any traditional art medium. Graphic software programs, which can be broadly grouped into vector graphics editors, raster graphics editors, and 3D modelers, are the primary tools with which a user may manipulate, enhance, and transform images. Many image editing programs are also used to render or create computer art from scratch.

Basics of Image Editing

Raster images are stored in a computer in the form of a grid of picture elements, or pixels. These pixels contain the image's color and brightness information. Image editors can change the pixels to enhance the image in many ways. The pixels can be changed as a group, or individually, by the sophisticated algorithms within the image editors. This article mostly refers to bitmap graphics editors, which are often used to alter photographs and other raster graphics. However, vector graphics software, such as Adobe Illustrator, CorelDRAW, Xara Designer Pro or Inkscape, are used to create and modify vector images, which are stored as descriptions of lines, Bézier curves, and text instead of pixels. It is easier to rasterize a vector image than to vectorize a raster image; how to go about vectorizing a raster image is the focus of much research in the field of computer vision. Vector images can be modified more easily because they contain descriptions of the shapes for easy rearrangement. They are also scalable, being rasterizable at any resolution.

Automatic Image Enhancement

Camera or computer image editing programs often offer basic automatic image enhancement features that correct color hue and brightness imbalances as well as other image editing features, such as red eye removal, sharpness adjustments, zoom features and automatic cropping. These are called automatic because generally they happen without user interaction or are offered with one click of a button or mouse button or by selecting an option from a menu. Additionally, some automatic editing features offer a combination of editing actions with little or no user interaction.

Digital Data Compression

Many image file formats use data compression to reduce file size and save storage space. Digital compression of images may take place in the camera, or can be done in the computer with the image editor. When images are stored in JPEG format, compression has already taken place. Both cameras and computer programs allow the user to set the level of compression.

Some compression algorithms, such as those used in PNG file format, are lossless, which means no information is lost when the file is saved. By contrast, the JPEG file format uses a lossy compression algorithm by which the greater the compression, the more information is lost, ultimately reducing image quality or detail that can not be restored. JPEG uses knowledge of the way the human brain and eyes perceive color to make this loss of detail less noticeable.

Image Editor Features

Listed below are some of the most used capabilities of the better graphics manipulation programs. The list is by no means all-inclusive. There are a myriad of choices associated with the application of most of these features.

Selection

One of the prerequisites for many of the applications mentioned below is a method of selecting part(s) of an image, thus applying a change selectively without affecting the entire picture. Most graphics programs have several means of accomplishing this, such as:

- A marquee tool for selecting rectangular or other regular polygon-shaped regions.

- A lasso tool for freehand selection of a region.

- A magic wand tool that selects objects or regions in the image defined by proximity of color or luminance.

- Vector-based pen tools.

as well as more advanced facilities such as edge detection, masking, alpha compositing, and color and channel-based extraction. The border of a selected area in an image is often animated with the marching ants effect to help the user to distinguish the selection border from the image background.

Layers

Another feature common to many graphics applications is that of layers, which are analogous to sheets of transparent acetate (each containing separate elements that make up a combined picture), stacked on top of each other, each capable of being individually positioned, altered and blended with the layers below, without affecting any of the elements on the other layers. This is a fundamental workflow which has become the norm for the majority of programs on the market today, and enables maximum flexibility for the user while maintaining non-destructive editing principles and ease of use.

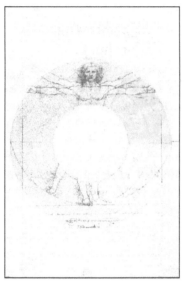

Leonardo da Vinci's Vitruvian Man overlaid with Goethe's Color Wheel using a screen layer in Adobe Photoshop. Screen layers can be helpful in graphic design and in creating multiple exposures in photography.

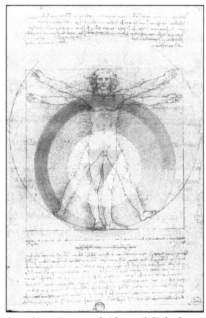

Leonardo da Vinci's Vitruvian Man overlaid a soft light layer Moses Harris's Color Wheel and a soft light layer of Ignaz Schiffermüller's Color Wheel. Soft light layers have a darker, more translucent look than screen layers.

Image Size Alteration

Image editors can resize images in a process often called image scaling, making them larger, or smaller. High image resolution cameras can produce large images which are often reduced in size for Internet use. Image editor programs use a mathematical process called resampling to calculate new pixel values whose spacing is larger or smaller than the original pixel values. Images for Internet use are kept small, say 640 x 480 pixels which would equal 0.3 megapixels.

Cropping an Image

Digital editors are used to crop images. Cropping creates a new image by selecting a desired rectangular portion from the image being cropped. The unwanted part of the image is discarded. Image cropping does not reduce the resolution of the area cropped. Best results are obtained when the original image has a high resolution. A primary reason for cropping is to improve the image composition in the new image.

Uncropped image from camera.

Lily cropped from larger image.

Cutting out a Part of an Image from the Background

Using a selection tool, the outline of the figure or element in the picture is traced/selected, and then the background is removed. Depending on how intricate the "edge" is this may be more or less difficult to do cleanly. For example, individual hairs can require a lot of work. Hence the use of the "green screen" technique (chroma key) which allows one to easily remove the background.

Histogram

Sunflower image.

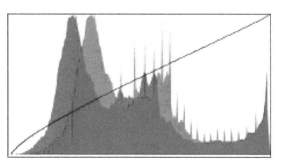
Histogram of Sunflower image.

Image editors have provisions to create an image histogram of the image being edited. The histogram plots the number of pixels in the image (vertical axis) with a particular brightness value (horizontal axis). Algorithms in the digital editor allow the user to visually adjust the brightness value of each pixel and to dynamically display the results as adjustments are made. Improvements in picture brightness and contrast can thus be obtained.

Noise Reduction

Image editors may feature a number of algorithms which can add or remove noise in an image. Some JPEG artifacts can be removed; dust and scratches can be removed and an image can be de-speckled. Noise reduction merely estimates the state of the scene without the noise and is not a substitute for obtaining a "cleaner" image. Excessive noise reduction leads to a loss of detail, and its application is hence subject to a trade-off between the undesirability of the noise itself and that of the reduction artifacts.

Noise tends to invade images when pictures are taken in low light settings. A new picture can be given an 'antiqued' effect by adding uniform monochrome noise.

Removal of Unwanted Elements

Most image editors can be used to remove unwanted branches, etc., using a "clone" tool. Removing these distracting elements draws focus to the subject, improving overall composition.

Notice the branch in the original.   The eye is drawn to the center of the globe.

Selective Color Change

Some image editors have color swapping abilities to selectively change the color of specific items in an image, given that the selected items are within a specific color range.

Selective color change.

Image Orientation

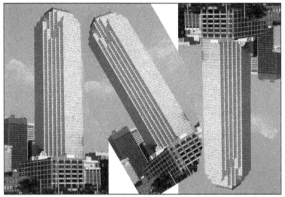
Image orientation (from left to right): original, 30° CCW rotation, and flipped.

Image editors are capable of altering an image to be rotated in any direction and to any degree. Mirror images can be created and images can be horizontally flipped or vertically flopped. A small rotation of several degrees is often enough to level the horizon, correct verticality (of a building, for example), or both. Rotated images usually require cropping afterwards, in order to remove the resulting gaps at the image edges.

Perspective Control and Distortion

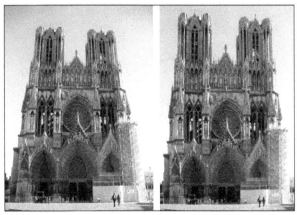
Perspective control: original (left), perspective distortion removed (right).

Some image editors allow the user to distort (or "transform") the shape of an image. While this might also be useful for special effects, it is the preferred method of correcting the typical perspective distortion which results from photographs being taken at an oblique angle to a rectilinear subject. Care is needed while performing this task, as the image is reprocessed using interpolation of adjacent pixels, which may reduce overall image definition. The effect mimics the use of a perspective control lens, which achieves a similar correction in-camera without loss of definition.

Lens Correction

Photo manipulation packages have functions to correct images for various lens distortions including pincushion, fisheye and barrel distortions. The corrections are in most cases subtle, but can improve the appearance of some photographs.

Enhancing Images

In computer graphics, the process of improving the quality of a digitally stored image by manipulating the image with software. It is quite easy, for example, to make an image lighter or darker, or to increase or decrease contrast. Advanced photo enhancement software also supports many filters for altering images in various ways. Programs specialized for image enhancement are sometimes called image editors.

Sharpening and Softening Images

Graphics programs can be used to both sharpen and blur images in a number of ways, such as unsharp masking or deconvolution. Portraits often appear more pleasing when selectively softened (particularly the skin and the background) to better make the subject stand out. This can be achieved with a camera by using a large aperture, or in the image editor by making a selection and then blurring it. Edge enhancement is an extremely common technique used to make images appear sharper, although purists frown on the result as appearing unnatural.

Image sharpening: original (top), image sharpened (bottom).

Another form of image sharpening involves a form of contrast. This is done by finding the average color of the pixels around each pixel in a specified radius, and then contrasting that pixel from that average color. This effect makes the image seem clearer, seemingly adding details. An example of this effect can be seen to the right. It is widely used in the printing and photographic industries for increasing the local contrasts and sharpening the images.

Selecting and Merging of Images

Photomontage of 16 photos which have been digitally manipulated in Photoshop to give the impression that it is a real landscape.

Many graphics applications are capable of merging one or more individual images into a single file. The orientation and placement of each image can be controlled.

When selecting a raster image that is not rectangular, it requires separating the edges from the background, also known as silhouetting. This is the digital-analog of cutting out the image from a physical picture. Clipping paths may be used to add silhouetted images to vector graphics or page layout files that retain vector data. Alpha compositing, allows for soft translucent edges when selecting images. There are a number of ways to silhouette an image with soft edges, including selecting the image or its background by sampling similar colors, selecting the edges by raster tracing, or converting a clipping path to a raster selection. Once the image is selected, it may be copied and pasted into another section of the same file, or into a separate file. The selection may also be saved in what is known as an alpha channel.

A popular way to create a composite image is to use transparent layers. The background image is used as the bottom layer, and the image with parts to be added are placed in a layer above that. Using an image layer mask, all but the parts to be merged are hidden from the layer, giving the impression that these parts have been added to the background layer. Performing a merge in this manner preserves all of the pixel data on both layers to more easily enable future changes in the new merged image.

Slicing of Images

A more recent tool in digital image editing software is the image slicer. Parts of images for graphical user interfaces or web pages are easily sliced, labeled and saved separately from whole images so the parts can be handled individually by the display medium. This is useful to allow dynamic swapping via interactivity or animating parts of an image in the final presentation.

Special Effects

An example of some special effects that can be added to a picture.

Image editors usually have a list of special effects that can create unusual results. Images may be skewed and distorted in various ways. Scores of special effects can be applied to an image which include various forms of distortion, artistic effects, geometric transforms and texture effects, or combinations thereof.

A complex effect in the first image from the right.

Using custom Curves settings in Image editors such as Photoshop, one can mimic the "pseudo-solarisation" effect, better known in photographic circles as the Sabattier-effect.

A pseudo-solarised color image.

Stamp Clone Tool

The Clone Stamp tool selects and samples an area of your picture and then uses these pixels to paint over any marks. The Clone Stamp tool acts like a brush so you can change the size, allowing cloning from just one pixel wide to hundreds. You can change the opacity to produce a subtle clone effect. Also, there is a choice between Clone align or Clone non-align the sample area. In Photoshop this tool is called Clone Stamp, but it may also be called a Rubber Stamp tool.

Image after stamp tool processed.

Change Color Depth

An example of converting an image from color to grayscale.

It is possible, using the software, to change the color depth of images. Common color depths are 2, 4, 16, 256, 65,536 and 16.7 million colors. The JPEG and PNG image formats are capable of storing 16.7 million colors (equal to 256 luminance values per color channel). In addition, grayscale images of 8 bits or less can be created, usually via conversion and down-sampling from a full-color image. Grayscale conversion is useful for reducing the file size dramatically when the original photographic print was monochrome, but a color tint has been introduced due to aging effects.

Contrast Change and Brightening

An example of contrast correction. Left side of the image is untouched.

Image editors have provisions to simultaneously change the contrast of images and brighten or darken the image. Underexposed images can often be improved by using this feature. Recent advances have allowed more intelligent exposure correction whereby only pixels below a particular luminosity threshold are brightened, thereby brightening underexposed shadows without affecting the rest of the image. The exact transformation that is applied to each color channel can vary from editor to editor. GIMP applies the following formula:

```
if (brightness < 0.0) value = value * ( 1.0 + brightness);

    else value = value + ((1 - value) * brightness);

value = (value - 0.5) * (tan ((contrast + 1) * PI/4) ) + 0.5;
```

where value is the input color value in the 0..1 range and brightness and contrast are in the −1..1 range.

Gamma Correction

In addition to the capability of changing the images' brightness and/or contrast in a non-linear fashion, most current image editors provide an opportunity to manipulate the images' gamma value.

Gamma correction is particularly useful for bringing details that would be hard to see on most computer monitors out of shadows. In some image editing software, this is called "curves", usually, a tool found in the color menu, and no reference to "gamma" is used anywhere in the program or the program documentation. Strictly speaking, the curves tool usually does more than simple gamma correction, since one can construct complex curves with multiple inflection points, but when no dedicated gamma correction tool is provided, it can achieve the same effect.

Color Adjustments

An example of color adjustment using raster graphics editor.

The color of images can be altered in a variety of ways. Colors can be faded in and out, and tones can be changed using curves or other tools. The color balance can be improved, which is important if the picture was shot indoors with daylight film, or shot on a camera with the white balance incorrectly set. Special effects, like sepia tone and grayscale, can be added to an image. In addition, more complicated procedures such as the mixing of color channels are possible using more advanced graphics editors.

The red-eye effect, which occurs when flash photos are taken when the pupil is too widely open (so that light from the flash that passes into the eye through the pupil reflects off the fundus at the back of the eyeball), can also be eliminated at this stage.

Dynamic Blending

Sunset Sky   Blue Hour City   Final Blended Image

Before and After example of Advanced Dynamic Blending Technique created by Elia Locardi.

Advanced Dynamic Blending is a concept introduced by photographer Elia Locardi in his blog Blame The Monkey to describe the photographic process of capturing multiple bracketed exposures of a land or cityscape over a specific span of time in a changing natural or artificial lighting environment. Once captured, the exposure brackets are manually blended together into a single High Dynamic Range image using post-processing software. Dynamic Blending images serve to display a consolidated moment. This means that while the final image may be a blend of a span of time, it visually appears to represent a single instant.

Printing

Control printed image by changing pixels-per-inch.

Controlling the print size and quality of digital images requires an understanding of the pixels-per-inch (ppi) variable that is stored in the image file and sometimes used to control the size of the printed image. Within Adobe Photoshop's Image Size dialog, the image editor allows the user to manipulate both pixel dimensions and the size of the image on the printed document. These parameters work together to produce a printed image of the desired size and quality. Pixels per inch of the image, pixel per inch of the computer monitor, and dots per inch on the printed document are related, but in use are very different. The Image Size dialog can be used as an image calculator of sorts. For example, a 1600 × 1200 image with a resolution of 200 ppi will produce a printed image of 8 × 6 inches. The same image with 400 ppi will produce a printed image of 4 × 3 inches. Change the resolution to 800 ppi, and the same image now prints out at 2 × 1.5 inches. All three printed images contain the same data (1600 × 1200 pixels), but the pixels are closer together on the smaller prints, so the smaller images will potentially look sharp when the larger ones do not. The quality of the image will also depend on the capability of the printer.

Facial Recognition System

A facial recognition system is a technology capable of identifying or verifying a person from a digital image or a video frame from a video source. There are multiple methods in which facial recognition systems work, but in general, they work by comparing selected facial features from given image with faces within a database. It is also described as a Biometric Artificial Intelligence based application that can uniquely identify a person by analysing patterns based on the person's facial textures and shape.

Swiss European surveillance: face recognition and vehicle make, model, color and license plate reader.

Close-up of the infrared illuminator. The light is invisible to the human eye, but creates a day-like environment for the surveillance cameras.

While initially a form of computer application, it has seen wider uses in recent times on mobile platforms and in other forms of technology, such as robotics. It is typically used as access control in security systems and can be compared to other biometrics such as fingerprint or eye iris recognition systems. Although the accuracy of facial recognition system as a biometric technology is lower than iris recognition and fingerprint recognition, it is widely adopted due to its contactless and non-invasive process. Recently, it has also become popular as a commercial identification and marketing tool. Other applications include advanced human-computer interaction, video surveillance, automatic indexing of images, and video database, among others.

Techniques for Face Acquisition

Essentially, the process of face recognition is performed in two steps. The first involves feature extraction and selection and the second is the classification of objects. Later developments introduced varying technologies to the procedure. Some of the most notable include the following techniques:

Traditional

Some face recognition algorithms identify facial features by extracting landmarks, or features, from an image of the subject's face. For example, an algorithm may analyze the relative position, size, and/or shape of the eyes, nose, cheekbones, and jaw. These features are then used to search for other images with matching features.

Other algorithms normalize a gallery of face images and then compress the face data, only saving the data in the image that is useful for face recognition. A probe image is then compared with the face data. One of the earliest successful systems is based on template matching techniques applied to a set of salient facial features, providing a sort of compressed face representation.

Recognition algorithms can be divided into two main approaches: geometric, which looks at distinguishing features, or photometric, which is a statistical approach that distills an image into values and compares the values with templates to eliminate variances. Some classify these algorithms into two broad categories: Holistic and feature-based models. The former attempts to recognize the face in its entirety while the feature-based subdivide into components such as according to features and analyze each as well as its spatial location with respect to other features.

Popular recognition algorithms include principal component analysis using eigenfaces, linear discriminant analysis, elastic bunch graph matching using the Fisherface algorithm, the hidden Markov model, the multilinear subspace learning using tensor representation, and the neuronal motivated dynamic link matching.

3-Dimensional Recognition

Three-dimensional face recognition technique uses 3D sensors to capture information about the shape of a face. This information is then used to identify distinctive features on the surface of a face, such as the contour of the eye sockets, nose, and chin.

One advantage of 3D face recognition is that it is not affected by changes in lighting like other techniques. It can also identify a face from a range of viewing angles, including a profile view. Three-dimensional data points from a face vastly improve the precision of face recognition. 3D research is enhanced by the development of sophisticated sensors that do a better job of capturing 3D face imagery. The sensors work by projecting structured light onto the face. Up to a dozen or more of these image sensors can be placed on the same CMOS chip—each sensor captures a different part of the spectrum.

Even a perfect 3D matching technique could be sensitive to expressions. For that goal a group at the Technion applied tools from metric geometry to treat expressions as isometries

A new method is to introduce a way to capture a 3D picture by using three tracking cameras that point at different angles; one camera will be pointing at the front of the subject, second one to the side, and third one at an angle. All these cameras will work together so it can track a subject's face in real time and be able to face detect and recognize.

Skin Texture Analysis

Another emerging trend uses the visual details of the skin, as captured in standard digital or scanned images. This technique, called Skin Texture Analysis, turns the unique lines, patterns, and spots apparent in a person's skin into a mathematical space.

Surface Texture Analysis works much the same way facial recognition does. A picture is taken of a patch of skin, called a skinprint. That patch is then broken up into smaller blocks. Using algorithms to turn the patch into a mathematical, measurable space, the system will then distinguish any lines, pores and the actual skin texture. It can identify the contrast between identical pairs, which are not yet possible using facial recognition software alone.

Tests have shown that with the addition of skin texture analysis, performance in recognizing faces can increase 20 to 25 percent.

Facial Recognition Combining Different Techniques

As every method has its advantages and disadvantages, technology companies have amalgamated the traditional, 3D recognition and Skin Textual Analysis, to create recognition systems that have higher rates of success.

Combined techniques have an advantage over other systems. It is relatively insensitive to changes in expression, including blinking, frowning or smiling and has the ability to compensate for mustache or beard growth and the appearance of eyeglasses. The system is also uniform with respect to race and gender.

Thermal Cameras

A different form of taking input data for face recognition is by using thermal cameras, by this procedure the cameras will only detect the shape of the head and it will ignore the subject accessories such as glasses, hats, or makeup. Unlike conventional cameras, thermal cameras can capture facial imagery even in low-light and nighttime conditions without using a flash and exposing the position of the camera. However, a problem with using thermal pictures for face recognition is that the databases for face recognition is limited. Diego Socolinsky and Andrea Selinger (2004) research the use of thermal face recognition in real life and operation sceneries, and at the same time build a new database of thermal face images. The research uses low-sensitive, low-resolution ferroelectric electrics sensors that are capable of acquiring long-wave thermal infrared (LWIR). The results show that a fusion of LWIR and regular visual cameras has greater results in outdoor probes. Indoor results show that visual has a 97.05% accuracy, while LWIR has 93.93%, and the fusion has 98.40%, however on the outdoor proves visual has 67.06%, LWIR 83.03%, and fusion has 89.02%. The study used 240 subjects over a period of 10 weeks to create a new database. The data was collected on sunny, rainy, and cloudy days.

In 2018, researchers from the U.S. Army Research Laboratory (ARL) developed a technique that would allow them to match facial imagery obtained using a thermal camera with those in databases that were captured using a conventional camera. This approach utilized artificial intelligence and machine learning to allow researchers to visibly compare conventional and thermal facial imagery. Known as a cross-spectrum synthesis method due to how it bridges facial recognition from two different imaging modalities, this method synthesize a single image by analyzing multiple facial regions and details. It consists of a non-linear regression model that maps a specific thermal image into a corresponding visible facial image and an optimization issue that projects the latent projection back into the image space.

ARL scientists have noted that the approach works by combining global information (i.e. features across the entire face) with local information (i.e. features regarding the eyes, nose, and mouth). In addition to enhancing the discriminability of the synthesized image, the facial recognition system can be used to transform a thermal face signature into a refined visible image of a face. According to performance tests conducted at ARL, researchers found that the multi-region cross-spectrum synthesis model demonstrated a performance improvement of about 30% over baseline methods and about 5% over state-of-the-art methods. It has also been tested for landmark detection for thermal images.

Application

Social media

Social media platforms have adopted facial recognition capabilities to diversify their functionalities in order to attract a wider user base amidst stiff competition from different applications.

Founded in 2013, Looksery went on to raise money for its face modification app on Kickstarter. After successful crowdfunding, Looksery launched in October 2014. The application allows video chat with others through a special filter for faces that modifies the look of users. While there is image augmenting applications such as FaceTune and Perfect365, they are limited to static images, whereas Looksery allowed augmented reality to live videos. In late 2015, SnapChat purchased Looksery, which would then become its landmark lenses function.

SnapChat's animated lenses, which used facial recognition technology, revolutionized and redefined the selfie, by allowing users to add filters to change the way they look. The selection of filters changes every day, some examples include one that makes users look like an old and wrinkled version of themselves, one that airbrushes their skin, and one that places a virtual flower crown on top of their head. The dog filter is the most popular filter that helped propel the continual success of SnapChat, with popular celebrities such as Gigi Hadid, Kim Kardashian and the likes regularly posting videos of themselves with the dog filter.

DeepFace is a deep learning facial recognition system created by a research group at Facebook. It identifies human faces in digital images. It employs a nine-layer neural net with over 120 million connection weights, and was trained on four million images uploaded by Facebook users. The system is said to be 97% accurate, compared to 85% for the FBI's Next Generation Identification system. One of the creators of the software, Yaniv Taigman, came to Facebook via their acquisition of Face.com.

ID Verification

The emerging use of facial recognition is in the use of ID verification services. Many companies and others are working in the market now to provide these services to banks, ICOs, and other e-businesses. In 2017, Time and Attendance company ClockedIn released facial recognition as a form of attendance tracking for businesses and organizations looking to have a more automated system of keeping track of hours worked as well as for security and health and safety control.

Face ID

Apple introduced Face ID on the flagship iPhone X as a biometric authentication successor to the Touch ID, a fingerprint based system. Face ID has a facial recognition sensor that consists of two parts: a "Romeo" module that projects more than 30,000 infrared dots onto the user's face, and a "Juliet" module that reads the pattern. The pattern is sent to a local "Secure Enclave" in the device's central processing unit (CPU) to confirm a match with the phone owner's face. The facial pattern is not accessible by Apple. The system will not work with eyes closed, in an effort to prevent unauthorized access.

The technology learns from changes in a user's appearance, and therefore works with hats, scarves, glasses, and many sunglasses, beard and makeup.

It also works in the dark. This is done by using a "Flood Illuminator", which is a dedicated infrared flash that throws out invisible infrared light onto the user's face to properly read the 30,000 facial points.

Additional Uses

In addition to being used for security systems, authorities have found a number of other applications for face recognition systems. While earlier post-9/11 deployments were well-publicized trials, more recent deployments are rarely written about due to their covert nature.

At Super Bowl XXXV in January 2001, police in Tampa Bay, Florida used Viisage face recognition software to search for potential criminals and terrorists in attendance at the event. 19 people with minor criminal records were potentially identified.

In the 2000 Mexican presidential election, the Mexican government employed face recognition software to prevent voter fraud. Some individuals had been registering to vote under several different names, in an attempt to place multiple votes. By comparing new face images to those already in the voter database, authorities were able to reduce duplicate registrations. Similar technologies are being used in the United States to prevent people from obtaining fake identification cards and driver's licenses.

Face recognition has been leveraged as a form of biometric authentication for various computing platforms and devices; Android 4.0 "Ice Cream Sandwich" added facial recognition using a smartphone's front camera as a means of unlocking devices, while Microsoft introduced face recognition login to its Xbox 360 video game console through its Kinect accessory, as well as Windows 10 via its "Windows Hello" platform (which requires an infrared-illuminated camera). Apple's iPhone X smartphone introduced facial recognition to the product line with its "Face ID" platform, which uses an infrared illumination system.

Face recognition systems have also been used by photo management software to identify the subjects of photographs, enabling features such as searching images by person, as well as suggesting photos to be shared with a specific contact if their presence were detected in a photo.

Facial recognition is used as added security in certain websites, phone applications, and payment methods.

The United States' popular music and country music celebrity Taylor Swift surreptitiously employed facial recognition technology at a concert in 2018. The camera was embedded in a kiosk near a ticket booth and scanned concert-goers as they entered the facility for known stalkers.

On August 18, 2019, The Times reported that the UAE-owned Manchester City hired a Texas-based firm, Blink Identity, to deploy facial recognition systems in a driver program. The club has planned a single super-fast lane for the supporters at the Etihad stadium. However, civil rights groups cautioned the club against the introduction of this technology, saying that it would risk "normalising a mass surveillance tool". The policy and campaigns officer at Liberty, Hannah Couchman said that Man City's move is alarming, since the fans will be obliged to share deeply sensitive personal information with a private company, where they could be tracked and monitored in their everyday lives.

Advantages and Disadvantages

Compared to other Biometric Systems

One key advantage of a facial recognition system that it is able to person mass identification as it does not require the cooperation of the test subject to work. Properly designed systems installed in airports, multiplexes, and other public places can identify individuals among the crowd, without passers-by even being aware of the system.

However, as compared to other biometric techniques, face recognition may not be most reliable and efficient. Quality measures are very important in facial recognition systems as large degrees of variations are possible in face images. Factors such as illumination, expression, pose and noise during face capture can affect the performance of facial recognition systems. Among all biometric systems, facial recognition has the highest false acceptance and rejection rates, thus questions have been raised on the effectiveness of face recognition software in cases of railway and airport security.

Weaknesses

Ralph Gross, a researcher at the Carnegie Mellon Robotics Institute in 2008, describes one obstacle related to the viewing angle of the face: "Face recognition has been getting pretty good at full frontal faces and 20 degrees off, but as soon as you go towards profile, there've been problems." Besides the pose variations, low-resolution face images are also very hard to recognize. This is one of the main obstacles of face recognition in surveillance systems.

Face recognition is less effective if facial expressions vary. A big smile can render the system less effective. For instance: Canada, in 2009, allowed only neutral facial expressions in passport photos.

There is also inconstancy in the datasets used by researchers. Researchers may use anywhere from several subjects to scores of subjects and a few hundred images to thousands of images. It is important for researchers to make available the datasets they used to each other, or have at least a standard dataset.

Data privacy is the main concern when it comes to storing biometrics data in companies. Data stores about face or biometrics can be accessed by the third party if not stored properly or hacked. In the Techworld, Parris adds (2017), "Hackers will already be looking to replicate people's faces to trick facial recognition systems, but the technology has proved harder to hack than fingerprint or voice recognition technology in the past."

Ineffectiveness

Critics of the technology complain that the London Borough of Newham scheme has, as of 2004, never recognized a single criminal, despite several criminals in the system's database living in the Borough and the system has been running for several years. "Not once, as far as the police know, has Newham's automatic face recognition system spotted a live target." This information seems to conflict with claims that the system was credited with a 34% reduction in crime (hence why it was rolled out to Birmingham also). However it can be explained by the notion that when the public is regularly told that they are under constant video surveillance with advanced face recognition technology, this fear alone can reduce the crime rate, whether the face recognition system technically works or does not. This has been the basis for several other face recognition based security systems, where the technology itself does not work particularly well but the user's perception of the technology does.

An experiment in 2002 by the local police department in Tampa, Florida, had similarly disappointing results.

A system at Boston's Logan Airport was shut down in 2003 after failing to make any matches during a two-year test period.

In 2014, Facebook stated that in a standardized two-option facial recognition test, its online system scored 97.25% accuracy, compared to the human benchmark of 97.5%.

In 2018, a report by the civil liberties and rights campaigning organisation Big Brother Watch revealed that two UK police forces, South Wales Police and the Metropolitan Police, were using live facial recognition at public events and in public spaces, in September 2019, South Wales Police use of facial recognition was ruled lawful.

Systems are often advertised as having accuracy near 100%; this is misleading as the studies often use much smaller sample sizes than would be necessary for large scale applications. Because facial recognition is not completely accurate, it creates a list of potential matches. A human operator must then look through these potential matches and studies show the operators pick the correct match out of the list only about half the time. This causes the issue of targeting the wrong suspect.

Color Mapping

Source image.   Reference image.

Color mapping is a function that maps (transforms) the colors of one (source) image to the colors of another (target) image. A color mapping may be referred to as the algorithm that results in the mapping function or the algorithm that transforms the image colors. Color mapping is also sometimes called color transfer or, when grayscale images are involved, brightness transfer function (BTF).

Source image color mapped using histogram matching.

Algorithms

There are two types of color mapping algorithms: Those that employ the statistics of the colors of two images, and those that rely on a given pixel correspondence between the images.

An example of an algorithm that employs the statistical properties of the images is histogram matching. This is a classic algorithm for color mapping, suffering from the problem of sensitivity to image content differences. Newer statistic-based algorithms deal with this problem. An example of such algorithm is adjusting the mean and the standard deviation of Lab channels of the two images.

A common algorithm for computing the color mapping when the pixel correspondence is given is building the joint-histogram of the two images and finding the mapping by using dynamic programming based on the joint-histogram values.

When the pixel correspondence is not given and the image contents are different (due to different point of view), the statistics of the image corresponding regions can be used as an input to statistics-based algorithms, such as histogram matching. The corresponding regions can be found by detecting the corresponding features.

Applications

Color mapping can serve two different purposes: one is calibrating the colors of two cameras for further processing using two or more sample images, the second is adjusting the colors of two images for perceptual visual compatibility.

Color calibration is an important pre-processing task in computer vision applications. Many applications simultaneously process two or more images and, therefore, need their colors to be calibrated. Examples of such applications are: Image differencing, registration, object recognition, multi-camera tracking, co-segmentation and stereo reconstruction.

Digital Image Processing

In computer science, digital image processing is the use of computer algorithms to perform image processing on digital images. As a subcategory or field of digital signal processing, digital image processing has many advantages over analog image processing. It allows a much wider range of algorithms to be applied to the input data and can avoid problems such as the build-up of noise and signal distortion during processing. Since images are defined over two dimensions (perhaps more) digital image processing may be modeled in the form of multidimensional systems. The generation and development of digital image processing are mainly affected by three factors: first, the development of computers; second, the development of mathematics (especially the creation and improvement of discrete mathematics theory); third, the demand for a wide range of applications in environment, agriculture, military, industry and medical science has increased.

Tasks

Digital image processing allows the use of much more complex algorithms, and hence, can offer both more sophisticated performance at simple tasks, and the implementation of methods which would be impossible by analog means.

In particular, digital image processing is the only practical technology for:

- Classification,
- Feature extraction,
- Multi-scale signal analysis,
- Pattern recognition,
- Projection.

Some techniques which are used in digital image processing include:

- Anisotropic diffusion,
- Hidden Markov models,
- Image editing,
- Image restoration,
- Independent component analysis,

- Linear filtering,

- Neural networks,

- Partial differential equations,

- Pixelation,

- Point feature matching,

- Principal components analysis,

- Self-organizing maps,

- Wavelets.

Digital Image Transformations

Filtering

Digital filters are used to blur and sharpen digital images. Filtering can be performed by:

- Convolution with specifically designed kernels (filter array) in the spatial domain.

- Masking specific frequency regions in the frequency (Fourier) domain.

The following examples show both methods:

Filter type	Kernel or mask	Example
Original Image	$$\begin{bmatrix} 0 & 0 & 0 \\ 0 & 1 & 0 \\ 0 & 0 & 0 \end{bmatrix}$$	Identity (Original)
Spatial Lowpass	$$\frac{1}{9} \times \begin{bmatrix} 1 & 1 & 1 \\ 1 & 1 & 1 \\ 1 & 1 & 1 \end{bmatrix}$$	3 × 3 Mean Blur

Spatial Highpass	$$\begin{bmatrix} 0 & -1 & 0 \\ -1 & 4 & -1 \\ 0 & -1 & 0 \end{bmatrix}$$	Laplacian Edge Detection
Fourier Representation	Pseudo-code: image = checkerboard F = Fourier Transform of image Show Image: log(1+Absolute Value(F))	FFT Representation
Fourier Lowpass	Lowpass Butterworth	FFT Lowpass Filtered
Fourier Highpass	Highpass Butterworth	FFT Highpass Filtered

Image Padding in Fourier Domain Filtering

Images are typically padded before being transformed to the Fourier space, the high-pass filtered images below illustrate the consequences of different padding techniques:

Zero padded	Repeated edge padded
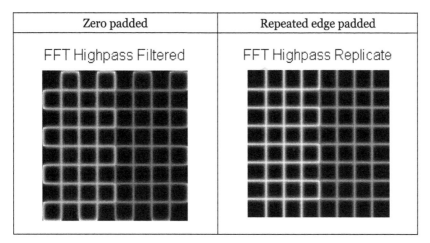	

Notice that the highpass filter shows extra edges when zero padded compared to the repeated edge padding.

Filtering Code Examples

MATLAB example for spatial domain highpass filtering.

```
img=checkerboard(20);          % generate checkerboard

% ********************** SPATIAL DOMAIN **************************

klaplace=[0 -1 0; -1 5 -1; 0 -1 0];     % Laplacian filter kernel

X=conv2(img,klaplace);        % convolve test img with

            % 3x3 Laplacian kernel

figure()

imshow(X,[])           % show Laplacian filtered

title('Laplacian Edge Detection')
```

Affine Transformations

Affine transformations enable basic image transformations including scale, rotate, translate, mirror and shear as is shown in the following examples:

To apply the affine matrix to an image, the image is converted to matrix in which each entry corresponds to the pixel intensity at that location. Then each pixel's location can be represented as a vector indicating the coordinates of that pixel in the image, [x, y], where x and y are the row and column of a pixel in the image matrix. This allows the co-ordinate to be multiplied by an affine-transformation matrix, which gives the position that the pixel value will be copied to in the output image.

Transformation Name	Affine Matrix	Example
Identity	$$\begin{bmatrix} 1 & 0 & 0 \\ 0 & 1 & 0 \\ 0 & 0 & 1 \end{bmatrix}$$	
Reflection	$$\begin{bmatrix} -1 & 0 & 0 \\ 0 & 1 & 0 \\ 0 & 0 & 1 \end{bmatrix}$$	
Scale	$$\begin{bmatrix} c_x = 2 & 0 & 0 \\ 0 & c_y = 1 & 0 \\ 0 & 0 & 1 \end{bmatrix}$$	
Rotate	$$\begin{bmatrix} \cos(\theta) & \sin(\theta) & 0 \\ -\sin(\theta) & \cos(\theta) & 0 \\ 0 & 0 & 1 \end{bmatrix}$$ where $\theta = \dfrac{\pi}{6} = 30°$	
Shear	$$\begin{bmatrix} 1 & c_x = 0.5 & 0 \\ c_y = 0 & 1 & 0 \\ 0 & 0 & 1 \end{bmatrix}$$	

However, to allow transformations that require translation transformations, 3 dimensional homogeneous coordinates are needed. The third dimension is usually set to a non-zero constant, usually 1, so that the new coordinate is [x, y, 1]. This allows the coordinate vector to be multiplied by a 3 by 3 matrix, enabling translation shifts. So the third dimension, which is the constant 1, allows translation.

Because matrix multiplication is associative, multiple affine transformations can be combined into a single affine transformation by multiplying the matrix of each individual transformation in the order that the transformations are done. This results in a single matrix that, when applied to a point vector, gives the same result as all the individual transformations performed on the vector [x, y, 1] in sequence. Thus a sequence of affine transformation matrices can be reduced to a single affine transformation matrix.

For example, 2 dimensional coordinates only allow rotation about the origin (0, 0). But 3 dimensional homogeneous coordinates can be used to first translate any point to (0, 0), then perform the rotation, and lastly translate the origin (0, 0) back to the original point (the opposite of the first translation). These 3 affine transformations can be combined into a single matrix, thus allowing rotation around any point in the image.

Digital Audio

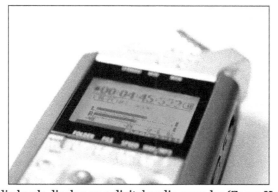
Audio levels display on a digital audio recorder (Zoom H4n).

Digital audio is sound that has been recorded in, or converted into, digital form. In digital audio, the sound wave of the audio signal is encoded as numerical samples in continuous sequence. For example, in CD audio, samples are taken 44100 times per second each with 16 bit sample depth. Digital audio is also the name for the entire technology of sound recording and reproduction using audio signals that have been encoded in digital form. Following significant advances in digital audio technology during the 1970s, it gradually replaced analog audio technology in many areas of audio engineering and telecommunications in the 1990s and 2000s.

In a digital audio system, an analog electrical signal representing the sound is converted with an analog-to-digital converter (ADC) into a digital signal, typically using pulse-code modulation. This digital signal can then be recorded, edited, modified, and copied using computers, audio playback machines, and other digital tools. When the sound engineer wishes to listen to the recording on headphones or loudspeakers (or when a consumer wishes to listen to a digital sound file), a digital-to-analog converter (DAC) performs the reverse process, converting a digital signal back into an analog signal, which is then sent through an audio power amplifier and ultimately to a loudspeaker.

Digital audio systems may include compression, storage, processing, and transmission components. Conversion to a digital format allows convenient manipulation, storage, transmission, and retrieval of an audio signal. Unlike analog audio, in which making copies of a recording results in generation loss and degradation of signal quality, digital audio allows an infinite number of copies to be made without any degradation of signal quality.

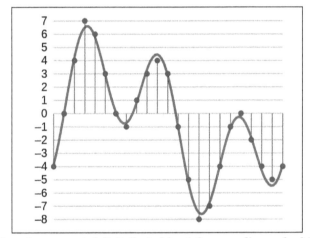

A sound wave, in red, represented digitally, in blue (after sampling and 4-bit quantization).

Digital audio technologies are used in the recording, manipulation, mass-production, and distribution of sound, including recordings of songs, instrumental pieces, podcasts, sound effects, and other sounds. Modern online music distribution depends on digital recording and data compression. The availability of music as data files, rather than as physical objects, has significantly reduced the costs of distribution. Before digital audio, the music industry distributed and sold music by selling physical copies in the form of records and cassette tapes. With digital-audio and online distribution systems such as iTunes, companies sell digital sound files to consumers, which the consumer receives over the Internet.

An analog audio system converts physical waveforms of sound into electrical representations of those waveforms by use of a transducer, such as a microphone. The sounds are then stored on an analog medium such as magnetic tape, or transmitted through an analog medium such as a telephone line or radio. The process is reversed for reproduction: the electrical audio signal is amplified and then converted back into physical waveforms via a loudspeaker. Analog audio retains its fundamental wave-like characteristics throughout its storage, transformation, duplication, and amplification.

Analog audio signals are susceptible to noise and distortion, due to the innate characteristics of electronic circuits and associated devices. Disturbances in a digital system do not result in error unless the disturbance is so large as to result in a symbol being misinterpreted as another symbol or disturb the sequence of symbols. It is therefore generally possible to have an entirely error-free digital audio system in which no noise or distortion is introduced between conversion to digital format, and conversion back to analog.

A digital audio signal may optionally be encoded for correction of any errors that might occur in the storage or transmission of the signal. This technique, known as channel coding, is essential for broadcast or recorded digital systems to maintain bit accuracy. Eight-to-fourteen modulation is a channel code used in the audio compact disc (CD).

Conversion Process

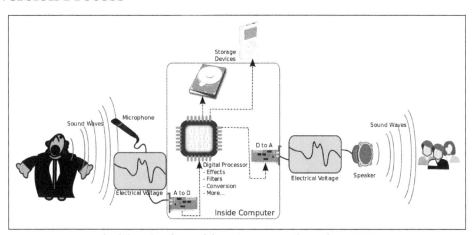

The lifecycle of sound from its source, through an ADC,
digital processing, a DAC, and finally as sound again.

A digital audio system starts with an ADC that converts an analog signal to a digital signal. The ADC runs at a specified sampling rate and converts at a known bit resolution. CD audio, for example, has a sampling rate of 44.1 kHz (44,100 samples per second), and has 16-bit resolution for each stereo channel. Analog signals that have not already been bandlimited must be passed through an anti-aliasing filter before conversion, to prevent the aliasing distortion that is caused by audio signals with frequencies higher than the Nyquist frequency (half the sampling rate).

A digital audio signal may be stored or transmitted. Digital audio can be stored on a CD, a digital audio player, a hard drive, a USB flash drive, or any other digital data storage device. The digital signal may be altered through digital signal processing, where it may be filtered or have effects applied. Sample-rate conversion including upsampling and downsampling may be used to conform signals that have been encoded with a different sampling rate to a common sampling rate prior to processing. Audio data compression techniques, such as MP3, Advanced Audio Coding, Ogg Vorbis, or FLAC, are commonly employed to reduce the file size. Digital audio can be carried over digital audio interfaces such as AES3 or MADI. Digital audio can be carried over a network using audio over Ethernet, audio over IP or other streaming media standards and systems.

For playback, digital audio must be converted back to an analog signal with a DAC which may use oversampling.

Audio Coding Format

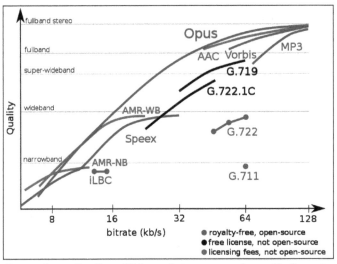

Comparison of coding efficiency between popular audio formats.

An audio coding format (or sometimes audio compression format) is a content representation format for storage or transmission of digital audio (such as in digital television, digital radio and in audio and video files). Examples of audio coding formats include MP3, AAC, Vorbis, FLAC, and Opus. A specific software or hardware implementation capable of audio compression and decompression to/from a specific audio coding format is called an audio codec; an example of an audio codec is LAME, which is one of several different codecs which implements encoding and decoding audio in the MP3 audio coding format in software.

Some audio coding formats are documented by a detailed technical specification document known as an audio coding specification. Some such specifications are written and approved by standardization organizations as technical standards, and are thus known as an audio coding standard. The term "standard" is also sometimes used for de facto standards as well as formal standards.

Audio content encoded in a particular audio coding format is normally encapsulated within a container format. As such, the user normally doesn't have a raw AAC file, but instead has a .m4a audio file, which is a MPEG-4 Part 14 container containing AAC-encoded audio. The container also contains metadata such as title and other tags, and perhaps an index for fast seeking. A notable exception is MP3 files, which are raw audio coding without a container format. De facto standards for adding metadata tags such as title and artist to MP3s, such as ID3, are hacks which work by appending the tags to the MP3, and then relying on the MP3 player to recognize the chunk as malformed audio coding and therefore skip it. In video files with audio, the encoded audio content is bundled with video (in a video coding format) inside a multimedia container format.

An audio coding format does not dictate all algorithms used by a codec implementing the format. An important part of how lossy audio compression works is by removing data in ways humans cannot hear, according to a psychoacoustic model; the implementer of an encoder has some freedom of choice in which data to remove (according to their psychoacoustic model).

Lossless, Lossy and Uncompressed Audio Coding Formats

A lossless audio coding format reduces the total data needed to represent a sound but can be de-coded to its original, uncompressed form. A lossy audio coding format additionally reduces the bit resolution of the sound on top of compression, which results in far less data at the cost of irretrievably lost information.

Consumer audio is most often compressed using lossy audio codecs as the smaller size is far more convenient for distribution. The most widely used audio coding formats are MP3 and Advanced Audio Coding (AAC), both of which are lossy formats based on modified discrete cosine transform (MDCT) and perceptual coding algorithms.

Lossless audio coding formats such as FLAC and Apple Lossless are sometimes available, though at the cost of larger files.

Uncompressed audio formats, such as pulse-code modulation (PCM, or .wav), are also sometimes used. PCM was the standard format for Compact Disc Digital Audio (CDDA), before lossy compression eventually became the standard after the introduction of MP3.

Solidyne 922: The world's first commercial audio bit compression sound card for PC.

In 1950, Bell Labs filed the patent on differential pulse-code modulation (DPCM). Adaptive DPCM (ADPCM) was introduced by P. Cummiskey, Nikil S. Jayant and James L. Flanagan at Bell Labs in 1973.

Perceptual coding was first used for speech coding compression, with linear predictive coding (LPC). Initial concepts for LPC date back to the work of Fumitada Itakura (Nagoya University) and Shuzo Saito (Nippon Telegraph and Telephone) in 1966. During the 1970s, Bishnu S. Atal and Manfred R. Schroeder at Bell Labs developed a form of LPC called adaptive predictive coding (APC), a perceptual coding algorithm that exploited the masking properties of the human ear, followed in the early 1980s with the code-excited linear prediction (CELP) algorithm which achieved a significant compression ratio for its time. Perceptual coding is used by modern audio compression formats such as MP3 and AAC.

Discrete cosine transform (DCT), developed by Nasir Ahmed, T. Natarajan and K. R. Rao in 1974, provided the basis for the modified discrete cosine transform (MDCT) used by modern audio compression formats such as MP3 and AAC. MDCT was proposed by J. P. Princen, A. W. Johnson and A. B. Bradley in 1987, following earlier work by Princen and Bradley in 1986. The MDCT is used by modern audio compression formats such as Dolby Digital, MP3, and Advanced Audio Coding (AAC).

Digital Recording

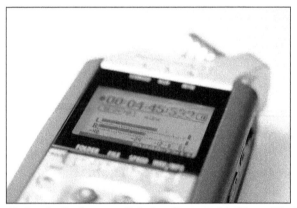

Audio levels display on a digital audio recorder (Zoom H4n).

In digital recording, audio signals picked up by a microphone or other transducer or video signals picked up by a camera or similar device are converted into a stream of discrete numbers, representing the changes over time in air pressure for audio, and chroma and luminance values for video, then recorded to a storage device. To play back a digital sound recording, the numbers are retrieved and converted back into their original analog waveforms so that they can be heard through a loudspeaker. To play back a digital video recording, the numbers are retrieved and converted back into their original analog waveforms so that they can be viewed on a video monitor, television or other display.

Process

Recording

- The analog signal is transmitted from the input device to an analog-to-digital converter (ADC).

- The ADC converts this signal by repeatedly measuring the momentary level of the analog (audio) wave and then assigning a binary number with a given quantity of bits (word length) to each measuring point.

- The frequency at which the ADC measures the level of the analog wave is called the sample rate or sampling rate.

- A digital audio sample with a given word length represents the audio level at one moment.

- The longer the word length the more precise the representation of the original audio wave level.

- The higher the sampling rate the higher the upper audio frequency of the digitized audio signal.

- The ADC outputs a sequence of digital audio samples that make up a continuous stream of 0s and 1s.

- These binary numbers are stored on recording media such as a hard drive, optical drive or in solid state memory.

Playback

- The sequence of numbers is transmitted from storage into a digital-to-analog converter (DAC), which converts the numbers back to an analog signal by sticking together the level information stored in each digital sample, thus rebuilding the original analog wave form.

- This signal is amplified and transmitted to the loudspeakers or video screen.

Recording of Bits

Even after getting the signal converted to bits, it is still difficult to record; the hardest part is finding a scheme that can record the bits fast enough to keep up with the signal. For example, to record two channels of audio at 44.1 kHz sample rate with a 16 bit word size, the recording software has to handle 1,411,200 bits per second.

Techniques to Record to Commercial Media

For digital cassettes, the read/write head moves as well as the tape in order to maintain a high enough speed to keep the bits at a manageable size.

For optical disc recording technologies such as CDs or DVDs, a laser is used to burn microscopic holes into the dye layer of the medium. A weaker laser is used to read these signals. This works because the metallic substrate of the disc is reflective, and the unburned dye prevents reflection while the holes in the dye permit it, allowing digital data to be represented.

Concerns with Digital Audio Recording

Word Size

The number of bits used to represent a sampled audio wave (the word size) directly affects the resulting noise in a recording after intentionally added dither, or the distortion of an undithered signal.

The number of possible voltage levels at the output is simply the number of levels that may be represented by the largest possible digital number (the number 2 raised to the power of the number of bits in each sample). There are no "in between" values allowed. If there are more bits in each sample the waveform is more accurately traced, because each additional bit doubles the number of possible values. The distortion is roughly the percentage that the least significant bit represents out of the average value. Distortion (as a percentage) in digital systems increases as signal levels decrease, which is the opposite of the behavior of analog systems.

Sample Rate

The sample rate is just as important a consideration as the word size. If the sample rate is too low, the sampled signal cannot be reconstructed to the original sound signal.

To overcome aliasing, the sound signal (or other signal) must be sampled at a rate at least twice that of the highest frequency component in the signal. This is known as the Nyquist–Shannon sampling theorem.

For recording music-quality audio the following PCM sampling rates are the most common: 44.1, 48, 88.2, 96, 176.4, and 192 kHz.

When making a recording, experienced audio recording and mastering engineers will normally do a master recording at a higher sampling rate (i.e. 88.2, 96, 176.4 or 192 kHz) and then do any editing or mixing at that same higher frequency. High resolution PCM recordings have been released on DVD-Audio (also known as DVD-A), DAD (Digital Audio Disc—which utilizes the stereo PCM audio tracks of a regular DVD), DualDisc (utilizing the DVD-Audio layer), or Blu-ray (Profile 3.0 is the Blu-ray audio standard, although as of mid-2009 it is unclear whether this will ever really be used as an audio-only format). In addition it is nowadays also possible and common to release a high resolution recording directly as either an uncompressed WAV or lossless compressed FLAC file (usually at 24 bits) without down-converting it.

However, if a CD (the CD Red Book standard is 44.1 kHz 16 bit) is to be made from a recording, then doing the initial recording using a sampling rate of 44.1 kHz is obviously one approach. Another approach that is usually preferred is to use a higher sample rate and then downsample to the final format's sample rate. This is usually done as part of the mastering process. One advantage to the latter approach is that way a high resolution recording can be released, as well as a CD and/or lossy compressed file such as mp3—all from the same master recording.

Beginning in the 1980s, music that was recorded, mixed and mastered digitally was often labelled using the SPARS code to describe which processes were analog and which were digital.

Error Rectification

One of the advantages of digital recording over analog recording is its resistance to errors.

Advancements of Digital Audio in Technology

Digital Audio Broadcasting

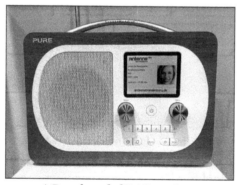

A Pure-branded DAB receiver.

Digital Audio Broadcasting (DAB) is a digital radio standard for broadcasting digital audio radio services, used in many countries around the world, though not North America where HD Radio is used instead.

The DAB standard was initiated as a European research project in the 1980s. The Norwegian Broadcasting Corporation (NRK) launched the first DAB channel in the world on 1 June 1995 (NRK Klassisk), and the BBC and Swedish Radio (SR) launched their first DAB digital radio broadcasts in 27 September 1995. DAB receivers have been available in many countries since the end of the 1990s.

DAB is generally more efficient in its use of spectrum than analogue FM radio, and thus can offer more radio services for the same given bandwidth. However the sound quality can be noticeably inferior if the bit-rate allocated to each audio program is not sufficient. DAB is more robust with regard to noise and multipath fading for mobile listening, although DAB reception quality degrades rapidly when the signal strength falls below a critical threshold, whereas FM reception quality degrades slowly with the decreasing signal, providing effective coverage over a larger area.

The original version of DAB used the MP2 audio codec. An upgraded version of the system was released in February 2007, called DAB+, which uses the modified discrete cosine transform (MDCT) based HE-AAC v2 (AAC+) audio codec. DAB is not forward compatible with DAB+, which means that DAB-only receivers are not able to receive DAB+ broadcasts. However, broadcasters can mix DAB and DAB+ programs inside the same transmission and so make a progressive transition to DAB+. DAB+ is approximately twice as efficient as DAB, and more robust.

In spectrum management, the bands that are allocated for public DAB services, are abbreviated with T-DAB, where the "T" stands for terrestrial.

As of 2018, 41 countries are running DAB services. The majority of these services are using DAB+, with only Ireland, UK, New Zealand, Romania and Brunei still using a significant number of DAB services. See Countries using DAB/DMB. In many countries, it is expected that existing FM services will switch over to DAB+. Norway is the first country to implement a national FM radio analog switchoff, in 2017; however that only applied to national broadcasters, not local ones.

Technology

Bands and Modes

DAB uses a wide-bandwidth broadcast technology and typically spectra have been allocated for it in Band III (174–240 MHz) and L band (1.452–1.492 GHz), although the scheme allows for operation between 30 and 300 MHz. The US military has reserved L-Band in the USA only, blocking its use for other purposes in America, and the United States has reached an agreement with Canada to restrict L-Band DAB to terrestrial broadcast to avoid interference.

DAB historically had a number of country specific transmission modes (I, II, III and IV).

- Mode I for Band III, Earth.

- Mode II for L-Band, Earth and satellite.

- Mode III for frequencies below 3 GHz, Earth and satellite.

- Mode IV for L-Band, Earth and satellite.

In January 2017, an updated DAB specification (2.1.1) removed Modes II, III and IV, leaving only Mode I.

Protocol Stack

From an OSI model protocol stack viewpoint, the technologies used on DAB inhabit the following layers: The audio codec inhabits the presentation layer. Below that is the data link layer, in charge of statistical time division multiplexing and frame synchronization. Finally, the physical layer contains the error-correction coding, OFDM modulation, and dealing with the over-the-air transmission and reception of data.

Audio Codec

DAB uses the MPEG-1 Audio Layer II audio codec, which is often referred to as MP2 because of the ubiquitous MP3 (MPEG-1 Audio Layer III).

The newer DAB+ standard adopted the HE-AAC version 2 audio codec, commonly known as 'AAC+' or 'aacPlus'. AAC+ uses a modified discrete cosine transform (MDCT) algorithm, and is approximately three times more efficient than MP2, which means that broadcasters using DAB+ are able to provide far higher audio quality or far more stations than they could with DAB, or a combination of both higher audio quality and more stations.

One of the most important decisions regarding the design of a digital radio broadcasting system is the choice of which audio codec to use, because the efficiency of the audio codec determines how many radio stations can be carried on a fixed capacity multiplex at a given level of audio quality.

Error-correction Coding

Error-correction coding (ECC) is an important technology for a digital communication system because it determines how robust the reception will be for a given signal strength – stronger ECC will provide more robust reception than a weaker form.

The old version of DAB uses punctured convolutional coding for its ECC. The coding scheme uses unequal error protection (UEP), which means that parts of the audio bitstream that are more susceptible to errors causing audible disturbances are provided with more protection (i.e. a lower code rate) and vice versa. However, the UEP scheme used on DAB results in there being a grey area in between the user experiencing good reception quality and no reception at all, as opposed to the situation with most other wireless digital communication systems that have a sharp "digital cliff", where the signal rapidly becomes unusable if the signal strength drops below a certain threshold. When DAB listeners receive a signal in this intermediate strength area they experience a "burbling" sound which interrupts the playback of the audio.

The DAB+ standard incorporates Reed-Solomon ECC as an "inner layer" of coding that is placed around the byte interleaved audio frame but inside the "outer layer" of convolutional coding used by the original DAB system, although on DAB+ the convolutional coding uses equal error protection (EEP) rather than UEP since each bit is equally important in DAB+. This combination of Reed-Solomon coding as the inner layer of coding, followed by an outer layer of convolutional coding – so-called "concatenated coding" – became a popular ECC scheme in the 1990s, and NASA adopted it for its deep-space missions. One slight difference between the concatenated coding used by the DAB+ system and that used on most other systems is that it uses a rectangular byte interleaver rather than Forney interleaving in order to provide a greater interleaver depth, which increases the distance over which error bursts will be spread out in the bit-stream, which in turn will allow the Reed-Solomon error decoder to correct a higher proportion of errors.

The ECC used on DAB+ is far stronger than is used on DAB, which, with all else being equal (i.e., if the transmission powers remained the same), would translate into people who currently experience reception difficulties on DAB receiving a much more robust signal with DAB+ transmissions. It also has a far steeper "digital cliff", and listening tests have shown that people prefer this when the signal strength is low compared to the shallower digital cliff on DAB.

Modulation

Immunity to fading and inter-symbol interference (caused by multipath propagation) is achieved without equalization by means of the OFDM and DQPSK modulation techniques.

Using values for Transmission Mode I (TM I), the OFDM modulation consists of 1,536 subcarriers that are transmitted in parallel. The useful part of the OFDM symbol period is 1 millisecond, which results in the OFDM subcarriers each having a bandwidth of 1 kHz due to the inverse relationship between these two parameters, and the overall OFDM channel bandwidth is 1,537 kHz. The OFDM guard interval for TM I is 246 microseconds, which means that the overall OFDM symbol duration is 1.246 milliseconds. The guard interval duration also determines the maximum separation between transmitters that are part of the same single-frequency network (SFN), which is approximately 74 km for TM I.

Single-frequency Networks

OFDM allows the use of single-frequency networks (SFN), which means that a network of transmitters can provide coverage to a large area – up to the size of a country – where all transmitters use the same transmission frequency. Transmitters that are part of an SFN need to be very accurately synchronised with other transmitters in the network, which requires the transmitters to use very accurate clocks.

When a receiver receives a signal that has been transmitted from the different transmitters that are part of an SFN, the signals from the different transmitters will typically have different delays, but to OFDM they will appear to simply be different multipaths of the same signal. Reception difficulties can arise, however, when the relative delay of multipaths exceeds the OFDM guard interval duration, and there are frequent reports of reception difficulties due to this issue when there is a lift, such as when there's high pressure, due to signals travelling farther than usual, and thus the signals are likely to arrive with a relative delay that is greater than the OFDM guard interval.

Low power gap-filler transmitters can be added to an SFN as and when desired in order to improve reception quality, although the way SFNs have been implemented in the UK up to now they have tended to consist of higher power transmitters being installed at main transmitter sites in order to keep costs down.

Bit Rates

An ensemble has a maximum bit rate that can be carried, but this depends on which error protection level is used. However, all DAB multiplexes can carry a total of 864 "capacity units". The number of capacity units, or CU, that a certain bit-rate level requires depends on the amount of error correction added to the transmission. In the UK, most services transmit using 'protection level three', which provides an average ECC code rate of approximately ½, equating to a maximum bit rate per multiplex of 1,184 kbit/s.

Services and Ensembles

Various different services are embedded into one ensemble (which is also typically called a multiplex). These services can include:

- Primary services, like main radio stations.

- Secondary services, like additional sports commentaries.

- Data services.

  - Electronic Programme Guide (EPG).

  - Collections of HTML pages and digital images (known as 'broadcast websites').

  - Slideshows, which may be synchronised with audio broadcasts. For example, a police appeal could be broadcast with the e-fit of a suspect or CCTV footage.

  - Video.

  - Java platform applications.

  - IP tunnelling.

  - Other raw data.

DAB

The term "DAB" most commonly refers both to a specific DAB standard using the MP2 audio codec, but can sometimes refer to a whole family of DAB-related standards, such as DAB+, DMB and DAB-IP.

DAB+

WorldDAB, the organisation in charge of the DAB standards, announced DAB+, a major upgrade to the DAB standard in 2006, when the HE-AAC v2 audio codec (also known as eAAC+) was adopted. AAC+ uses a modified discrete cosine transform (MDCT) algorithm. The new standard, which is called DAB+, has also adopted the MPEG Surround audio format and stronger error correction coding in the form of Reed-Solomon coding. DAB+ has been standardised as European Telecommunications Standards Institute (ETSI) TS 102 563.

As DAB is not forward compatible with DAB+, older DAB receivers cannot receive DAB+ broadcasts. However, DAB receivers that will be able to receive the new DAB+ standard via a firmware upgrade went on sale in July 2007. If a receiver is DAB+ compatible, there will be a sign on the product packaging.

DAB+ broadcasts have launched in several countries like Australia, Czech Republic, Denmark, Germany, Hong Kong (now terminated), Italy, Malta, Norway, Poland, Switzerland, Belgium (October 2017), the United Kingdom and the Netherlands. Malta was the first country to launch DAB+ in Europe. Several other countries are also expected to launch DAB+ broadcasts over the next few years, such as Austria, Hungary, Thailand, Vietnam and Indonesia. South Africa began a DAB+ technical pilot in November 2014 on channel 13F in Band 3. If DAB+ stations launch in established DAB countries, they can transmit alongside existing DAB stations that use the older MPEG-1 Audio Layer II audio format, and most existing DAB stations are expected to continue broadcasting until the vast majority of receivers support DAB+.

Ofcom in the UK published a consultation for a new national multiplex containing a mix of DAB and DAB+ services, with the intention of moving all services to DAB+ in the long term. In February 2016, the new national network Sound Digital launched with three DAB+ stations.

DMB

Digital multimedia broadcasting (DMB) and DAB-IP are both suitable for mobile radio and TV because they support MPEG 4 AVC and WMV9 respectively as video codecs. However, a DMB video subchannel can easily be added to any DAB transmission, as it was designed to be carried on a DAB subchannel. DMB broadcasts in Korea carry conventional MPEG 1 Layer II DAB audio services alongside their DMB video services.

Countries using DAB

More than 40 countries provide DAB, DAB+ or DMB broadcasts, either as a permanent technology or as test transmissions.

DAB is not used in the United States. The United States' FCC argues that stations on such a national DAB Band would be more difficult to control from signal interference than AM/FM/TV because of the continent's large land mass; and corporations who sell DAB radio in North America could find it more expensive to market these types of radio to consumers. There are no DAB radio stations that operate in North America as of 2018.

DAB and AM/FM Compared

Traditionally, radio programmes were broadcast on different frequencies via AM and FM, and the radio had to be tuned into each frequency as needed. This used up a comparatively large amount of spectrum for a relatively small number of stations, limiting listening choice. DAB is a digital radio broadcasting system that, through the application of multiplexing and compression, combines multiple audio streams onto a relatively narrow band centred on a single broadcast frequency called a DAB ensemble.

Within an overall target bit rate for the DAB ensemble, individual stations can be allocated different bit rates. The number of channels within a DAB ensemble can be increased by lowering average bit rates, but at the expense of the quality of streams. Error correction under the DAB standard makes the signal more robust but reduces the total bit rate available for streams.

FM HD Radio versus DAB

Some countries have implemented Eureka-147 digital audio broadcasting (DAB). DAB broadcasts a single multiplex that is approximately 1,500 kilohertz wide ($\approx$1,000 kilobits per second). That multiplex is then subdivided into multiple digital streams of between 9 and 12 programs. In contrast, FM HD Radio adds its digital carriers to the traditional 270 kilohertz-wide analog channels, with capability of up to 300 kbit/s per station (pure digital mode). The full bandwidth of the hybrid mode approaches 400 kHz.

The first generation DAB uses the MPEG-1 Audio Layer II (MP2) audio codec, which has less efficient compression than newer codecs. The typical bitrate for DAB stereo programs is only 128 kbit/s or less, and as a result, most radio stations on DAB have a lower sound quality than FM, prompting a number of complaints among the audiophile community. As with DAB+ or T-DMB in Europe, FM HD Radio uses a codec based upon the MPEG-4 HE-AAC standard.

HD Radio is a proprietary system from the company IBiquity. DAB is an open standard deposited at ETSI.

Use of Frequency Spectrum and Transmitter Sites

DAB can give substantially higher spectral efficiency, measured in programmes per MHz and per transmitter site, than analogue systems. In many places, this has led to an increase in the number of stations available to listeners, especially outside of the major urban areas. This can be further improved with DAB+ which uses a much more efficient codec, allowing a lower bitrate per channel with little to no loss in quality. If some stations transmit in mono, their bitrate can be reduced compared to stereo broadcasts, further improving the efficiency.

Numerical example: Analog FM requires 0.2 MHz per programme. The frequency reuse factor in most countries is approximately 15 for stereo transmissions (with lesser factors for mono FM networks), meaning (in the case of stereo FM) that only one out of 15 transmitter sites can use the same channel frequency without problems with co-channel interference, i.e. crosstalk. Assuming a total availability of 102 FM channels at a bandwidth of 0.2MHz over the Band II spectrum of 87.5 to 108.0 MHz, an average of 102/15 = 6.8 radio channels are possible on each transmitter site (plus lowerpower local transmitters causing less interference). This results in a system spectral efficiency of $1/15/(0.2 \text{ MHz}) = 0.30$ programmes/transmitter/MHz. DAB with 192 kbit/s codec requires 1.536 MHz * 192 kbit/s/1,136 kbit/s = 0.26 MHz per audio programme. The frequency reuse factor for local programmes and multifrequency broad-casting networks (MFN) is typically 4 or 5, resulting in 1/4/ (0.26 MHz) = 0.96 programmes/transmitter/MHz. This is 3.2 times as efficient as analog FM for local stations. For single frequency network (SFN) transmission, for example of national programmes, the channel reuse factor is 1, resulting in 1/1/0.25 MHz = 3.85 programmes/transmitter/MHz, which is 12.7 times as efficient as FM for national and regional networks.

Note the above capacity improvement may not always be achieved at the L-band frequencies, since these are more sensitive to obstacles than the FM band frequencies, and may cause shadow fading for hilly terrain and for indoor communication. The number of transmitter sites or the transmission power required for full coverage of a country may be rather high at these frequencies, to avoid the system becoming noise limited rather than limited by co-channel interference.

Sound Quality

The original objectives of converting to digital transmission were to enable higher fidelity, more stations and more resistance to noise, co-channel interference and multipath than in analogue FM radio. However, many countries in implementing DAB on stereo radio stations use compression to such a degree that it produces lower sound quality than that received from FM broadcasts. This is because of the bit rate levels being too low for the MPEG Layer 2 audio codec to provide high fidelity audio quality.

Benefits of DAB

Improved Features for Users

DAB devices perform band-scans over the entire frequency range, presenting all stations from a single list for the user to select from.

DAB can carry "radiotext" (in DAB terminology, Dynamic Label Segment, or DLS) from the station giving real-time information such as song titles, music type and news or traffic updates, of up to 128 characters in length. This is similar to a feature of FM RDS, which enables a radiotext of up to 64 characters.

The DAB transmission contains a local time of day and so a device may use this to automatically correct its internal clock when travelling between time zones and when changing to or from Daylight Saving.

More Stations

DAB is not more bandwidth efficient than analogue measured in programmes per MHz of a specific transmitter (the so-called link spectral efficiency), but it is less susceptible to co-channel interference (cross talk), which makes it possible to reduce the reuse distance, i.e., use the same radio frequency channel more densely. The system spectral efficiency (the average number of radio programmes per MHz and transmitter) is a factor three more efficient than analogue FM for local radio stations. For national and regional radio networks, the efficiency is improved by more than an order of magnitude due to the use of SFNs. In that case, adjacent transmitters use the same frequency.

In certain areas – particularly rural areas – the introduction of DAB gives radio listeners a greater choice of radio stations. For instance, in Southern Norway, radio listeners experienced an increase in available stations from 6 to 21 when DAB was introduced in November 2006.

Reception Quality

The DAB standard integrates features to reduce the negative consequences of multipath fading and signal noise, which afflict existing analogue systems.

Also, as DAB transmits digital audio, there is no hiss with a weak signal, which can happen on FM. However, radios in the fringe of a DAB signal can experience a "bubbling mud" sound interrupting the audio or the audio cutting out altogether.

Due to sensitivity to doppler shift in combination with multipath propagation, DAB reception range (but not audio quality) is reduced when travelling speeds of more than 120 to 200 km/h, depending on carrier frequency.

Less Unlicensed "Pirate" Station Interference

The specialised nature, limited spectrum and higher cost of DAB broadcasting equipment provides barriers to unlicensed ("pirate") stations broadcasting on DAB. In cities such as London with large numbers of unlicensed radio stations broadcasting on FM, this means that some stations can be reliably received via DAB in areas where they are regularly difficult or impossible to receive on FM because of interference from unlicensed radio stations.

Variable Bandwidth

Mono talk radio, news and weather channels and other non-music programs need significantly less bandwidth than a typical music radio station, which allows DAB to carry these programmes at lower bit rates, leaving more bandwidth to be used for other programs.

However, this led to the situation where some stations are being broadcast in mono.

Transmission Costs

DAB transmitters are inevitably more expensive than their FM counterparts. DAB uses higher frequencies than FM and therefore there may be a need to compensate with more transmitters to achieve the same coverage as a single FM transmitter. DAB is commonly transmitted by a different company from the broadcaster who then sells the capacity to a number of radio stations. This shared cost can work out cheaper than operating an individual FM transmitter.

This efficiency originates from the ability a DAB network has in broadcasting more channels per transmitter/network. One network can broadcast 6–10 channels (with MP2 audio codec) or 10–18 channels (with HE AAC codec). Hence, it is thought that the replacement of FM-radios and FM-transmitters with new DAB-radios and DAB-transmitters will not cost any more compared with new FM facilities. It is also argued that the power consumption will be lower for stations transmitted on a single DAB multiplex compared with individual analog transmitters.

Once applied, one operator has claimed that DAB transmission is as low as one-nineteenth of the cost of FM transmission.

Disadvantages of DAB

Reception Quality

The reception quality during the early stage of deployment of DAB was poor even for people who live well within the coverage area. The reason for this is that DAB uses weak error correction coding, so that when there are a lot of errors with the received data not enough of the errors can be corrected and a "bubbling mud" sound occurs. In some cases a complete loss of signal can happen. This situation has been improved upon in the newer DAB+ version that uses stronger error correction coding and as additional transmitters are built.

As with other digital systems, when the signal is weak or suffers severe interference, it will not work at all. DAB reception may also be a problem for receivers when the wanted signal is adjacent to a stronger one. This was a particular issue for early and low cost receivers.

Audio Quality

A common complaint by listeners is that broadcasters 'squeeze in' more stations per ensemble than recommended by:

- Minimizing the bit-rate, to the lowest level of sound-quality that listeners are willing to tolerate, such as 112 kbit/s for stereo and even 48 kbit/s for mono speech radio (LBC 1152 and the Voice of Russia are examples).

- Having few digital channels broadcasting in stereo.

Signal Delay

The nature of a single-frequency network (SFN) is such that the transmitters in a network must broadcast the same signal at the same time. To achieve synchronization, the broadcaster must counter any differences in propagation time incurred by the different methods and distances involved in carrying the signal from the multiplexer to the different transmitters. This is done by applying a delay to the incoming signal at the transmitter based on a timestamp generated at the multiplexer, created taking into account the maximum likely propagation time, with a generous added margin for safety. Delays in the audio encoder and the receiver due to digital processing (e.g. deinterleaving) add to the overall delay perceived by the listener. The signal is delayed, usually by around 1 to 4 seconds and can be considerably longer for DAB+. This has disadvantages:

- DAB radios are out of step with live events, so the experience of listening to live commentaries on events being watched is impaired;

- Listeners using a combination of analogue (AM or FM) and DAB radios (e.g. in different rooms of a house) will hear a mixture when both receivers are within earshot.

Time signals, on the contrary, are not a problem in a well-defined network with a fixed delay. The DAB multiplexer adds the proper offset to the distributed time information. The time information is also independent from the (possibly varying) audio decoding delay in receivers since the time is not embedded inside the audio frames. This means that built in clocks in receivers can be precisely correct.

Transmission Costs

DAB can provide savings for networks of several stations. The original development of DAB was driven by national network operators with a number of channels to transmit from multiple sites. However, for individual stations such as small community or local stations which traditionally operate their own FM transmitter on their own building the cost of DAB transmission will be much higher than analog. Operating a DAB transmitter for a single station is not an efficient use of spectrum or power. With that said, this can be solved to some degree by combining multiple local stations in one DAB/DAB+ mux, similar to what is done on DVB-T/DVB-T2 with local TV stations.

Coverage

Although FM coverage still exceeds DAB coverage in most countries implementing any kind of DAB services, a number of countries moving to digital switchover have undergone significant DAB network rollouts.

As of 2019, the following coverages were given by WorldDAB:

Country	Coverage (% of population)
Norway	99.7
Switzerland	99.5
Denmark	98
UK	97.3
Germany	97
Belgium	95
Netherlands	95
Italy	84
Czech Republic	73
Australia	65
Sweden	41.8
France	21.3
Spain	20

Compatibility

In 2006 tests began using the much improved HE-AAC codec for DAB+. Hardly any of the receivers made before 2008 support the newer codec, however, making them partially obsolete once DAB+ broadcasts begin and completely obsolete once all MP2 encoded stations are gone. Most new receivers are both DAB and DAB+ compatible; however, the issue is exacerbated by some manufacturers disabling the DAB+ features on otherwise compatible radios to save on licensing fees when sold in countries without current DAB+ broadcasts.

Power Requirements

Portable DAB/DAB+ and FM receiver, circa 2016. This unit requires
two "AA" size batteries. (Headphones not shown).

As DAB requires digital signal processing techniques to convert from the received digitally encoded signal to the analogue audio content, the complexity of the electronic circuitry required to do this is higher. This translates into needing more power to effect this conversion than compared to an analogue FM to audio conversion, meaning that portable receiving equipment will have a much shorter battery life, and require higher power (and hence more bulk). This means that they use more energy than analogue Band II VHF receivers. However, thanks to increased integration (radio-on-chip), DAB receiver power usage has been reduced dramatically, making portable receivers far more usable.

Digital Radio Mondiale

Digital Radio Mondiale (DRM; mondiale being Italian and French for "worldwide") is a set of digital audio broadcasting technologies designed to work over the bands currently used for analogue radio broadcasting including AM broadcasting, particularly shortwave, and FM broadcasting. DRM is more spectrally efficient than AM and FM, allowing more stations, at higher quality, into a given amount of bandwidth, using various MPEG-4 audio coding formats.

Digital Radio Mondiale is also the name of the international non-profit consortium that has designed the platform and is now promoting its introduction. Radio France Internationale, TéléDiffusion de France, BBC World Service, Deutsche Welle, Voice of America, Telefunken (now Transradio) and Thomcast (now Ampegon) took part at the formation of the DRM consortium.

The principle of DRM is that bandwidth is the limited element, and computer processing power is cheap; modern CPU-intensive audio compression techniques enable more efficient use of available bandwidth, at the expense of processing resources.

Features

DRM can deliver up to FM-comparable sound quality on frequencies below 30 MHz (long wave, medium wave and short wave), which allow for very-long-distance signal propagation. The modes for these lower frequencies are often collectively known under the term "DRM30". In the VHF bands, the term "DRM+" is used. DRM+ is able to use available broadcast spectra between 30 and 300 MHz; generally this means band I (47 to 68 MHz), band II (87.5 to 108 MHz) and band III (174 to 230 MHz). DRM has been designed to be able to re-use portions of existing analogue transmitter facilities such as antennas, feeders, and, especially for DRM30, the transmitters themselves, avoiding major new investment. DRM is robust against the fading and interference which often plague conventional broadcasting in these frequency ranges.

The encoding and decoding can be performed with digital signal processing, so that a cheap embedded computer with a conventional transmitter and receiver can perform the rather complex encoding and decoding.

As a digital medium, DRM can transmit other data besides the audio channels (datacasting) — as well as RDS-type metadata or program-associated data as Digital Audio Broadcasting (DAB) does. DRM services can be operated in many different network configurations, from a traditional AM one-service one-transmitter model to a multi-service (up to four) multi-transmitter model, either as a single-frequency network (SFN) or multi-frequency network (MFN). Hybrid operation, where the same transmitter delivers both analogue and DRM services simultaneously is also possible.

DRM incorporates technology known as Emergency Warning Features that can override other programming and activates radios which are in standby in order to receive emergency broadcasts.

Audio Source Coding

Useful bitrates for DRM30 range from 6.1 kbit/s (Mode D) to 34.8 kbit/s (Mode A) for a 10 kHz bandwidth (±5 kHz around the central frequency). It is possible to achieve bit rates up to 72 kbit/s (Mode A) by using a standard 20 kHz (±10 kHz) wide channel. (For comparison, pure digital HD Radio can broadcast 20 kbit/s using channels 10 kHz wide and up to 60 kbit/s using 20 kHz channels.) Useful bitrate depends also on other parameters, such as:

- Desired robustness to errors (error coding),

- Power needed (modulation scheme),

- Robustness in regard to propagation conditions (multipath propagation, doppler effect), etc.

When DRM was originally designed, it was clear that the most robust modes offered insufficient capacity for the then state-of-the-art audio coding format MPEG-4 HE-AAC (High Efficiency Advanced Audio Coding). Therefore, the standard launched with a choice of three different audio coding systems (source coding) depending on the bitrate:

- MPEG-4 HE-AAC (High Efficiency Advanced Audio Coding). AAC is a perceptual coder suited for voice and music and the High Efficiency is an optional extension for reconstruction of high frequencies (SBR: spectral bandwidth replication) and stereo image (PS: Parametric Stereo). 24 kHz or 12 kHz sampling frequencies can be used for core AAC (no SBR) which correspond respectively to 48 kHz and 24 kHz when using SBR oversampling.

- MPEG-4 CELP which is a parametric coder suited for voice only (vocoder) but that is robust to errors and needs a small bit rate.

- MPEG-4 HVXC which is also a parametric coder for speech programs that uses an even smaller bitrate than CELP.

However, with the development of MPEG-4 xHE-AAC, which is an implementation of MPEG Unified Speech and Audio Coding, the DRM standard was updated and the two speech-only coding formats, CELP and HVXC, were replaced. USAC is designed to combine the properties of a speech and a general audio coding according to bandwidth constraints and so is able to handle all kinds of programme material. Given that there were few CELP and HVXC broadcasts on-air, the decision to drop the speech-only coding formats has passed without issue.

Many broadcasters still use the HE-AAC coding format because it still offers an acceptable audio quality, somewhat comparable to FM broadcast at bitrates above about 15 kbit/s. However, it is anticipated that in future, most broadcasters will adopt xHE-AAC.

Additionally, as of v2.1, the popular Dream software can broadcast using the Opus coding format. Whilst not within the current DRM standard the inclusion of this codec is provided for experimentation. Aside from perceived technical advantages over the MPEG family such as low latency (delay between coding and decoding), the codec is royalty-free and has an open source implementation. It is an alternative to the proprietary MPEG family whose use is permitted at the discretion of the patent holders. Unfortunately it has a substantially lower audio quality than xHE-AAC at low bitrates, which are a key to conserve bandwidth. In fact, at 8 Kbps Opus actually sounds worse than analog shortwave radio. A video showing the comparison between. Equipment manufacturers currently pay royalties for incorporating the MPEG codecs.

Bandwidth

DRM broadcasting can be done using a choice of different bandwidths:

- 4.5 kHz: Gives the ability for the broadcaster to do a simulcast and use the lower-sideband area of a 9 kHz raster channel for AM, with a 4.5 kHz DRM signal occupying the area traditionally taken by the upper-sideband. However the resulting bit rate and audio quality is not good.

- 5 kHz: Gives the ability for the broadcaster to do a simulcast and use the lower-sideband area of a 10 kHz raster channel for AM, with a 5 kHz DRM signal occupying the area traditionally taken by the upper-sideband. However the resulting bit rate and audio quality is marginal (7.1–16.7 kbit/s for 5 kHz). This technique could be used on the shortwave bands throughout the world.

- 9 kHz: Occupies half the standard bandwidth of a region 1 long wave or medium wave broadcast channel.

- 10 kHz: Occupies half the standard bandwidth of a region 2 broadcast channel. could be used to simulcast with analogue audio channel restricted to NRSC5. Occupies a full worldwide short wave broadcast channel (giving 14.8–34.8 kbit/s).

- 18 kHz: Occupies full bandwidth of region 1 long wave or medium wave channels according to the existing frequency plan. This offers better audio quality.

- 20 kHz: Occupies full bandwidth of region 2 or region 3 AM channel according to the existing frequency plan. This offers highest audio quality of the DRM30 standard (giving 30.6–72 kbit/s).

- 100 kHz for DRM+: This bandwidth can be used in band I, II, and III and DRM+ can transmit four different programs in this bandwidth or even one low definition digital video channel.

Modulation

The modulation used for DRM is coded orthogonal frequency division multiplexing (COFDM), where every carrier is modulated with quadrature amplitude modulation (QAM) with a selectable error coding.

The choice of transmission parameters depends on signal robustness wanted and propagation conditions. Transmission signal is affected by noise, interference, multipath wave propagation and Doppler effect.

It is possible to choose among several error coding schemes and several modulation patterns: 64-QAM, 16-QAM and 4-QAM. OFDM modulation has some parameters that must be adjusted depending on propagation conditions. This is the carrier spacing which will determine the robustness against Doppler effect (which cause frequencies offsets, spread: Doppler spread) and OFDM guard interval which determine robustness against multipath propagation (which cause delay offsets, spread: delay spread). The DRM consortium has determined four different profiles corresponding to typical propagation conditions:

- A: Gaussian channel with very little multipath propagation and Doppler effect. This profile is suited for local or regional broadcasting.

- B: multipath propagation channel. This mode is suited for medium range transmission. It is nowadays frequently used.

- C: similar to mode B, but with better robustness to Doppler (more carrier spacing). This mode is suited for long distance transmission.

- D: similar to mode B, but with a resistance to large delay spread and Doppler spread. This case exists with adverse propagation conditions on very long distance transmissions. The useful bit rate for this profile is decreased.

The trade-off between these profiles stands between robustness, resistance in regards to propagation conditions and useful bit rates for the service. This table presents some values depending on these profiles. The larger the carrier spacing, the more the system is resistant to Doppler effect (Doppler spread). The larger the guard interval, the greater the resistance to long multipath propagation errors (delay spread).

The resulting low-bit rate digital information is modulated using COFDM. It can run in simulcast mode by switching between DRM and AM, and it is also prepared for linking to other alternatives (e.g., DAB or FM services).

DRM has been tested successfully on shortwave, mediumwave (with 9 as well as 10 kHz channel spacing) and longwave.

Mode	OFDM carrier spacing (Hz)	Number of carriers				Symbol length (ms)	Guard interval length (ms)	Nb symbols per frame
		9 kHz	10 kHz	18 kHz	20 kHz			
A	41.66	204	228	412	460	26.66	2.66	15
B	46.88	182	206	366	410	26.66	5.33	15
C	68.18	-	138	-	280	20.00	5.33	20
D	107.14	-	88	-	178	16.66	7.33	24

There is also a lower bandwidth two-way communication version of DRM as a replacement for SSB communications on HF - note that it is not compatible with the official DRM specification. It may be possible in some future time for the 4.5 kHz bandwidth DRM version used by the Amateur Radio community to be merged with the existing DRM specification.

The Dream software will receive the commercial versions and also limited transmission mode using the FAAC AAC encoder.

Error Coding

Error coding can be chosen to be more or less robust.

This table shows an example of useful bitrates depending on protection classes:

- OFDM propagation profiles (A or B).
- Carrier modulation (16QAM or 64QAM).
- Channel bandwidth (9 or 10 kHz).

Bitrates, kbit/s								
Protec-tion class	A (9 kHz)	B (9 kHz)	B (10 kHz)		C (10 kHz)		D (10 kHz)	
	64-QAM	16-QAM	16-QAM	64-QAM	16-QAM	64-QAM	16-QAM	64-QAM
0	19.6	7.6	8.7	17.4	6.8	13.7	4.5	9.1
1	23.5	10.2	11.6	20.9	9.1	16.4	6.0	10.9
2	27.8	-	-	24.7	-	19.4	-	12.9
3	30.8	-	-	27.4	-	21.5	-	14.3

The lower the protection class the higher the level of error correction.

DRM+

While the initial DRM standard covered the broadcasting bands below 30 MHz, the DRM consortium voted in March 2005 to begin the process of extending the system to the VHF bands up to 108 MHz.

On 31 August 2009, DRM+ (Mode E) became an official broadcasting standard with the publication of the technical specification by the European Telecommunications Standards Institute; this is effectively a new release of the whole DRM spec with the additional mode permitting operation above 30 MHz up to 174 MHz.

Wider bandwidth channels are used, which allows radio stations to use higher bit rates, thus providing higher audio quality. A 100 kHz DRM+ channel has sufficient capacity to carry one low-definition 0.7 megabit/s wide mobile TV channel: it would be feasible to distribute mobile TV over DRM+ rather than DMB or DVB-H. However, DRM+ (DRM Mode E) as designed and standardized only provides bitrates between 37.2 and 186.3 kbit/s depending on robustness level, using 4-QAM or 16-QAM modulations and 100 kHz bandwidth.

DRM+ bitrates [kbit/s]			
Mode	MSC modulation	Robustness level	Bandwidth 100 kHz
E	4-QAM	Max	37.2
		Min	74.5
	16-QAM	Max	99.4
		Min	186.3

DRM+ has been successfully tested in all the VHF bands, and this gives the DRM system the widest frequency usage; it can be used in band I, II and III. DRM+ can coexist with DAB in band III. but also the present FM-band can be utilized. The ITU has published three recommendations on DRM+, known in the documents as Digital System G. This indicate the introduction of the full DRM system (DRM 30 and DRM+). ITU-R Rec. BS.1114 is the ITU recommendation for sound broadcasting in the frequency range 30 MHz to 3 GHz. DAB, HD-Radio and ISDB-T were already recommended in this document as Digital Systems A, C and F respectively.

In 2011, the pan-European organisation Community Media Forum Europe has recommended to the European Commission that DRM+ should rather be used for small scale broadcasting (local radio, community radio) than DAB/DAB+.

Digital Video

Digital video is an electronic representation of moving visual images (video) in the form of encoded digital data. This is in contrast to analog video, which represents moving visual images with analog signals. Digital video comprises a series of digital images displayed in rapid succession.

Digital video was first introduced commercially in 1986 with the Sony D1 format, which recorded an uncompressed standard definition component video signal in digital form. In addition to uncompressed formats, popular compressed digital video formats today include H.264 and MPEG-4. Modern interconnect standards for digital video include HDMI, DisplayPort, Digital Visual Interface (DVI) and serial digital interface (SDI).

Digital video can be copied with no degradation in quality. In contrast, when analog sources are copied, they experience generation loss. Digital video can be stored on digital media such as Blu-ray Disc, on computer data storage or streamed over the Internet to end users who watch content on a desktop computer screen or a digital smart TV. In everyday practice, digital video content such as TV shows and movies also includes a digital audio soundtrack.

Digital video comprises a series of digital images displayed in rapid succession. In the context of video these images are called frames. The rate at which frames are displayed is known as the frame rate and is measured in frames per second (FPS). Every frame is an orthogonal bitmap digital image and so comprises a raster of pixels. Pixels have only one property, their color. The color of a pixel is represented by a fixed number of bits. The more bits the more subtle variations of colors can be reproduced. This is called the color depth of the video.

Interlacing

In interlaced video each frame is composed of two halves of an image. The first half contains only the odd-numbered lines of a full frame. The second half contains only the even-numbered lines. Those halves are referred to individually as fields. Two consecutive fields compose a full frame. If an interlaced video has a frame rate of 30 frames per second the field rate is 60 fields per second. All the properties discussed here apply equally to interlaced video but one should be careful not to confuse the fields-per-second rate with the frames-per-second rate.

Bit Rate and BPP

By its definition, bit rate is a measure of the rate of information content of the digital video stream. In the case of uncompressed video, bit rate corresponds directly to the quality of the video as bit rate is proportional to every property that affects the video quality. Bit rate is an important property when transmitting video because the transmission link must be capable of supporting that bit rate. Bit rate is also important when dealing with the storage of video because, as shown above, the video size is proportional to the bit rate and the duration. Video compression is used to greatly reduce the bit rate while having a lesser effect on quality.

Bits per pixel (BPP) is a measure of the efficiency of compression. A true-color video with no compression at all may have a BPP of 24 bits/pixel. Chroma subsampling can reduce the BPP to 16 or 12 bits/pixel. Applying jpeg compression on every frame can reduce the BPP to 8 or even 1 bits/pixel. Applying video compression algorithms like MPEG1, MPEG2 or MPEG4 allows for fractional BPP values.

Constant Bit Rate versus Variable Bit Rate

BPP represents the average bits per pixel. There are compression algorithms that keep the BPP almost constant throughout the entire duration of the video. In this case, we also get video output with a constant bitrate (CBR). This CBR video is suitable for real-time, non-buffered, fixed bandwidth video streaming (e.g. in videoconferencing). As not all frames can be compressed at the same level, because quality is more severely impacted for scenes of high complexity, some algorithms try to constantly adjust the BPP. They keep it high while compressing complex scenes and low for less demanding scenes. This way, one gets the best quality at the smallest average bit rate (and the smallest file size, accordingly). This method produces a variable bitrate because it tracks the variations of the BPP.

Technical Details

Standard film stocks typically record at 24 frames per second. For video, there are two frame rate standards: NTSC, at 30/1.001 (about 29.97) frames per second (about 59.94 fields per second), and PAL, 25 frames per second (50 fields per second). Digital video cameras come in two different image capture formats: Interlaced and progressive scan. Interlaced cameras record the image in alternating sets of lines: The odd-numbered lines are scanned, and then the even-numbered lines are scanned, then the odd-numbered lines are scanned again, and so on. One set of odd or even lines is referred to as a field, and a consecutive pairing of two fields of opposite parity is called a frame. Progressive scan cameras record all lines in each frame as a single unit. Thus, interlaced video captures samples the scene motion twice as often as progressive video does, for the same frame rate. Progressive-scan generally produces a slightly sharper image. However, motion may not be as smooth as interlaced video.

Digital video can be copied with no generation loss which degrades quality in analog systems. However a change in parameters like frame size or a change of the digital format can decrease the quality of the video due to image scaling and transcoding losses. Digital video can be manipulated and edited on a non-linear editing systems frequently implemented using commodity computer hardware and software.

Digital video has a significantly lower cost than 35 mm film. In comparison to the high cost of film stock, the tape stock (or other electronic media used for digital video recording, such as flash memory or hard disk drive) used for recording digital video is very inexpensive. Digital video also allows footage to be viewed on location without the expensive chemical processing required by film. Also physical deliveries of tapes and broadcasts do not apply anymore. Digital television (including higher quality HDTV) started to spread in most developed countries in early 2000s. Digital video is also used in modern mobile phones and video conferencing systems. Digital video is also used for Internet distribution of media, including streaming video and peer-to-peer movie distribution. However even within Europe are lots of TV-Stations not broadcasting in HD, due to restricted budgets for new equipment for processing HD.

Many types of video compression exist for serving digital video over the internet and on optical disks. The file sizes of digital video used for professional editing are generally not practical for these purposes, and the video requires further compression with codecs such as Sorenson, H.264 and more recently Apple ProRes especially for HD. Probably the most widely used formats for delivering video over the internet are MPEG4, Quicktime, Flash and Windows Media, while MPEG2 is used almost exclusively for DVDs, providing an exceptional image in minimal size but resulting in a high level of CPU consumption to decompress.

As of 2011, the highest resolution demonstrated for digital video generation is 35 megapixels (8192 x 4320). The highest speed is attained in industrial and scientific high speed cameras that are capable of filming 1024x1024 video at up to 1 million frames per second for brief periods of recording.

Properties

An example video can have a duration (T) of 1 hour (3600sec), a frame size of 640x480

(WxH) at a color depth of 24 bits and a frame rate of 25fps. This example video has the following properties:

- Pixels per frame = 640 * 480 = 307,200.

- Bits per frame = 307,200 * 24 = 7,372,800 = 7.37 Mbits.

- Bit rate (BR) = 7.37 * 25 = 184.25 Mbits/sec.

- Video size (VS) = 184 Mbits/sec * 3600 sec = 662,400 Mbits = 82,800 Mbytes = 82.8 Gbytes.

The most important properties are bit rate and video size. The formulas relating those two with all other properties are:

```
BR = W * H * CD * FPS

VS = BR * T = W * H * CD * FPS * T

(units are: BR in bit/s, W and H in pixels, CD in bits, VS in bits, T
in seconds)
```

while some secondary formulas are:

```
pixels_per_frame = W * H

pixels_per_second = W * H * FPS

bits_per_frame = W * H * CD
```

The above are accurate for uncompressed video. Because of the relatively high bit rate of uncompressed video, video compression is extensively used. In the case of compressed video each frame requires a small percentage of the original bits. Assuming a compression algorithm that shrinks the input data by a factor of **CF**, the bit rate and video size would equal to:

```
BR = W * H * CD * FPS/CF

VS = BR * T/CF
```

Note that it is not necessary that all frames are equally compressed by a factor of CF. In practice they are not, so CF is the average factor of compression for all the frames taken together.

The above equation for the bit rate can be rewritten by combining the compression factor and the color depth like this:

```
BR = W * H * ( CD/CF ) * FPS
```

The value (CD/CF) represents the average bits per pixel (BPP). As an example, if there is a color depth of 12 bits/pixel and an algorithm that compresses at 40x, then

BPP equals 0.3 (12/40). So in the case of compressed video the formula for bit rate is:

```
BR = W * H * BPP * FPS
```

The same formula is valid for uncompressed video because in that case one can assume that the "compression" factor is 1 and that the average bits per pixel equal the color depth.

Fundamentals of Video

Different Types of Video

There are several broad attributes that can be used to describe video. For example, video can be categorized as real time or pre-recorded, streaming or pre-positioned, and high resolution or low resolution. The network load is dependent on the type of video being sent. Pre-recorded, pre-positioned, low resolution video is little more than a file transfer while real-time streaming video demands a high performance network. Many generic video applications fall somewhere in between. This allows non-real-time streaming video applications to work acceptably over the public Internet. Tuning the network and media encoders are both important aspects of deploying video on an IP network.

H.264 Coding and Decoding Implications

Video codecs have been evolving over the last 15 years. Today's codecs take advantage of the increased processing power to better optimize the stream size. The general procedure has not changed much since the original MPEG1 standard was released. Pictures consist of a matrix of pixels which are grouped into blocks. Blocks combine into macro blocks. A row of macro blocks is a slice. Slices form pictures which are combined into groups of pictures (GOPs).

Each pixel has a red, green, and blue component. The encoding process starts by color sampling the RGB into a luma and two-color components, commonly referred to as YCrCb. Small amounts of color information can be ignored during encoding and then replaced later by interpolatation. Once in YCrCb form, each component is passed through a transform. The transform is reversible and does not compress the data. Instead, the data is represented differently to allow more efficient quantization and compression. Quantization is then used to round out small details in the data. This rounding is used to set the quality. Reduced quality allows better compression. Following quantization, lossless compression is applied by replacing common bit sequences with binary codes. Each macro block in the picture goes through this process resulting in an elementary stream of bits. This stream is sliced into 188-byte packets known as a Packetized Elementary Stream (PES). This stream is then loaded into IP packets. Because IP packets have a 1500 byte MTU and PES packets are fixed at 188 bytes, only 7 PES can fit into an IP packet. The resulting IP packet will be 1316 bytes, not including headers. As a result, IP fragmentation is not a concern. An entire frame of high definition video may require 100 IP packets to carry all of the elementary stream packets, although 45 to 65 packets are more common. Quantization and picture complexity are the primary factors in determining the number of packets required for transmission. Forward error correction can be used to estimate some lost information. However in many cases, multiple IP packets are dropped in sequence. This makes the frame almost impossible to decompress. The packets that were successfully sent represent wasted bandwidth. RTCP can be used to request a new frame. Without a valid initial frame, subsequent frames will not decode properly.

Frame Types

The current generation of video coding is known by three names; H.264, MPEG4 part 10, and Advanced Video Coding (AVC). As with earlier codecs, H.264 employs spatial and temporal compression. Spatial compression is used on a single frame of video as described previously. These types of frames are known as I-frames. An I-Frame is the first picture in a GOP. Temporal compression takes advantage of the fact that little information changes between subsequent frames. Changes are a result of motion, although changes in zoom or camera movement can result in almost every pixel changing. Vectors are used to describe this motion and are applied to a block. A global vector is used if the encoder determines all pixels moved together, as is the case with camera panning. In addition, a difference signal is used to fine tune any error that results. H.264 allows variable block sizes and is able to code motion as fine as a ¼ pixel. The decoder uses this information to determine how the current frame should look based on the previous frame. Packets that contain the motion vectors and error signals are known as P-Frames. Lost P-Frames usually results in artifacts that are folded into subsequent frames. If an artifact persists over time, then the likely cause is a lost P-Frame.

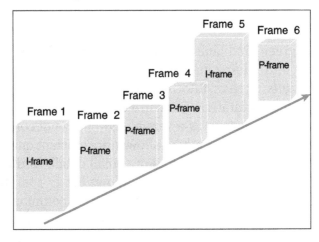

H.264 also implements B-Frames. This type of frame fills in information between P-Frames. This means that the B-Frame will need to be held until the next P-frame arrives before the information can be used. B-Frames are not used in all modes of H.264. The encoder decides what type of frame is best suited. There are typically more P-frames than I-frames. Lab analysis has shown TelePresence I-frames to generally be 64K wide (50 packets @ 1316 bytes), while P- frames average 8K wide (9 packets at 900 bytes).

Motion JPEG – MJPEG

Another type of video compression is MJPEG. Temporal compression is not used with this coding. There are some advantageous and disadvantages. First, the resulting video stream is larger but the packet sizes are more consistent at 1316 bytes (payload). Quantization can be used to mitigate the increased bandwidth but at the cost of picture quality. The advantage that MJPEG offers is that each frame of video is independent of the previous frame. If a several packets from a particular frame are dropped, the artifact is not carried forward. Another advantage is that a single frame is easily extracted from the stream without the need for the reference I-Frame and prior PandB Frames. This is useful in some applications such as video Surveillance where a single frame may be extracted and sent as a JPG via email.

Voice versus Video

Voice and video are often thought of as close cousins. Although they are both real time protocol (RTP) applications, the similarities stop there. They do not even use the same codec to encode audio information. Voice uses G.711 or G.729 while video uses MP3 or AAC. Voice is generally considered well behaved because each packet is a fixed size and fixed rate. Video frames are spread over multiple packets that travel as a group. Because one lost packet can ruin a P-frame, and one bad P-frame can cause a persistent artifact, video generally has a tighter loss requirement than audio. Video is asymmetrical. Voice can also be but typically is not. Even on mute, an IP phone will send and receive the same size flow. Video uses a separate camera and viewer so there is no assurance of symmetry. In the case of broadcast video, the asymmetrical load on the network can be substantial. Network policies may be necessary to manage potential senders. For example, if a branch is presenting a video, the WAN aggregation router may be receiving more data than it is sending. Video will increase the average real time packet size, and has the capacity to quickly alter the traffic profile of networks. Without planning, this could be detrimental to network performance.

Resolution

The sending station determines the video's resolution and consequently, the load on the network. This is irrespective of the size of the monitor used to display the video. Observing the video is not a reliable method to estimate load. Common high definition formats are 720i, 1080i, 1080p, etc. The numerical value of the format represents the number of rows in the frame. The aspect ratio of high definition is 16:9 which results in 1920 columns. There is work underway on 2160p resolution and UHDV (7,680 x 4320). This format was first demonstrated by NHK over an IP network and used 600 Mb/s of bandwidth. Video load on the network is likely to increase over time due to the demand for high quality images. In addition to high resolution, there is also a proliferation of lower quality video that is often tunneled in HTTP or in some cases, HTTPS, and SSL. Typical resolutions include CIF (352x288) and 4CIF (704x576). These numbers were chosen as integers of the 16x16 macro blocks that is used by the DCT (22x18) and (44x36) macro blocks respectively.

Format	Resolution	Typical BW
QCIF (1/4 CIF)	176x144	260K
CIF	352x288	512K
4CIF	704x576	1 Mb/s
SD NTSC	720x480	Analog, 4.2Mhz
720 HD	1280x720	1-8 mb/s
1080 HD	1080x1920	5-8 mb/s h.264 12+ mb/s mpg2
CUPC	640x480 max	
YouTube	320x240	Flash(H.264)
Skype	Camera limits	128 - 512K+

Network Load

The impact of resolution on the network load is generally a squared term. An image that is twice as big will require four times the bandwidth. In addition, the color sampling, quantization and the frame rate also impact the amount of network traffic. Standard rates are 30 frames per second (actually 29.97) but this is an arbitrary value chosen based on the frequency of AC power. In Europe, analog video is traditionally 25 FPS. Cineplex movies are shot at 24 FPS. As the frame rate is decreased, the network load is also decrease and the motion becomes less life like. Video above 24 FPS does not noticeable improve motion. Finally the sophistication of the encoder has a large impact on video load. H.264 encoders have great flexibility in determining how best to encode video and with this comes complexity in determining the best method. For example, MPEG4.10 allows the encoder to select the most appropriate block size depending on the surrounding pixels. Because efficient encoding is more difficult then decoding, and because the sender determines the load on the network, low cost encoders will usually require more bandwidth then high end encoders. H.264 coding of real time CIF video will drive all but the most powerful laptops well into the 90% CPU range without dedicated media processors.

Multicast

Broadcast video lends itself well to take advantage of the bandwidth savings offered by multicast. This has been in place in many networks for years. Recent improvements to multicast simplify the deployment on the network. Multicast will play a role going forward. However, multicast is not used in all situations. Some applications such as multipoint TelePresence use a dedicated MCU to replicate video. The MCU can make decisions concern which participants are viewing each sender. The MCU can also quench senders that are not being viewed.

Transports

MPEG4 uses the same transport as MPEG2. A PES consists of 188-byte datagrams that are loaded into IP. The video packets can be loaded into RTP/UDP/IP or HTTP(S)/TCP/IP.

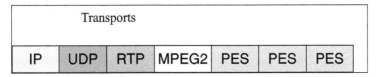

Video over UDP is found with dedicated real time applications such as teleconferencing or TelePresence. In this case, a RTCP channel can be setup from the receiver towards the sender. This is used to manage the video session, and is implementation specific. RTCP can be used to request I-frames or report capabilities to the sender. UDP and RTP each provide a method to multiplex channels together. Audio and Video typically use different UDP ports, but also have unique RTP payload types. Deep packet inspection (DPI) can be used on the network to identify the type of video and audio that is present. Note that H.264 also provides a mechanism to multiplex together layers of the video. This could be used to handle a scrolling ticker at the bottom of the screen without sending a continuous stream of motion vectors.

Buffering

Jitter and delay are present in all IP networks. Jitter is the variation in delay. Delay is generally caused by interface queuing. Video decoders can employ a play out buffer to smooth out jitter found in the network. There are limitations to the depth of this buffer. If it is too small, then drops will result. If it is too deep, then the video will be time delayed which could be a problem in real time applications such as TelePresence. Another limitation is handling dropped packets which often accompany deep play out buffers. If RTCP is used to request a new I-Frame, then more frames will be skipped over at the time of resync. The result is that dropped packets have a slightly greater impact in video degradation then they would have if the missing packet was discovered earlier. Most codecs employ a dynamic play out buffer.

Reconstructing 3D Scenes from 2D Images

3D video captures two fundamental kinds of information about real-world scenes which dynamically changes over time: Three-dimensional geometry and appearance of surface materials.

For a fixed viewpoint, appearance can be acquired completely using conventional video cameras. This may be simply extended to 3D video by recording all possible viewpoints at the same time, resulting in a so-called light field representation. Although this is the most generic approach, yielding high-quality output images for most scenes, it has several practical limitations. The desired viewing range has to be densely sampled using a lot of cameras. As a result, the amount of produced image data is huge and difficult to handle. Moreover, no inherent knowledge about the scene besides images is captured, making post-processing difficult and constraining the application to virtual replay and synthetic aperture and lens effects only.

Instead, we opt for a different approach including explicit information about scene geometry. By acquiring not only images but also depth maps, novel views can be interpolated from a sparse set of input viewpoints. A consistent three-dimensional model can be built easily by back projecting pixels from all views into three-dimensional space using their individual depth values. Such a scene model allows for applications beyond virtual camera control.

Our view interpolation requires one fundamental assumption: Each surface point has to have an identical appearance from all possible viewing directions. As a consequence, novel views of that point can be computed easily as soon as its position in three-space and its appearance from one viewing direction is known. Moreover, its appearance under the present lighting conditions can be captured from a single viewpoint by using a color camera. Thus, we impose the following requirements on the acquired scene and our applications:

- We are only interested in surfaces of objects, not in their interior structure.

- All surface materials have to be Lambertian, i.e. they scatter all incoming light evenly in all possible directions. There are no effects such as specular reflections or transparencies.

- There is no visible medium like smoke or fog between surfaces and acquisition cameras.

For such cases, reconstruction of depth maps is a heavily researched topic in the field of computer vision. A variety of methods exist, differing in the required hardware, reconstruction quality, and additional scene constraints. After surveying those approaches and discussing the needed theoretical concepts, we present our chosen method of depth from stereo on structured light. Especially, we discuss our extension for increasing fidelity at depth discontinuities. As a result, we are able to obtain decent-quality depth maps in a robust way.

Depth Acquisition Methods

All depth map acquisition methods we examine are based on some imaging device acquiring a two-dimensional view of light reflected or emitted by the scene. However, such information is generally not enough for reconstructing three-dimensional geometry. Thus, additional techniques are used for obtaining more data. These form the main differences between the examined methods and determine the complexity of the performed computations. Most approaches are based on triangulation. They can be separated in active methods which illuminate the scene with specialized light sources and passive methods which do not influence the environment. Different approaches are used by time-of-flight and shape-from-silhouette methods. The first performs temporal measurements instead of triangulation, the latter reconstructs an approximate geometry based on the silhouettes of an object seen from multiple viewpoints.

We define a set of requirements an optimal reconstruction algorithms should fulfill for recording 3D video of dynamic scenes:

- Quality: The acquired depth values should be of high quality, accurately representing the real scene without too much noise and outliers.

- Density: The depth maps should be dense, i.e. they should contain a valid depth value at almost every image pixel.

- Dynamics: The algorithm should be able to robustly capture moving scenes.

- Scalability: The system using the depth reconstruction algorithm should be scalable to an arbitrary number of acquisition viewpoints. As a consequence, multiple depth acquisition devices should not interfere with each other.

- Generality: The depth reconstruction method should be applicable to a large variety of scenes.

- Practicability: The acquisition system should comprise an acceptable amount of hardware that can be set up easily.

Existing methods are surveyed under these constraints.

Stereo Vision

Stereo vision algorithms are inspired by human depth perception. By finding pixel correspondences in two camera images captured from different but nearby viewpoints, the depth of the projected object point can be calculated via triangulation. The pixel search is essentially a minimization problem optimizing the matches for all pixels. A survey of different methods and their implementations can be found in the paper by Scharstein and Szeliski. They can be divided into two fundamentally different categories. Local methods do a matching search for each pixel individually, whereas global methods try to solve the problem for the whole image at once. Moreover, one could distinguish sparse methods providing depth values only at feature points from dense methods providing depth values at every pixel. As we require dense depth maps, we concentrate on the second category.

Local matching algorithms are based on correlation of small pixel neighborhoods within a usually rectangular window in both images. Due to their local view, they have difficulties at ambiguities occurring in regions with uniform color or repetitive texture. Hence, they require input images with highly varying textures. A second issue are depth discontinuities which cannot be modeled if they occur inside the correlation window. Thus, the core algorithms are not capable of accurately capturing object silhouettes without further extensions. On the other hand, they can easily find matches with sub-pixel accuracy, which is important for obtaining a high depth resolution.

Global stereo algorithms based on Markov random fields try to find all pixel matches at the same time with respect to some overall consistency constraints. By minimizing an energy composed of a correlation term and an edge-preserving smoothness term, they are able to handle both ambiguities and depth discontinuities. However, obtaining accurate depth values in texture-less regions still remains difficult because they are just interpolated by the smoothness function. In texture-rich regions, global algorithms are in general not better than local methods. Depth resolution can be even worse because many global algorithms such as the one by Boykov et al. cannot easily handle sub-pixel accuracy.

More recently, segmentation-based stereo algorithms have been developed. Correlation of whole color segments performs much better at depth discontinuities than pixel-based matching and is able to accurately reconstruct sharp boundaries. Global solvers again produce the best quality. However, those methods require a color segmentation as input that reliably represents discontinuities and that is consistent in both camera images. This is an additional nontrivial computer vision problem.

Matching ambiguities in homogeneous regions can be avoided by producing artificial textures using structured light illumination. Because the light patterns can be random, such an approach scales well with overlapping projections. Window-based algorithms show a great improvement with structured light. Their only remaining instability is in matching depth discontinuities. Global methods, on the other hand, showed to behave very unstable in our experiments. This is due to their build-in smoothness function which assumes correlation between depth and texture discontinuities, which is not true with the employed light patterns.

All stereo algorithms are in principle able to handle dynamic input data because they only require one image pair recorded at one point in time. To improve coherence, matching can be extended to the temporal domain by considering a whole stack of successive images at once. With local approaches, this usually improves stability at slow but not at fast motions, because the latter tend to create additional depth discontinuities in time.

Stereo vision can theoretically reconstruct arbitrary scenes as long as enough texture information is available. If the latter is generated by structured light projections, acquisition is naturally constrained to indoor scenes only. The acquisition setup consists of pairs of calibrated cameras and, optionally, uncalibrated structured light projectors, which have to be synchronized in the case of dynamic recording. The resulting matching quality largely depends on the number and complexity of occlusions which should be minimized. Besides changing the scene itself, this can be achieved by choosing small baselines between corresponding cameras of the stereo pairs. Between independent camera pairs, large baselines can be used to cover a large viewing range. On the other hand, specialized wide-baseline stereo vision methods exist, but they largely depend on distinct image features and, thus, rather belong to the category of sparse matching algorithms.

Structured Light

Structured light scanning systems are similar to stereo vision systems but replace one camera with a projector. Thus, they are naturally constrained to indoor scenes. Stereo matching is performed between camera and projector pixels. In contrast to the aforementioned stereo vision on structured light, the projector has to be calibrated. The camera-projector baselines should be small in order to minimize occlusions. To find correct correlations, the algorithms have to uniquely identify light from distinct projector pixels in the camera images. Therefore, the projected patterns have to be well defined and should be more prominent than the scene textures. Compared to stereo vision, this improves the quality of correlation and generally yields superior results. On the other hand, it constrains the setup of multiple projectors and impairs scalability, as the pattern determinateness gets destroyed as soon as multiple projections overlap.

Structured light algorithms can be categorized into single-shot and multi-shot methods. Single-shot methods such as the one by Vuylsteke and Oosterlinck only need one image of the scene under one pattern illumination, making them suitable for capturing dynamic scenes. However, due to ambiguities in the pattern, they are only able to uniquely identify some specific projector pixels, yielding sparse depth maps only. Multi-shot methods resolve for those ambiguities by capturing multiple images of the scene under a sequence of different lighting conditions. They are able to reconstruct dense depth maps but cannot easily cope with motions. A special case of multi-shot approaches are laser range scanners which replace the pattern projection with a laser line that is constantly swept over the recorded object.

Time-of-flight

Time-of-flight systems such as the one by Iddan and Yahav are based on a completely different approach. Instead of computing triangulations they measure the time light needs to travel from a calibrated source to an imaging sensor. This is achieved by measuring either directly the time of light pulses or phase shifts of modulated light. In the latter case, multiple devices can be combined without interference by using different modulation frequencies.

Shape-from-silhouettes

Shape-from-silhouette methods reconstruct an approximate geometry of distinct objects by backprojecting their silhouettes from multiple viewpoints into three-space and intersecting the resulting generalized cones. The acquisition setup consists of multiple calibrated cameras covering a convex viewing range. In order to be able to extract the silhouettes, only one or very few clearly separated objects but no complex scenes can be captured. They are usually placed in front of a background with a defined color. The reconstruction method is very robust but needs many cameras to create a good approximation to the real geometry. Even in the theoretical limit, when using an infinite amount of cameras covering all possible viewing directions, it cannot reconstruct the real geometry but only its visual hull which does not capture surface concavities.

Summary of the capabilities of various depth map acquisition methods (+ good, ∘ average, – bad).

	Stereo vision				Structured light		Time of flight	Shape from silh.
	Local		Global		Single-shot	Multi-shot		
	Passive	St. light	Passive	St. light				
Quality	-	+	∘	-	+	+	∘	∘
Density	+	+	+	+	-	+	+	+
Scalability	+	+	+	+	-	-	∘	+
Dynamics	+	+	+	+	+	-	+	+
Generality	+	∘	+	∘	∘	∘	∘	-
Practicability	+	∘	+	∘	-	-	+	+

Mathematical Concepts of Image Acquisition

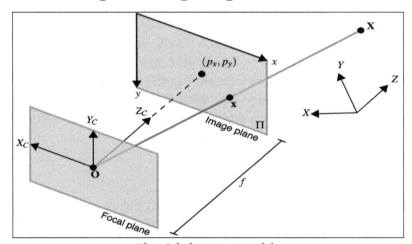

The pinhole camera model.

All traditional image acquisition devices capture projections of light rays emanating from three-dimensional space onto a two-dimensional image plane. Methods reconstructing three-dimensional geometry from imagery perform the inverse projection based on the image data and known internal and external camera parameters. Here, we present the mathematical foundations for computing those projections. The pinhole camera model provides a simple but powerful mathematical abstraction which can be applied to images of real-world cameras after compensating for effects of their optical systems. Epipolar geometry makes the transition from one to multiple cameras that acquire the same scene from different viewpoints by describing relations between the different images. For two cameras, the epipolar geometry can be greatly simplified by postprocessing their images with the presented rectification method.

The Pinhole Camera Model

The pinhole camera model, as illustrated in figure, describes how a point $\mathbf{X}$ in three-dimensional world coordinates (X,Y,Z) is projected on a two-dimensional image plane Π, yielding a pixel x with coordinates (x,y). It is an abstraction of real-world cameras, replacing the optical lens system by an infinitesimal small pinhole which is the center of projection $\mathbf{O}$ where all light rays pass through. $\mathbf{O}$ is lying on the focal plane which is parallel to the image plane. The distance f between both planes is called the focal length of the camera. In contrast to real cameras, we use the common approach of placing the image plane in front of the center of projection instead behind it. This is valid due to symmetry. For convenience, points $\mathbf{X}$ are first transformed into 3D camera coordinates $\mathbf{X}_C = (X_C, Y_C, Z_C)$ before performing the projection. The origin of the camera coordinate system is placed at the center of projection $\mathbf{O}$, its XC- and YC-axes span the focal plane. Transformation of world coordinates into camera coordinates can be described by a 3 × 3 rotation matrix R and a translation to the center of projection $\mathbf{O}$ as

$$\mathbf{X}_C = R \cdot (\mathbf{X} - \mathbf{O})$$

or by using homogeneous coordinates as

$$\tilde{\mathbf{X}}_C = \begin{pmatrix} R & -R\mathbf{O} \\ 0 & 1 \end{pmatrix} \cdot \tilde{\mathbf{X}}.$$

R and $\mathbf{O}$ are the so-called extrinsic parameters of the camera. They encode all external characteristics like camera position and orientation. For convenience, we mainly use the notation of $\mathbf{X}_C = R \cdot (\mathbf{X} - \mathbf{O})$.

The main step for projecting $\mathbf{X}_C$ into a pixel x = (x,y) on the image plane is the perspective division by its third coordinate Z_C scaled with the focal length f:

$$x = f \cdot \frac{X_C}{Z_C},$$

$$y = f \cdot \frac{X_C}{Z_C}.$$

It can be written in homogeneous matrix notation as:

$$\tilde{\mathbf{x}} = \begin{pmatrix} f & 0 & 0 \\ 0 & f & 0 \\ 0 & 0 & 1 \end{pmatrix} \cdot \mathbf{X}_C.$$

However, in this example, image coordinates are measured in the same length units as camera coordinates. For image processing, it is practical to transform them into pixel coordinates by scaling the focal length f differently in the x- and y-directions, yielding separate coefficients f_x and f_y:

$$\tilde{\mathbf{x}} = \begin{pmatrix} f_x & 0 & 0 \\ 0 & f_y & 0 \\ 0 & 0 & 1 \end{pmatrix} \cdot \mathbf{X}_C.$$

Having separate scaling factors for the two image coordinate axes allows for modeling of non-square pixels as they occur in some image sensors. So far, the origin of the pixel coordinate system is located at the orthogonal projection of the pinhole onto the image plane. To comply with standard pixel coordinate notations that define the origin at an image corner, we add two more shifting coefficients p_x and p_y to equation $\tilde{\mathbf{x}} = \begin{pmatrix} f_x & 0 & 0 \\ 0 & f_y & 0 \\ 0 & 0 & 1 \end{pmatrix} \cdot \mathbf{X}_C.$ that describe the so-called principal point of the camera:

$$\tilde{\mathbf{x}} = \begin{pmatrix} f_x & 0 & p_y \\ 0 & f_x & p_y \\ 0 & 0 & 1 \end{pmatrix} \cdot \mathbf{X}_C.$$

Ideally, the principal point is located in the image center. Thus for an image of width w and height h its coordinates would be $p_x = w/2$ and $p_y = h/2$. However, lens systems of real-world cameras often introduce some small displacement there which is measured along with the other parameters by standard camera calibration tools.

The final matrix of equation $\tilde{\mathbf{x}} = \begin{pmatrix} f_x & 0 & p_y \\ 0 & f_x & p_y \\ 0 & 0 & 1 \end{pmatrix} \cdot \mathbf{X}_C.$ encodes all internal parameters of

the camera responsible for image projection. It is called the intrinsic matrix P. Putting it all together, any point $\mathbf{X}$ in Cartesian world coordinates can be projected to its homogeneous pixel coordinates $\tilde{\mathbf{x}}$ via

$$\tilde{\mathbf{x}} = \mathbf{P} \cdot \mathbf{R} \cdot (\mathbf{X} - \mathbf{O}).$$

As a side effect, the resulting homogeneous coordinate z of a pixel $\tilde{\mathbf{x}} = z \cdot (x, y, 1)^{\mathrm{T}}$ contains the so-called pixel depth that is the distance of the corresponding 3D point to the focal plane, i.e. $z = Z_C$. The three orthogonal coordinates x, y, and z define the so-called ray space of the camera. If, for a specific pixel, z is known, the 3D point can be reconstructed by inverting equation $\tilde{\mathbf{x}} = \mathbf{P} \cdot \mathbf{R} \cdot (\mathbf{X} - \mathbf{O})$:

$$\mathbf{X} = \mathbf{R}^{-1} \cdot \mathbf{P}^{-1} \cdot z \begin{pmatrix} x \\ y \\ 1 \end{pmatrix} + \mathbf{O}.$$

Real-world Cameras

Optical systems of real-world cameras show some additional effects that are not covered by the pinhole model. They include depth-of-field effects caused by the spatial extent of the aperture, chromatic aberration due to varying light refraction depending on the wavelength, and lens distortion. Chromatic aberration and depth-of-field effects cannot be handled easily without prior knowledge of the scene geometry. They have to be avoided during acquisition by choosing highquality lenses and a small aperture. Lens distortion can be compensated by applying two-dimensional post-processing to the acquired image. As result, we obtain an image looking similar to one that would have been captured using a corresponding pinhole camera.

We use the common Brown-Conrady model describing radial and tangential distortion of camera lenses. Given a pixel at coordinates (x, y) in an ideal image, the model describes the distorted pixel coordinates (x_D, y_D) as:

$$x_D = \left(1 + r_1 \rho^2 + r_2 \rho^4\right) \cdot x + 2t_1 xy + t_2 \left(\rho^2 + 2x^2\right),$$

$$x_D = \left(1 + r_1 \rho^2 + r_2 \rho^4\right) \cdot x + t_1 \left(\rho^2 + 2y^2\right) + 2t_2 xy,$$

where $\rho^2 = x^2 + y^2$.

Epipolar Geometry

Having two cameras with image planes Π_L, Π_R and centers of projection $\mathbf{O}_L$, $\mathbf{O}_R$ acquiring the same scene, there is a linear relationship between coordinates of corresponding pixels that is described by the epipolar geometry. Consider an object point $\mathbf{X}$. Together with both centers of projections, the point forms a triangle $\Delta(\mathrm{X}, \mathrm{O}_L, \mathrm{O}_R)$ as shown in figure Its edges $\overline{\mathbf{X},\mathbf{O}_L}$ and $\overline{\mathbf{O},\mathbf{O}_R}$ intersect the image planes at the respective projections $\mathbf{x}_L$ and $\mathbf{x}_R$ of $\mathbf{X}$. The projections of the epipolar plane into the camera images form so-called epipolar lines. For a varying $\mathbf{X}$ the epipolar plane rotates around the baseline of the camera pair building the epipolar pencil. All epipolar lines of the pencil intersect in one point $\mathbf{e}_L$ and $\mathbf{e}_R$, respectively, for each image, the so-called epipoles. The epipoles are located at the intersections of the camera baseline with the image planes.

Projections onto the two image planes corresponding to the same object point are always located on corresponding epipolar lines. This greatly reduces the search space in the stereo matching process. For a given pixel in the left image, the matching pixel in the right image can be found on the corresponding epipolar line. Intuitively, the search is performed on the projection of the viewing ray of the left image into the right image. Thus, stereo matching of two-dimensional images can be reduced to a one-dimensional search per pixel.

Mathematically, for each given camera setup, there exists a 3×3-matrix F such that for each object point $\mathbf{X}$ its two projections $\tilde{\mathbf{x}}_L$ and $\tilde{\mathbf{x}}_R$ fulfill the equation:

$$\tilde{\mathbf{x}}_L^T \cdot F \cdot \tilde{\mathbf{x}}_R = 0.$$

F is the so-called fundamental matrix which even holds for uncalibrated cameras. It is of rank 2 having 6 degrees of freedom. In the calibrated case, F can be reduced to the special case of the so-called essential matrix describing the relationship of points in camera coordinates by encoding the difference of orientation and position of both cameras. Those matrices can be used to compute the epipolar lines.

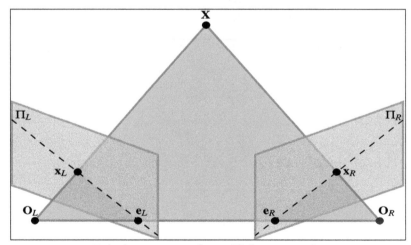

Epipolar geometry of a rectified camera pair.

For stereo matching, we use a different approach instead. By applying a rectification algorithm, the camera images are post-processed in a way that makes their epipolar geometry as simple as possible, alleviating the needed computations.

Image Rectification

Generally, epipolar lines form a pencil in each image. Image rectification warps and resamples both images in such a way that all epipolar lines are parallel and corresponding lines lie on the same scan line. In that case, the epipoles of both cameras are located at infinity and the image planes are coplanar and parallel to the baseline, as illustrated in figure. We use the rectification method by Fusiello et al. Given the intrinsic and extrinsic matrices of the input cameras, it computes a new rectified camera configuration and a transformation that warps the images from the input cameras into the rectified cameras.

Consider a pair of pinhole cameras defined by their projection matrices P_L, P_R, rotation matrices RL, RR and centers of projection $\mathbf{O}_L, \mathbf{O}_R,$. They can be transformed into a rectified pair as follows:

First, the rectified cameras have to have the same intrinsic matrices $\overline{P}_L = \overline{P}_R$.

They can be defined arbitrarily, e.g.,

$$\overline{P}_L = \overline{P}_R = \frac{1}{2} \cdot (P_L + P_R).$$

Second, their image planes should have the same orientation, parallel to their baseline. This is achieved by building a new orthonormal camera coordinate system defined by the three vectors:

$$\mathbf{V}_1 = \frac{\mathbf{O}_L, \mathbf{O}_R}{\|\mathbf{O}_L, \mathbf{O}_R\|},$$

$$\mathbf{V}_2 = \mathbf{V}_1 \times \mathbf{W},$$

And

$$\mathbf{V}_3 = \mathbf{V}_1 \times \mathbf{V}_2,$$

where $\mathbf{W}$ is an arbitrary vector and $\times$ denotes the cross product. A new, common rotation matrix can then be built as:

$$\overline{R}_L = \overline{R}_R = \begin{pmatrix} \mathbf{V}_1^T \\ \mathbf{V}_2^T \\ \mathbf{V}_3^T \end{pmatrix}.$$

Finally, the center of projections remains unchanged, i.e.,

$$\overline{\mathbf{O}}_L = \mathbf{O}_L$$

and,

$$\overline{\mathbf{O}}_R = \mathbf{O}_R.$$

Keeping the camera positions permits the computation of rectified images using a 2D linear warping function. Warping matrices can be computed as:

$$T_L = \overline{P}_L \, \overline{R}_L \, R_L^{-1} \, P_L^{-1}$$

and,

$$T_R = \overline{P}_R \, \overline{R}_R \, R_R^{-1} \, P_R^{-1}.$$

Figure shows the original camera images and the resulting rectified images with augmented epipolar lines.

From now on, if not mentioned otherwise, all matrices and images from stereo camera pairs are assumed to be rectified, without using the bar notation.

Stereo image pair with augmented epipolar lines. Top: original images. Bottom: rectified images.

Stereo Triangulation

If projections $\mathbf{x}_L, \mathbf{x}_R$ of an object point $\mathbf{X}$ onto two different camera planes Π_L, Π_R are known, one can reconstruct the coordinates of $\mathbf{X}$ via triangulation. Depth from stereo algorithms typically first compute pixel disparities, i.e. the coordinate deviations of corresponding pixels in two images. They can be directly transformed into depth maps that store for each image pixel the distance from its corresponding object point to the focal plane. Finally, three-dimensional geometry can be computed by back projecting the pixels using the inverse camera projection matrix.

The pixel disparity d is defined as the deviation of the pixel coordinates, measured relative to the principal points of the cameras:

$$d = \left(x_R - p_{x,R} \right) - \left(x_L - p_{x,L} \right).$$

To compute the pixel depth, note that the triangles $\Delta(\mathbf{X}, \mathbf{O}_L, \mathbf{O}_R)$ and $\Delta(\mathbf{X}, x_L, x_R)$ in figure are similar and it holds that:

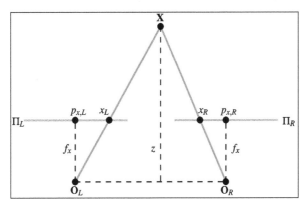

$$\frac{\|\mathbf{O}_R - \mathbf{O}_L\|}{z} = \frac{\|\mathbf{O}_R - \mathbf{O}_L\| + (x_R - p_{x,R}) - (x_L - p_{x,L})}{z - f_x}.$$

Simple calculations and substitution of d yields:

$$z = -\|\mathbf{O}_R - \mathbf{O}_L\| \cdot \frac{f_x}{d}.$$

With the gained pixel depths, the object point can be reconstructed from e.g., the left camera by back projection:

$$\mathbf{X} = \mathbf{R}_L^{-1} \cdot \mathbf{P}_L^{-1} \cdot z \begin{pmatrix} x_L \\ y \\ 1 \end{pmatrix} + \mathbf{O}_L.$$

Stereo Matching

Stereo reconstruction is a one-dimensional search for corresponding pixels in two images along corresponding epipolar lines. Hence, for two rectified grayscale or color images C_L and C_R one has to find for every pixel (x, y) its disparity d such that $C_L(x, y) = C_R(x + d, y)$. This can be expressed as a minimization of an energy:

$$E_M(d) = e_M\left(C_L(x, y), C_R(x + d, y)\right),$$

where e_M is an error function describing the difference between two pixels, for example the absolute difference metric $e_M(a, b) = |a - b|$. It employs absolute differences on intensity functions that are linearly interpolated from small pixel neighbourhoods and is therefore independent from image sampling.

Because all real images are augmented by acquisition noise, the colors of two corresponding pixels will never be the same and the above pixel-wise minimization will not succeed. This problem is solved by minimizing over a small rectangular window $\mathcal{W}(x_0, y_0) = \{x_0 - \Delta x, \ldots, x_0 + \Delta x\} \times \{y_0 - \Delta y, \ldots, y_0 + \Delta y\}$ of size $2\Delta x + 1 \times 2\Delta y + 1$ around one pixel of interest (x_0, y_0):

$$E_M(d) = \sum_{(x,y) \in \mathcal{W}(x_0, y_0)} e(C_L(x, y), C_R(x + d, y)).$$

However, this assumes a constant disparity over the whole correlation window which is only correct for planar surfaces parallel to the image plane. If this is not the case, the computed disparities may deviate a few pixels from the ground truth. To obtain more accurate results, Zhang et al. extend the minimization by also searching for the gradient (dx, dy) of the disparity:

$$E_M(d, d_x, d_y) = \sum_{(x,y) \in \mathcal{W}(x_0, y_0)} e(C_L(x, y), C_R(x + d', y)).$$

Where,

$$d' = d + d_x(x - x_0) + d_y(y - y_0).$$

This corresponds to linearly changing disparities in the matching window which is exact for all planar surfaces and a good local approximation of the scene geometry.

If not only still images but videos are used as input, temporal coherence can be improved by extending the matching window over multiple successive frames, yielding a so-called spacetime stereo algorithm. Furthermore, it can be used to reconstruct static scenes under varying illumination conditions, increasing the robustness of the matching. In both cases, equation $E_M(d, d_x, d_y) = \sum_{(x,y) \in \mathcal{W}(x_0, y_0)} e(C_L(x, y), C_R(x + d', y))$ is extended to:

$$E_M(d, d_x, d_y) = \sum_{(x,y) \in \mathcal{W}(x_0, y_0)} e(C_L(x, y), C_R(x + d', y)).$$

With,

$$d' = d + d_x(x - x_0) + d_y(y - y_0) + d_t(t - t_0).$$

There, t_0 denotes position of the current frame along the temporal axis t. Minimizing for the temporal derivative d_t of the disparities permits linear motions of objects perpendicular to the image plane.

According to Scharstein and Szeliski, most stereo matching algorithms can be subdivided into the following successive stages:

S1	Matching cost computation
S2	Cost aggregation
S3	Minimization
S4	Disparity refinement

For efficiency, steps 1 to 3 usually only compute disparities at integer pixel accuracy. They are finally refined in the optional stage 4 up to a desired subpixel level. In the following, we explain those stages for our stereo matching implementation for a single pair of images. Extension to spacetime stereo is straightforward by adding the additional temporal domain.

- Matching cost computation does a pixel-wise correlation by evaluating equation $E_M(d) = e_M\left(C_L(x,y), C_R(x+d,y)\right)$, for all pixels (x,y) and a set of integer disparities d within a specific range. For each disparity d, all pixels of the left image are compared with those of the right image that has been shifted about d pixels along the x-direction. The result of the comparison using the error metric e_M is stored in a new image. Iteration over all disparities produces a whole stack of difference images, a so-called three-dimensional disparity space image (DSI).

- Cost aggregation does the averaging over the matching window W by computing the sum of equation $E_M(d) = \sum_{(x,y) \in W(x_0,y_0)} e\left(C_L(x,y), C_R(x+d,y)\right)$. For a rectangular window, this can simply be achieved by applying a box filter to each DSI layer of constant disparity.

- Minimization computes the final pixel-accurate disparities by identifying for each pixel in the DSI the layer with minimal cost.

- Disparity refinement computes a subpixel-accurate result by minimizing equation $E_M(d, d_x, d_y) = \sum_{(x,y) \in W(x_0,y_0)} e\left(C_L(x,y), C_R(x+d',y)\right)$. By constraining the search space of d to a small region around the previously computed coarse disparities, the optimization problem can be solved efficiently using the Levenberg-Marquardt algorithm. Besides allowing for skew surfaces by optimizing for dx and dy, we also handle discontinuities by masking those pixels in the correlation window whose coarse disparities differ too much from the one of the center pixel. This yields a non-rectangular window at depth boundaries. The additionally computed disparity gradients can be also used later to compute the 3D scene representation.

Stereo on Structured Light

The presented stereo matching algorithm requires a highly textured scene to find good correlations between different views. It generally fails in reconstructing simple geometry of uniformly colored objects, e.g. white walls. Additionally, the textures should be non-periodic to guarantee unique matches. As a consequence, we add artificial textures to the scene by projecting structured light patterns, as originally proposed by Kang et al. We use a binary vertical stripe pattern with randomly varying stripe widths. It yields strong and unique correlations in the horizontal direction of the stereo baseline and is at the same time insensitive to vertical deviations which may occur from inaccuracies in the camera calibration.

Rectified stereo camera images of a scene under uniform
illumination (top) and under structured light illumination (bottom).

If spacetime stereo is used, temporally changing patterns can further increase the matching quality. To avoid untextured shadows, multiple overlapping projections can be used for illumination. Unlike pure structured light approaches or stereo matching between a single camera and a projector, our approach has the advantage of also working robustly within those overlap regions up to a certain extent: The dynamic range of the imaging sensors should be high enough to cover both single and overlapping projections with a sufficient contrast. Due to the linearity of light reflection, the minimum pattern contrast of an overlap region is actually equal to the one of a single projection. Practical experience has shown that our acquisition equipment is able to robustly handle up to four overlapping projections, which should be sufficient to cover a whole scene. Moreover, stereo on structured light does not need a projector calibration. Figure shows a stereo pair of images from the same scene under uniform and under structured light illumination.

As a result, stereo matching is much more robust, even in untextured regions of the scene. Figure shows a comparison of reconstructions of the same scene under uniform illumination and with structured light projections.

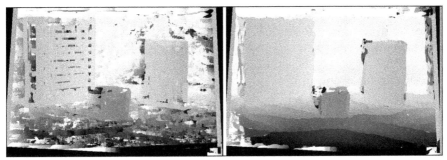

Depth map of the scene shown in figure reconstructed by local stereo matching
under uniform illumination (left) and by stereo on structured light (right).
In both cases, a matching window of 25×25 pixels was used.

Handling Depth Discontinuities

Local stereo matching algorithms generally have difficulties in properly handling depth discontinuities, as illustrated in figure. Due to occlusions, pixels in one image may not have corresponding partners in the other image. Furthermore, disparities are assumed to change only linearly within the matching window, which is not the case at discontinuities. In the following, two extensions for handling those issues are presented.

Symmetric Stereo Matching

The algorithm presented so far is asymmetric in a sense that it performs matching search only in the right image for fixed pixels of the left image. As a consequence, it assumes that each pixel in the left image should have a corresponding partner in the right image. This is, however, not the case at occlusions. In those situations, the algorithm finds matches that do not exist in reality. A good stereo algorithm should detect those situations and mask all occluded pixels.

Illustration of difficulties in correlating depth discontinuities. Left to right: Correlation window in left image, disparity image and right image. Upper row: occlusion. Lower row: Sharp color boundary.

This can be achieved by a simple extension called cross-checking. There, the coarse stereo matching in steps one to three is performed twice: search in the right image for pixels corresponding to left image, and vice versa. Corresponding pixels in both disparity maps should have the same values, otherwise they belong to occlusions. A result of symmetric stereo matching is presented in figure.

As a drawback, time for computing the coarse matching is doubled. This can be overcome by symmetric stereo algorithms which search for matches on both sides in one step. However, because processing time of coarse matching can be neglected over the time for sub pixel matching, we have chosen cross-checking for simplicity.

Symmetric stereo matching. Original scene (left) and computed occlusion mask (right).

Multi-window Matching

Due to the spatial extend of the correlation window, a second issue arises at discontinuities. Because discontinuities generally come along with sharp color boundaries, they cause a strong correlation. This yields a low matching cost as soon as the pixel window overlaps the color edge, no matter if the center pixel itself is part of that edge. Thus, the matching algorithm tends to find similar disparities in neighbourhoods on both sides of color boundaries, which cannot be correct at depth discontinuities.

To solve that, we extend our matching algorithm to a multi-window approach. At each pixel we consider all matching windows of equal size that still contain the pixel of interest and choose the one with the best correlation by extending equation

$$E_M(d) = \sum_{(x,y)\in W(x_0,y_0)} e\big(C_L(x,y),C_R(x+d,y)\big) \text{ to}$$

$$E_M(d) = \min_{(x',y')\in W(x_0,y_0)} \sum_{(x,y)\in W(x',y')} e\big(C_L(x,y),C_R(x+d,y)\big).$$

The chosen window usually has minimal overlaps with possible depth discontinuities, yielding a more reliable disparity value. A similar algorithm has already been proposed by Fusiello et al. who considered five different dilated windows around each pixel at the cost of a five times higher computation time. By sharing computations among neighbouring pixels, our algorithm is able to consider all possible dilated windows containing the pixel of interest with low computational costs. It is implemented as a minimum filter on the DSI layers of equal disparity, using the shape of the matching window as structuring element. The filter is applied after the cost aggregation, yielding a new five-step stereo pipeline:

S1	Matching cost computation
S2	Cost aggregation
S3	Minimum filter for discontinuity preservation
S4	Minimization
S5	Disparity refinement

As a result, our algorithm achieves a better reconstruction quality at depth discontinuities with only a small overhead in computational costs. A comparison of conventional window-based stereo and our multi-window approach is presented in figure.

References

- Multimedia-basics, certification-tutorial-html: vskills.in, Retrieved 10 March, 2019

- Hajnal JV, Hill DL (June 2001). Medical image registration. CRC press. ISBN 978-1-4200-4247-4

- Zhang, Jian, Yan, Ke, He, Zhen-Yu, and Xu, Yong (2014). "A Collaborative Linear Discriminative Representation Classification Method for Face Recognition. In 2014 International Conference on Artificial Intelligence and Software Engineering (AISE2014). Lancaster, PA: DEStech Publications, Inc. p.21 ISBN 9781605951508

- Stump, David (2014). Digital Cinematography: Fundamentals, Tools, Techniques, and Workflows. CRC Press. pp. 19–22. ISBN 978-1-136-04042-9

- Digital-images, computing-news-wires-white-papers-and-books: encyclopedia.com, Retrieved 14 June, 2019

- Murray, Susan (August 2008). "Digital Images, Photo-Sharing, and Our Shifting Notions of Everyday Aesthetics". Journal of Visual Culture. 7 (2): 147–163. doi:10.1177/1470412908091935

- Williams, J. B. (2017). The Electronics Revolution: Inventing the Future. Springer. pp. 245–8. ISBN 9783319490885

3
Multimedia Compression Technologies

Image compression, audio compression and video compression fall within the compression technologies of multimedia. It also involves transform coding, discrete cosine and wavelet transform, run length encoding, Huffman coding, etc. All these compression technologies used in multimedia have been carefully analyzed in this chapter.

Image Compression

Image compression is an application of data compression that encodes the original image with few bits. The objective of image compression is to reduce the redundancy of the image and to store or transmit data in an efficient form. Figure shows the block diagram of the general image storage system. The main goal of such system is to reduce the storage quantity as much as possible, and the decoded image displayed in the monitor can be similar to the original image as much as can be.

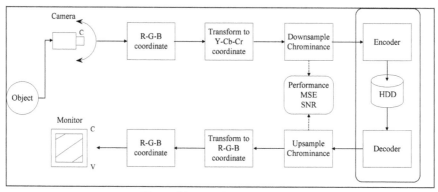

General image storage system.

Color Specification

The Y, Cb, and Cr components of one color image are defined in YUV color coordinate, where Y is commonly called the luminance and Cb, Cr are commonly called the chrominance. The meaning of luminance and chrominance is described as follows:

- Luminance: Received brightness of the light, which is proportional to the total energy in the visible band.

- Chrominance: Describe the perceived color tone of a light, which depends on the wavelength composition of light chrominance is in turn characterized by two attributes – hue and saturation.

  - Hue: Specify the color tone, which depends on the peak wavelength of the light.

  - Saturation: Describe how pure the color is, which depends on the spread or bandwidth of the light spectrum.

The RGB primary commonly used for color display mixes the luminance and chrominance attributes of a light. In many applications, it is desirable to describe a color in terms of its luminance and chrominance content separately, to enable more efficient processing and transmission of color signals. Towards this goal, various three-component color coordinates have been developed, in which one component reflects the luminance and the other two collectively characterize hue and saturation. One such coordinate is the YUV color space. The [Y Cb Cr]^T values in the YUV coordinate are related to the [R G B]T values in the RGB coordinate by:

$$\begin{pmatrix} Y \\ Cb \\ Cr \end{pmatrix} = \begin{pmatrix} 0.299 & 0.587 & 0.587 \\ -0.169 & -0.334 & 0.500 \\ 0.500 & -0.419 & -0.081 \end{pmatrix} \begin{pmatrix} R \\ G \\ B \end{pmatrix} + \begin{pmatrix} 0 \\ 128 \\ 128 \end{pmatrix}$$

Similarly, if we would like to transform the YUV coordinate back to RGB coordinate, the inverse matrix can be calculated from

$$\begin{pmatrix} Y \\ Cb \\ Cr \end{pmatrix} = \begin{pmatrix} 0.299 & 0.587 & 0.587 \\ -0.169 & -0.334 & 0.500 \\ 0.500 & -0.419 & -0.081 \end{pmatrix} \begin{pmatrix} R \\ G \\ B \end{pmatrix} + \begin{pmatrix} 0 \\ 128 \\ 128 \end{pmatrix},$$

and the inverse transform is taken to obtain the corresponding RGB components.

Spatial Sampling of Color Component

Because the eyes of human are more sensitive to the luminance than the chrominance, the sampling rate of chrominance components is half that of the luminance component. This will result in good performance in image compression with almost no loss of characteristics in visual perception of the new upsampled image. There are three color formats in the baseline system:

- 4:4:4 format: The sampling rate of the luminance component is the same as those of the chrominance.

- 4:2:2 format: There are 2 Cb samples and 2 Cr samples for every 4 Y samples. This leads to half number of pixels in each line, but the same number of lines per frame.

- 4:2:0 format: Sample the Cb and Cr components by half in both the horizontal and vertical directions. In this format, there are also 1 Cb sample and 1 Cr sample for every 4 Y samples.

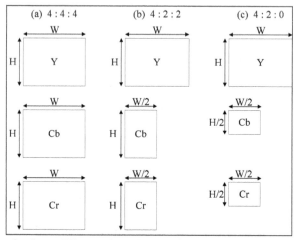

The three different chrominance downsampling format.

At the decoder, the downsampled chrominance components of 4:2:2 and 4:2:0 formats should be upsampled back to 4:4:4 format.

The Flow of Image Compression Coding

Image compression coding is to store the image into bit-stream as compact as possible and to display the decoded image in the monitor as exact as possible. Now consider an encoder and a decoder as shown in figure. When the encoder receives the original image file, the image file will be converted into a series of binary data, which is called the bit-stream. The decoder then receives the encoded bit-stream and decodes it to form the decoded image. If the total data quantity of the bit-stream is less than the total data quantity of the original image, then this is called image compression. The full compression flow is as shown in figure.

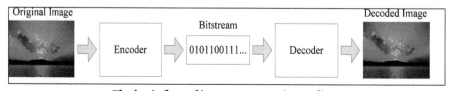

The basic flow of image compression coding.

The compression ratio is defined as follows:

$$Cr = \frac{n1}{n2},$$

where n1 is the data rate of original image and n2 is that of the encoded bit-stream.

In order to evaluate the performance of the image compression coding, it is necessary to define a measurement that can estimate the difference between the original image and the decoded image. Two common used measurements are the Mean Square Error (MSE) and the Peak Signal to Noise Ratio (PSNR), which are defined in

$$MSE = \sqrt{\frac{\sum_{x=0}^{W-1}\sum_{y=0}^{H-1}\left[f(x,y)-f'(x,y)\right]^2}{WH}} \quad \text{and} \quad PSNR = 20\log_{10}\frac{255}{MSE},$$

respectively. f(x,y) is the pixel value of the original image, and f'(x,y) is the pixel value of the decoded image. Most image compression systems are designed to minimize the MSE and maximize the PSNR.

$$MSE = \sqrt{\frac{\sum_{x=0}^{W-1}\sum_{y=0}^{H-1}\left[f(x,y)-f'(x,y)\right]^2}{WH}}$$

$$PSNR = 20\log_{10}\frac{255}{MSE}.$$

The general encoding architecture of image compression system is shown is figure.

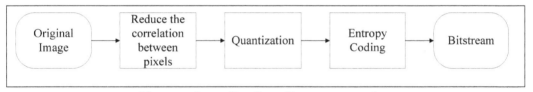

The general encoding flow of image compression.

Reduce the Correlation between Pixels

The reason is that the correlation between one pixel and its neighbor pixels is very high, or we can say that the values of one pixel and its adjacent pixels are very similar. Once the correlation between the pixels is reduced, we can take advantage of the statistical characteristics and the variable length coding theory to reduce the storage quantity. This is the most important part of the image compression algorithm; there are a lot of relevant processing methods being proposed. The best-known methods are as follows:

- Predictive Coding: Predictive Coding such as DPCM (Differential Pulse Code Modulation) is a lossless coding method, which means that the decoded image and the original image have the same value for every corresponding element.

- Orthogonal Transform: Karhunen-Loeve Transform (KLT) and Discrete Cosine

Transform (DCT) are the two most well-known orthogonal transforms. The DCT-based image compression standard such as JPEG is a lossy coding method that will result in some loss of details and unrecoverable distortion.

- Subband Coding: Subband Coding such as Discrete Wavelet Transform (DWT) is also a lossy coding method. The objective of subband coding is to divide the spectrum of one image into the lowpass and the highpass components. JPEG 2000 is a 2-dimension DWT based image compression standard.

Quantization

The objective of quantization is to reduce the precision and to achieve higher compression ratio. For instance, the original image uses 8 bits to store one element for every pixel; if we use less bits such as 6 bits to save the information of the image, then the storage quantity will be reduced, and the image can be compressed. The shortcoming of quantization is that it is a lossy operation, which will result into loss of precision and unrecoverable distortion.

Entropy Coding

The main objective of entropy coding is to achieve less average length of the image. Entropy coding assigns codewords to the corresponding symbols according to the probability of the symbols. In general, the entropy encoders are used to compress the data by replacing symbols represented by equal-length codes with the codewords whose length is inverse proportional to corresponding probability.

Image Compression Standard

JPEG – Joint Picture Expert Group

Figure below shows the Encoder and Decoder model of JPEG.

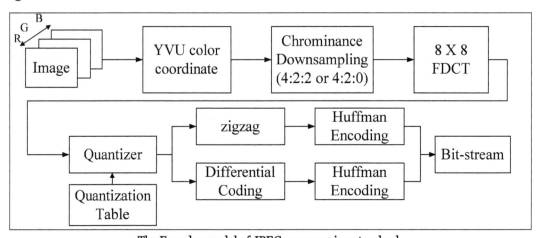

The Encoder model of JPEG compression standard.

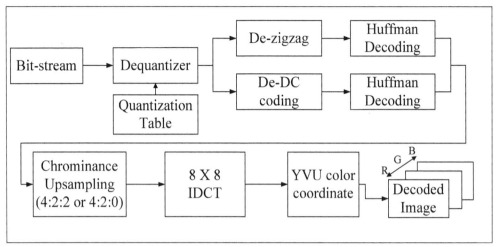

The Decoder model of JPEG compression standard.

Discrete Cosine Transform

The next step after color coordinate conversion is to divide the three color components of the image into many 8×8 blocks. The mathematical definition of the Forward DCT and the Inverse DCT are as follows:

Forward DCT:

$$F(u,v) = \frac{1}{2}C(u)C(v)\sum_{x=0}^{N-1}\sum_{y=0}^{N-1}f(x,y)\cos\left[\frac{\pi(2x+1)u}{2N}\right]\cos\left[\frac{\pi(2y+1)v}{2N}\right]$$

For $u = 0,...,N-1$ and $v = 0,...,N-1$

Where $N = 8$ and $C(k) = \begin{cases} 1/\sqrt{2} & \text{for } k = 0 \\ 1 & \text{otherwise} \end{cases}$

Inverse DCT:

$$f(x,y) = \frac{2}{N}\sum_{x=0}^{N-1}\sum_{y=0}^{N-1}C(u)C(v)F(u,v)\cos\left[\frac{\pi(2x+1)u}{2N}\right]\cos\left[\frac{\pi(2y+1)v}{2N}\right]$$

for $x = 0,...,N-1$ and $0,...,N-1$ where $N = 8$.

The $f(x,y)$ is the value of each pixel in the selected 8×8 block, and the $F(u,v)$ is the DCT coefficient after transformation. The transformation of the 8×8 block is also a 8×8 block composed of $F(u,v)$.

The DCT is closely related to the DFT. Both of them taking a set of points from the spatial domain and transform them into an equivalent representation in the frequency domain. However, why DCT is more appropriate for image compression than DFT? The two main reasons are:

- The DCT can concentrate the energy of the transformed signal in low frequency, whereas the DFT can not. According to Parseval's theorem, the energy is the same in the spatial domain and in the frequency domain. Because the human eyes are less sensitive to the low frequency component, we can focus on the low frequency component and reduce the contribution of the high frequency component after taking DCT.

- For image compression, the DCT can reduce the blocking effect than the DFT.

After transformation, the element in the upper most left corresponding to zero frequency in both directions is the "DC coefficient" and the rest are called "AC coefficients."

Quantization in JPEG

Quantization is the step where we actually throw away data. The DCT is a lossless procedure. The data can be precisely recovered through the IDCT (this isn't entirely true because in reality no physical implementation can compute with perfect accuracy). During Quantization every coefficients in the 8×8 DCT matrix is divided by a corresponding quantization value.

The quantized coefficient is defined in $F\left(u\ v\right)_{Quantization} = round\left(\dfrac{F\left(u,v\right)}{Q\left(u,v\right)}\right)$, and the reverse the process can be achieved by the $F\left(u,v\right)_{deQ} = F\left(u\ v\right)_{Quantization} \times Q\left(u,v\right)$.

$$F\left(u\ v\right)_{Quantization} = round\left(\dfrac{F\left(u,v\right)}{Q\left(u,v\right)}\right)$$

$$F\left(u,v\right)_{deQ} = F\left(u\ v\right)_{Quantization} \times Q\left(u,v\right).$$

The goal of quantization is to reduce most of the less important high frequency DCT coefficients to zero, the more zeros we generate the better the image will compress. The matrix Q generally has lower numbers in the upper left direction and large numbers in the lower right direction. Though the high-frequency components are removed, the IDCT still can obtain an approximate matrix which is close to the original 8×8 block matrix. The JPEG committee has recommended certain Q matrix that work well and the performance is close to the optimal condition, the Q matrix for luminance and chrominance components is defined in below 2 equations.

$$Q_Y = \begin{pmatrix} 16 & 11 & 10 & 16 & 24 & 40 & 51 & 61 \\ 12 & 12 & 14 & 19 & 26 & 58 & 60 & 55 \\ 14 & 13 & 16 & 24 & 40 & 57 & 69 & 56 \\ 14 & 17 & 22 & 29 & 51 & 87 & 80 & 62 \\ 18 & 22 & 37 & 56 & 68 & 109 & 103 & 77 \\ 24 & 35 & 55 & 64 & 81 & 104 & 113 & 92 \\ 49 & 64 & 78 & 87 & 103 & 121 & 120 & 101 \\ 72 & 92 & 95 & 98 & 112 & 100 & 103 & 99 \end{pmatrix}$$

$$Q_C = \begin{pmatrix} 17 & 18 & 24 & 47 & 99 & 99 & 99 & 99 \\ 18 & 21 & 26 & 66 & 99 & 99 & 99 & 99 \\ 24 & 26 & 56 & 99 & 99 & 99 & 99 & 99 \\ 47 & 66 & 99 & 99 & 99 & 99 & 99 & 99 \\ 99 & 99 & 99 & 99 & 99 & 99 & 99 & 99 \\ 99 & 99 & 99 & 99 & 99 & 99 & 99 & 99 \\ 99 & 99 & 99 & 99 & 99 & 99 & 99 & 99 \\ 99 & 99 & 99 & 99 & 99 & 99 & 99 & 99 \end{pmatrix}$$

Zigzag Scan

After quantization, the DC coefficient is treated separately from the 63 AC coefficients. The DC coefficient is a measure of the average value of the original 64 image samples. Because there is usually strong correlation between the DC coefficients of adjacent 8×8 blocks, the quantized DC coefficient is encoded as the difference from the DC term of the previous block. This special treatment is worthwhile, as DC coefficients frequently contain a significant fraction of the total image energy. The other 63 entries are the AC components. They are treated separately from the DC coefficients in the entropy coding process.

0	1	5	6	14	15	27	28
2	4	7	13	16	26	29	42
3	8	12	17	25	30	41	43
9	11	18	24	31	40	44	53
10	19	23	32	39	45	52	54
20	22	33	38	46	51	55	60
21	34	37	47	50	56	59	61
35	36	48	49	57	58	62	63

The zigzag scan order.

Entropy Coding in JPEG

Differential Coding

The mathematical representation of the differential coding is:

$$\text{Diffi}_i = DC_i - DC_{i-1}$$

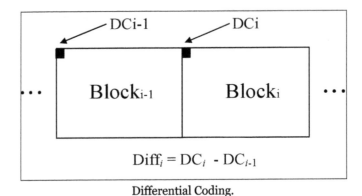

Differential Coding.

We set $DC_0 = 0$. DC of the current block DC_i will be equal to $DC_{i-1} + \text{Diff}_i$. Therefore, in the JPEG file, the first coefficient is actually the difference of DCs. Then the difference is encoded with Huffman coding algorithm together with the encoding of AC coefficients.

Zero-run-length Coding

After quantization and zigzag scanning, we obtain the one-dimensional vectors with a lot of consecutive zeroes. We can make use of this property and apply zero-run-length coding, which is variable length coding. Let us consider the 63 AC coefficients in the original 64 quantized vectors first. For instance, we have:

$$57, 45, 0, 0, 0, 0, 23, 0, -30, -16, 0, 0, 1, 0, 0, 0, 0, 0, 0, 0, ..., 0$$

We encode then encode the vector:

$57, 45, 0, 0, 0, 0, 23, 0, -30, -16, 0, 0, 1, 0, 0, 0, 0, 0, 0, 0, ..., 0$ into vector

$$(0, 57); (0, 45); (4, 23); (1, -30); (0, -16); (2, 1); EOB.$$

$$(0, 57); (0, 45); (4, 23); (1, -30); (0, -16); (2, 1); EOB.$$

The notation (L,F) means that there are L zeros in front of F, and EOB (End of Block) is a special coded value means that the rest elements are all zeros. If the last element of the vector is not zero, then the EOB marker will not be added. On the other hand, EOC is equivalent to (0,0), so we can express $(0, 57); (0, 45); (4, 23); (1, -30); (0, -16); (2, 1); EOB$ as $(0, 57); (0, 45); (4, 23); (1, -30); (0, -16); (2, 1); (0, 0)$.

$$(0,57);(0,45);(4,23);(1,-30);(0,-16);(2,1);(0,0)$$

We give a special case that L is larger than 15. See the following example.

$$57, eighteen\ zeroes, 3,0,0,0,0,2, thirty-three\ zeroes, 895, EOB$$

The JPEG Huffman coding restricts the number of previous zero(s) within 15 because the length of the encoded data is 4 bits. Hence,

we can encode $57, eighteen\ zeroes, 3,0,0,0,0,2, thirty-three\ zeroes, 895, EOB$ into $(0,57);(15,0);(2,3);(4,2);(15,0);(15,0);(1,895);(0,0)$.

$$(0,57);(15,0);(2,3);(4,2);(15,0);(15,0);(1,895);(0,0)$$

(15,0) is a special coded value which indicates that there are 16 consecutive zeroes. Therefore, the both of the values 18 and 33 are converted to 15.

Now back to the example $57,45,0,0,0,0,23,0,-30,-16,0,0,1,0,0,0,0,0,0,0,...,0$. The right value of the bracket is called category, and the left value of the bracket is called run. We can encode the category by looking up table which is specified in the JPEG standard. For example, 57 is in the category 6 and the bits for the value is 111001, so we encode it as 6,111001. The full encoded sequence of $57,45,0,0,0,0,23,0,-30,-16,0,0,1,0,0,0,0,0,0,0,...,0$ is as $(0,6,111001);(0,6,101101);(4,5,10111);(1,5,00001);(0,4,0111);(2,1,1);(0,0)$.

$$(0,6,111001);(0,6,101101);(4,5,10111);(1,5,00001);(0,4,0111);(2,1,1);(0,0)$$

Table of the category and bit-coded values.

Category	Values	Bits for the value
1	-1,1	0,1
2	-3,-2,2,3	00,01,10,11
3	-7,-6,-5,-4,4,5,6,7	000,001,010,011,100,101,110,111
4	-15,...,-8,8,...,15	0000,...,0111,1000,...,1111
5	-31,...,-16,16,...31	00000,...,01111,10000,...,11111
6	-63,...,-32,32,...63	000000,...,011111,100000,...,111111
7	127,...,-64,64,...,127	0000000,...,0111111,1000000,...,1111111
8	-255,..,-128,128,..,255	...
9	-511,..,-256,256,..,511	...
10	-1023,..,-512,512,..,1023	...
11	-2047,...,-1024,1024,...,2047	...

The first two values in bracket parenthesis can be represented on a byte because of the fact that each of the two values is 0,1,2,...,15. In this byte, the higher 4-bit (run) represents the number of previous zeros, and the lower 4-bit (category) represents the the value which is not 0.

The JPEG standard specifies the Huffman table for encoding the AC coefficients which is listed in table The final step is to encode

$(0,6,111001);(0,6,101101);(4,5,10111);(1,5,00001);(0,4,0111);(2,1,1);(0,0)$ by using the Huffman table defined in table.

Huffman Table of AC Coefficients

Run/Category	Code Length	Code Word
0/0 (EOB)	4	1010
15/0 (ZRL)	11	11111111001
0/1	2	00
...		
0/6	7	1111000
...		
0/10	16	1111111110000011
1/1	4	1100
1/2	5	11011
...		
1/10	16	1111111110001000
2/1	5	11100
...		
4/5	16	1111111110011000
...		
15/10	16	1111111111111110

The encoding method is quite easy and straight forward. For instance, the code (0,6) is encoded as 1111000, and the code (4,5) is encoded as 1111111110001000. The final bit-stream stored in the JPEG file for example $57,45,0,0,0,0,23,0,-30,-16,0,0,1,0,0,0,0,0,0,...,0$ is as (2.14).

> 1111000 1111001,111000 101101,1111111110011000 10111,
>
> 11111110110 00001,1011 0111,11100 1,1010

JPEG 2000

The JPEG standard has been used for many years and provided satisfactory quality for the users, but the quality of JPEG cannot fulfill the advanced requirement for image coding today. JPEG 2000 outperforms JPEG in many aspects, the major features of the JPEG 2000 standard is outlined as follows:

- High compression efficiency.

- Lossless color transformation.

- Region-of-Interest Coding.

- Lossless and lossy compression.

- Random code stream access and processing.

- Error resilience.

Figure below show the Encoder and Decoder architecture of JPEG 2000. We will introduce the operation and theory of each block in the following sections.

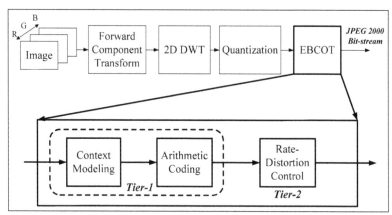

The encoder architecture of JPEG 2000.

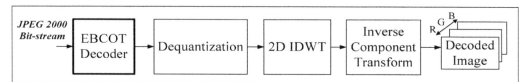

The decoder architecture of JPEG 2000.

Color Space Conversion

Instead of using the Irreversible Color Transform, JPEG 2000 adopts the Reversible Color Transform (RCT), which is a modified YUV color transform that does not contribute to quantization errors, so it is fully reversible. Proper implementation of the RCT requires that numbers are rounded as specified that cannot be expressed exactly in matrix form. The transformation is:

$$Yr = \left[\frac{R+2G+B}{4} \right]; Ur = B - G; Vr = R - G \cdot$$

The Inverse transformation can be obtained by:

$$G = Yr - \left(\frac{Ur + Vr}{4}\right); R = Ur + G; B = Vr + G.$$

$$G = Yr - \left(\frac{Ur + Vr}{4}\right); R = Ur + G; B = Vr + G$$

Quantization in JPEG 2000

To reduce the number of bits needed to represent the transform coefficients, the coefficient ab(u,v) of subband b is quantized to value qb(u,v) using:

$$q_b(u,v) = sign\left[a_u(u,v)\right] \cdot floor\left[\frac{\left|a_{b(u,v)}\right|}{\Delta_b}\right]$$

$$q_b(u,v) = sign\left[a_u(u,v)\right] \cdot floor\left[\frac{\left|a_{b(u,v)}\right|}{\Delta_b}\right]$$

where the quantization step size is $\Delta_b = 2^{R_b - \varepsilon_b}\left(1 + \frac{\mu_b}{2^{11}}\right)$

Rb is the nominal dynamic range of subband b, and ε band μ_b are the number of bits allotted to the exponent and mantissa of the subband's coefficients, respectively.

The nominal dynamic range of subband b is the sum of the number of bits used to represent the original image and the analysis gain bits for subband b.

Quantization operation is defined by the step size Δb, the selection of the step size is quite flexible, but there are a few restrictions imposed by the JPEG 2000 standard.

- Reversible wavelets: When reversible wavelets are utilized in JPEG 2000, uniform deadzone scalar quantization with a step size of $\Delta b = 1$ must be used.

- Irreversible wavelets: When irreversible wavelets are utilized in JPEG 2000, the step size selection is restricted only by the signaling syntax itself. The step size is specified in terms of an exponent εb, ε_b, $0 \le \varepsilon b < 2^5$, and a mantissa $\mu b, 0 \le \mu b < 2^{11}$.

EBCOT in JPEG 2000

Embedded Block Coding with Optimized Truncation (EBCOT) is adopted for the entropy coding of JPEG 2000. The EBCOT can be divided into two steps: Tier-1 and Tier-2 as shown in figure. The Tier-1 part is composed of the context formation and Arithmetic Coding. The Tier-1 encoder divides the input DWT coefficients into separate code blocks and encodes each block into block-based bit-stream. After Tier-1 coding operation, the Tier-2 truncates the embedded bit-stream to minimize the embedded bit-stream.

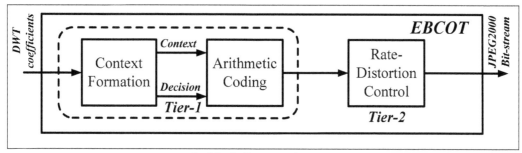

The block diagram of EBCOT.

Context Formation

The objective of context formation is to generate the context decision pairs for the arithmetic coder. We introduce some relevant concept in advance.

- Bit-plan scanning: The decimal DWT coefficients can be converted into signed binary format, so the DWT coefficients are decomposed into many 1-bit planes. Take one DWT coefficient for example, a bit is called significant after the first bit '1' is met from MSB to LSB, and the bits '0' before this bit '1' are insignificant, as shown in figure.

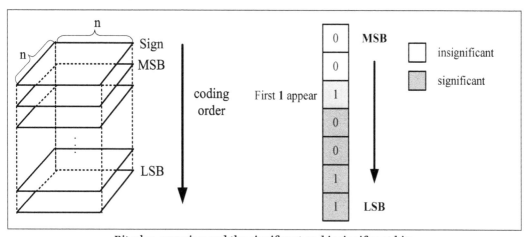

Bit-plan scanning and the significant and insignificant bits.

The scanning order of the bit-plane is shown as figure. Each element of the bit-plane is called a sample, and four vertical samples can form one column stripe. The 16 column stripes in the horizontal direction can form a full stripe.

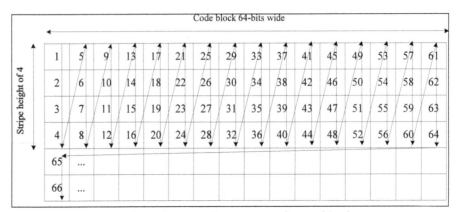

Context formation scanning sequence for one bit-plane.

The context window: The context window of JPEG 2000 is shown in figure, the "curr" is the sample which is to be coded, and the other 8 samples are its neighbor samples. The samples 1d, 3d, 6d, and 8d are the diagonal ones. The samples 2v and 7v are the vertical ones. The samples 4h and 5h are the horizontal ones.

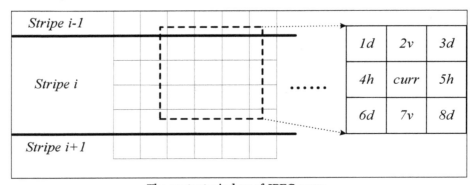

The context window of JPEG 2000.

Three coding passes:

- Significance Propagation Pass (pass1): Scanning all insignificant samples which have at least one of the neighbors become significant to determine whether it will become significant at current bit plane.

- Magnitude Refinement Pass (pass2): The coefficients-bits have become significant in previous bit-plane will be coded in pass2.

- Cleanup Pass (pass3): The remained coefficients rejected by pass1 and pass2 are coded in pass3.

Four Types of coding operations for Arithmetic coding:

- Zero Coding (ZC): This coding method is used to code the new significance. The context is determined according to the significance of the neighbors. The context assignment table for zero coding is defined in table.

Context Assignment Table for Zero Coding

LL and LH subbands			HL subband			HH subband		
ΣH	ΣV	ΣD	ΣH	ΣV	ΣD	$\Sigma(H+V)$	ΣD	Context Label
2	x	x	x	2	x	x	≥ 3	8
1	≥ 1	x	≥ 1	1	x	≥ 1	2	7
1	0	≥ 1	0	1	≥ 1	0	2	6
1	0	0	0	1	0	≥ 2	1	5
0	2	x	2	0	x	1	1	4
0	1	x	1	0	x	0	1	3
0	0	≥ 2	0	0	≥ 2	≥ 2	0	2
0	0	1	0	0	1	1	0	1
0	0	0	0	0	0	0	0	0

Sign Coding (SC): This coding method is used to code the sign samples right after the corresponding coefficient is identified significant. The context is determined by the sign of the four neighbors in the vertical and horizontal directions. There are two relevant tables defined in Table below, respectively: (a) Sign contribution of the H and V neighbors for sign coding. (b) Context assignment table for sign coding. The value of the decision can be obtained form $D = \oplus$ sign bit XOR bit.

Sign Contribution of the H and V Neighbors for Sign Coding

Sign Distribution	Significant (+)	Significant (-)	Insignificant
Significant (+)	1	0	1
Significant (-)	0	-1	-1
Insignificant	1	-1	0

Context Assignment Table for Sign Coding

Horizontal Contribution	Vertical Contribution	Context Label	XOR bit
1	1	13	0
1	0	12	0
1	-1	11	0
0	1	10	0
0	0	9	0
0	-1	10	1
-1	1	11	1
-1	0	12	1
-1	-1	13	1

Magnitude Refinement (MR): The context depends on the significance of its neighbors and whether it is the first time for refinement. The context is determined by the summation of the significance state of the horizontal, vertical, and diagonal neighbors.

Context Assignment Table for Magnitude Refinement

$\Sigma H + \Sigma V + \Sigma D$	1st refinement for this coefficient	Context label
X	False	16
≥1	True	15
0	True	14

Run-Length Coding (RLC): This coding method is used to reduce the average number of symbols needed to be coded. RLC must satisfy the following two conditions:

• Four consecutive coefficients in the same stripe must be insignificant.

• All consecutive neighbors for the four coefficients must be insignificant.

Only one context is needed when all the four samples are insignificant. If any one of the four samples becomes significant, more than one context is needed to indicate the location of the significant.

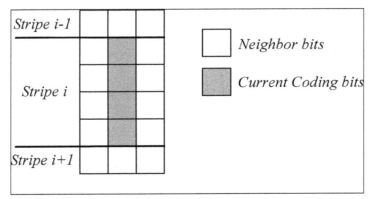

Current coding bits and their neighbors for RLC operation.

Arithmetic Coding

The decision and context data generated from context formation is coded in the arithmetic encoder (AE). The arithmetic encoder used by JPEG 2000 standard is a binary adaptive MQ coder. The basis of the binary arithmetic coding is a recursive probability interval subdivision process. Since it is a binary AE, there are only two sub-intervals. With each decision, the current probability interval is subdivided into two sub-intervals. If the value of decision is 1 then it means that it is More Possible Symbol (MPS). Otherwise, the value of decision is 0 and it means that it is Less Possible Symbol. The data distribution is shown in figure. The probability of MPS and LPS is represented by the gray interval and the white interval, respectively. The basic operation of the arithmetic encoder is calculating the new MPS and LPS according to the context and the decision form context formation. Because the AE of EBCOT is an adaptive encoder, the intervals of MPS and LPS will dynamically change with the value of decision. For example, if the context and the decision are equal to the value of MPS, then code MPS; otherwise, code LPS. The process is shown in figure. The operation stops until all context and decision are coded.

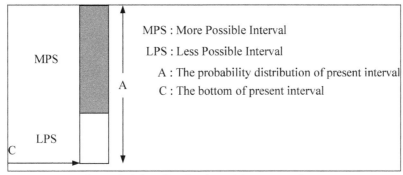

The probability distribution of the MPS and LPS.

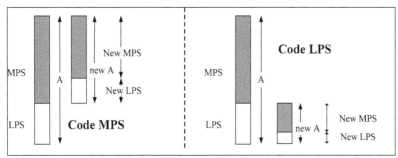

The MPS and LPS of the arithmetic encoder.

Rate Distortion Optimization

Each coding from tier-1 is a candidate truncation point of a code-block and the coding pass information is packaged into data units called packets in tier-2 coding. For meeting a target bit-rate or transmission time, the packaging process imposes a particular organization of coding pass data in the output code-stream. The rate-control assures that the desired number of bytes used by the code-stream while assuring the highest image quality possible.

Shape-adaptive Image Compression

Both the JPEG and JPEG 2000 image compression standard can achieve great compression ratio, however, both of them do not take advantage of the local characteristics of the given image effectively. Here is one new image compression algorithm proposed by Huang [4], it is called Shape Adaptive Image Compression, which is abbreviated as SAIC. Instead of taking the whole image as an object and utilizing transform coding, quantization, and entropy coding to encode this object, the SAIC algorithm segments the whole image into several objects, and each object has its own local characteristic and color. Because of the high correlation of the color values in each image segment, the SAIC can achieve better compression ratio and quality than conventional image compression algorithm.

The architecture of the shape-adaptive image compression is shown in figure. There are three parts of operation. First, the input image is segmented into boundary part and internal texture part. The boundary part contains the boundary information of the object, while the internal texture part contains the internal contents of the object such as color value. The two parts of the object is transformed and encoded, respectively. Finally, the two separate encoded data will be combined into the full bit-stream, and the processing of shape-adaptive image compression is finished. The theory and operation of each part will be introduced in the following sections.

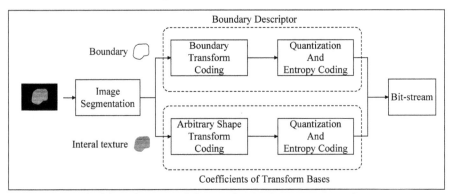

The block diagram of shape-adaptive image compression.

Boundary Description and Compression

First we obtain the boundary of the each object from the given image by means of image segmentation algorithm. Secondly, the boundary must be divided into two parts, and each part forms a non-closed boundary. We can make use of a second order polynomial to approximate the non-closed boundary. The equation of the second order polynomial is represented in $yk = Ax^2_k - Ax_{k-1}x_k$, for $k = 0,1,...,k-1$ and

$$A = -\frac{\sum_{k=0}^{K-1}\left[s_3(k)\left(-x_k^2 + x_{k-1}x_k\right)\right]}{\sum_{k=0}^{K-1}\left[\left(-x_k^2 + x_{k-1}x_k\right)^2\right]}.$$ The original and the approximate curve are shown in figure.

$$yk = Ax^2_k - Ax_{k-1}x_k, \text{for} k = 0,1,...,k-1$$

$$A = -\frac{\sum_{k=0}^{K-1}\left[s_3(k)\left(-x_k^2 + x_{k-1}x_k\right)\right]}{\sum_{k=0}^{K-1}\left[\left(-x_k^2 + x_{k-1}x_k\right)^2\right]}$$

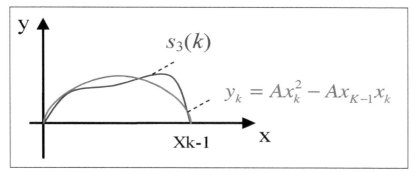

The original boundary $s_3(k)$ and the approximate 2ndorder curve y_k.

After the approximation of the boundary obtained, we express the coordinate of each points in the approximation as a complex number so the two dimensional data can be transformed into one dimensional data.

The mathematical expression is in $s(k) = x(k) + jy(k)$ for $k = 0, 1, 2, ..., K-1$.

$$s(k) = x(k) + jy(k) \text{ for } k = 0, 1, 2, ..., K-1$$

s(k) can be transformed into frequency domain by means of Fourier descriptor. The frequency components are expressed by a(u), and the forward transform is:

$$a(u) = \sum_{k=0}^{K-1} s(k) e^{-j2\pi uk/k} \text{ for } u = 0, 1, 2, ..., K-1.$$

In order to reduce the amount of data required to save the boundary, we truncate the less necessary high-frequency components. However, this may result in distortion, and the recovery boundary will be closed as shown in figure.

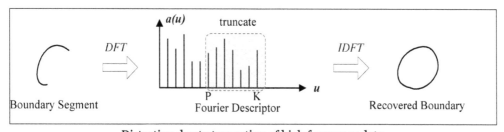

Distortion due to truncation of high frequency data.

The steps of the method is shown in figure and listed as follows:

- Record the coordinate of two end points of the non-closed boundary.

- Shift the boundary points linearly according to the distance on the curve between the two end points.

- Add a boundary segment which is odd-symmetric to the original one, and transform the two-dimensional data into one-dimensional complex number.

- Transform the one-dimensional complex data from spatial domain into frequency domain.

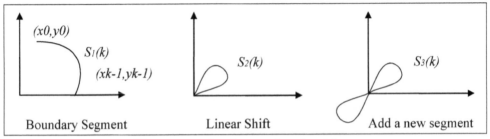

The steps to solve the non-closed problem.

Odd-symmetry property of DFT:

$$-s(-k) \xrightarrow{DFT} -a(-u) \cdot$$

Therefore, if the signal s(k) is odd-symmetric, its DFT a(u) is also odd-symmetric.

$$s(k) = -s(-k) \xrightarrow{DFT} a(u) = -a(-u) \cdot$$

Since the expanded data is odd symmetric to the original data, we can obtain the symmetric part from the original boundary by $s(k) = -s(-k) \xrightarrow{DFT} a(u) = -a(-u)$. Therefore, the odd symmetric part is useless and can be truncated, and the boundary can achieve compression of the boundary segments successfully. The frequency data can be encoded with entropy coding algorithm afterward.

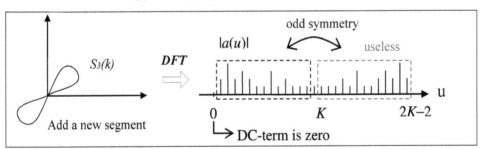

The new boundary segment and its Fourier descriptor.

Shape-adaptive Transform Coding

After the internal texture of one image segment is obtained, we can take DCT of the data of the internal texture. However, the height and width of one image segment are usually not equal. Hence, we redefine the DCT as:

Forward Shape-adaptive DCT:

$$F(k) = \sum_{x=0}^{W-1} \sum_{y=0}^{H-1} f(x,y) \omega'_{x,y}(k), \text{ for } k = 1, 2, ..., M$$

$$C(k) = \begin{cases} 1/\sqrt{2} \text{ for } k = 0 \\ 1 \quad \text{otherwise} \end{cases}$$

Inverse Shape-adaptive DCT:

$$f(x,y) = \frac{2}{\sqrt{H*W}} \sum_{k=1}^{M} F(k)\omega'_{x,y}(k), \text{ for } x = 0,...,W-1 \text{ and } y = 0,...,H-1$$

$$C(k) = \begin{cases} 1/\sqrt{2} \text{ for } k = 0 \\ 1 \quad \text{otherwise} \end{cases}$$

where W and H are the width and height of the image segment, respectively. M is the length of the DCT coefficients.

The F(u,v) is called the Shape-Adaptive DCT coefficient, and the DCT basis is:

$$\omega_{x,y}{}'(u,v) = \frac{2C(u)C(v)}{\sqrt{H*W}} \cos\left[\frac{\pi(2x+1)u}{2W}\right] \cos\left[\frac{\pi(2y+1)v}{2H}\right].$$

Because the number of points M is less than or equal to H×W, we can know that the H×W bases may not be orthogonal. We can obtain the M orthogonal bases by means of Gram-Schmidt process. After obtaining the orthogonal bases, we can take Shape-Adaptive DCT afterward.

Shape-adaptive Quantization

After the transform coefficients are obtained, we quantize the coefficients to compress the data. Because the length of the coefficients of the arbitrary shape is not fixed, the quantization table for JPEG in equations must be modified. Huang propose the unfixed quantization array as follows:

$$Q(k) = Q_a k + Q_c, \qquad \text{for } k = 1, 2, ..., M$$

where the two parameters Q_a and Q_c are the slope and the intercept of the line, respectively. And M is the length of the DCT coefficients.

Each DCT coefficient F(k) is divided by the corresponding quantization array Q(k) and rounded to the nearest integer as $F_q(k) = Round\left(\dfrac{F(k)}{Q(k)}\right)$, where $k = 1, 2, ..., M$:

$$F_q(k) = Round\left(\frac{F(k)}{Q(k)}\right), \quad \text{where } k = 1, 2, ..., M$$

Shape-adaptive Entropy Coding

Before introducing the theory of Shape-Adaptive entropy coding, here is one problem must be solved. Because the variation of color around the boundary is large, if we truncate these high frequency components, the original image may be corrupted by some unnecessary noise.

Since most of the variation is around the boundary region, we can divide the internal texture segments into internal part and boundary region part.

The way to divide the image segment is making use of morphological erosion. For two binary image set A and B, the erosion of A by B, denote $A \ominus B$, is defined as:

$$A \ominus B = \left\{ z \big| (B)_z \subseteq A \right\}$$

where the translation of set B by point $z = (z_1, z_2)$, denoted $(B)_z$, is defined as:

$$(B)_z = \left\{ c \big| c = b + z, \quad \text{for } b \in B \right\}$$

That is, the erosion of A by B is the set of all points z such that B which is translated by z is contained in A. Base on the definition described above, we erode the shapes of image segments by a 5×5 disk-shape image and we get the shape of the internal region. Then we subtract it from the original shape and we get the shape of boundary region. The process is illustrated in figure.

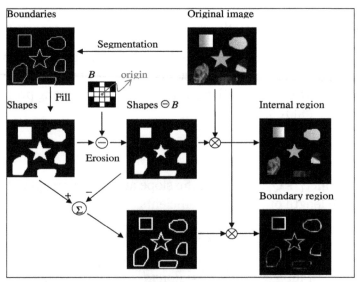

Divide the image segment by morphological erosion.

After transforming and quantizing the internal texture, we can encode the quantized coefficients and combine these encoded internal texture coefficients with the encoded boundary bit-stream. The full encoding process is shown in figure.

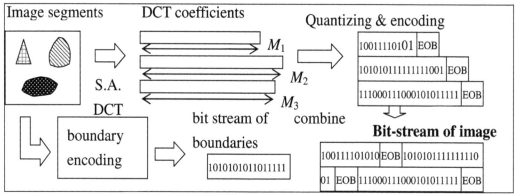

Process of shape-adaptive coding method.

Lossy Compression

Lossy compression aims at achieving a good compression ratio, but the cost for it is the loss of some original information. How much source information can be lost depends very much on the nature of applications. Nevertheless, the measure of a lossy compression algorithm or a lossy compression system normally includes a measure of the quality of reconstructed images compared with the original ones.

Distortion Measure

Although the best measure of the closeness or fidelity of a reconstructed image is to ask a person familiar with the work to look at the image and provide an opinion; this is not always practical because it is not useful in mathematical design approaches.

Here we introduce the more usual approach in which we try to measure the difference between the reconstructed image and the original one.

There are mathematical tools that measure the distortion in value of two variables, also called difference distortion measure. Considering an image to be a matrix of values; the measure of compression algorithm normally uses a standard matrix to measure the difference between reconstructed images and the original ones.

Let P_i be the pixels of reconstructed image and Q_i be the ones of the original, where i = 1, $\cdots$, N. We have the following commonly used measures:

- Squared error measure matrix (this is a measure of the difference):

$$D_i = \left(P_i - Q_i\right)^2$$

- Absolute difference measure matrix:

$$D_i = \left|P_i - Q_i\right|$$

- Mean squared error measure (MSE) matrix (this is an average measure):

$$\sigma^2 = \frac{1}{N}\sum_{i=1}^{N}(P_i - Q_i)^2$$

- Signal-to-noise-ratio (SNR) matrix (this is the ratio of the average squared value of the source output σ_x^2 the MSE σ_d^2):

$$SNR = \frac{\sigma_x^2}{\sigma_d^2}$$

- This is often in logarithmic scale (dB):

$$SNR = 10\log_{10}\frac{\sigma_x^2}{\sigma_d^2}$$

- Peak-signal-to-noise-ratio (PSNR) matrix (this measures the error relative to the average squared value of the signal, again normally in logarithmic scale (dB)):

$$SNR = 10\log_{10}\frac{\max_i |p_i|}{\sigma_d^2}$$

- Average of the absolute difference matrix:

$$D_i = \frac{1}{N}\sum_{i}^{N}|P_i - Q_i|$$

- Maximum value of the error magnitude matrix:

$$D_{i\infty} = \max_n D_i = |P_i - Q_i|$$

Progressive Image Compression

The main idea of progressive image compression is to gradually compress an image following a underlined order of priority. For example, compress the most important image information first, then compress the next most important information and append it to the compressed file, and so on.

This is an attractive choice when the compressed images are transmitted over a communication channel, and are decompressed and viewed in real time. The receiver would be able to view a development process of the image on the screen from a low to a high quality. The person can usually recognise most of the image features on completion of only 5–10% of the decompression.

The main advantages of progressive image compression are that:

- The user can control the amount of loss by means of telling the encoder when to stop the encoding process.

- The viewer can stop the decoding process early since she or he can recognise the image's feature at an early stage.

- As the compressed file has to be decompressed several times and displayed with different resolution, the decoder can, in each case, stop the decompression process once the device resolution has been reached.

There are several ways to implement the idea of progressive image compression:

- Using so-called SNR progressive or quality progressive compression (i.e. encode spatial frequency data progressively).

- Compress the grey image first and then add the colour. Such a method normally features slow encoding and fast decoding.

- Encode the image in layers. Early layers are large low-resolution pixels followed by smaller high-resolution pixels. The progressive compression done in this way is also called pyramid coding or hierarchical coding.

Example:

The following methods are often used in JPEG:

- Sequential coding (baseline encoding): This is a way to send data units following a left-to-right, top-to-bottom fashion.

- Progressive encoding: This transmits every nth line before filling the data in the middle.

- Hierarchical encoding: This is a way to compress the image at several different resolutions.

Transform Coding

Transform coding is used to convert spatial image pixel values to transform coefficient values. Since this is a linear process and no information is lost, the number of coefficients produced is equal to the number of pixels transformed.

The desired effect is that most of the energy in the image will be contained in a few large transform coefficients. If it is generally the same few coefficients that contain most of the energy in most pictures, then the coefficients may be further coded by lossless entropy coding. In addition, it is likely that the smaller coefficients can be coarsely quantized or deleted (lossy coding) without doing visible damage to the reproduced image.

Note: The energy of a pixel may be defined as the square of its value times some scaling factor. Similarly, the energy of a transform coefficient may be defined as the square of its value times some scaling factor. With the proper scaling factor, the total energy of the pixels in a picture will always equal the total energy in the transform coefficients. The transform process simply concentrates the energy into particular coefficients, generally the "low frequency" ones.

Many types of transforms have been tried for picture coding, including for example Fourier, Karhonen-Loeve, Walsh-Hadamard, lapped orthogonal, discrete cosine (DCT), and recently, wavelets. The various transforms differ among themselves in three basic ways that are of interest in picture coding:

- The degree of concentration of energy in a few coefficients;

- The region of influence of each coefficient in the reconstructed picture;

- The appearance and visibility of coding noise due to coarse quantization of the coefficients.

Karhunen-Loeve is a statistically based transform method that can be tailored to one image or group of images, and therefore has the optimum energy concentration. However, it generally will not have this optimum concentration for images not in the basis set.

Fourier transforms (discrete) have good energy concentration characteristics, but become unwieldy when dealing with large images requiring large numbers of coefficients. Block transforms, which work on a small portion of the image at a time, are therefore preferred. The discrete Fourier transform may be applied to a block of pixels. Other transforms which fall in this category are Walsh-Hadamard, and the DCT. The lapped orthogonal transforms are a special case in which the coefficients' influence is confined to a few adjacent blocks, with a tapering-off influence toward the edges.

Because of ease of hardware computation and generally very good energy concentration for a wide range of natural images, the DCT has become the transform of choice for many image coding schemes, including MPEG. The DCT, unlike the Fourier transform, is spatially variant. A portion of a sine wave coded with a Fourier transform has all the energy concentrated at the same frequency coefficients regardless of the phase of the sinusoid (although the energy will be apportioned differently between the sine and cosine components). The DCT, on the other hand, is sensitive to phase, so that an object moving across the screen will have different frequency content from frame to frame. This also means that the visibility of coding artifacts due to coefficient quantization will vary somewhat depending on the position of an object (edge) in the image. Also, because the DCT is a strictly bounded block transform, lossy coding will produce block-edge mismatch which will be visible at some level of quantization even if there is only low frequency content in that area.

Discrete Cosine Transform

The discrete cosine transform (DCT) is a technique for converting a signal into elementary frequency components. It is widely used in image compression.

The One-dimensional Discrete Cosine Transform

The discrete cosine transform of a list of n real numbers $s(x), x = 0, ..., n-1$, is the list of length n given by:

$$S(u) = \sqrt{2/n}\, C(u) \sum_{x=0}^{n-1} s(x) \cos \frac{(2x+1)u\pi}{2_n} \qquad u = 0, ..., n$$

$$C(u) = 2^{-1/2} \quad \text{for } u = 0$$
$$1 \qquad \text{otherwise}$$

Each element of the transformed list S(u) is the inner (dot) product of the input list s(x) and a basis vector. The constant factors are chosen so that the basis vectors are orthogonal and normalized. The eight basis vectors for n = 8 are shown in figure. The DCT can be written as the product of a vector (the input list) and the n x n orthogonal matrix whose rows are the basis vectors. This matrix, for n = 8, can be computed as follows:

```
DCTMatrix =

Table[ If[ k==0,

Sqrt[1/8],

Sqrt[2/8] Cos[Pi (2j + 1) k/16] ],

{k, 0, 7}, {j, 0, 7}] // N;
```

We can check that the matrix is orthogonal:

```
DCTMatrix . Transpose[DCTMatrix] // Chop // MatrixForm
```

1.	0	0	0	0	0	0	0
0	1.	0	0	0	0	0	0
0	0	1.	0	0	0	0	0
0	0	0	1.	0	0	0	0
0	0	0	0	1.	0	0	0
0	0	0	0	0	1.	0	0
0	0	0	0	0	0	1.	0
0	0	0	0	0	0	0	1.

Each basis vector corresponds to a sinusoid of a certain frequency:

```
Show[GraphicsArray[Partition[

    ListPlot[#, PlotRange -> {-.5, .5}, PlotJoined -> True, Dis-
        playFunction -> Identity]&

    /@ DCTMatrix, 2] ]];
```

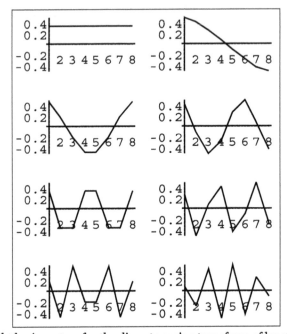

The eight basis vectors for the discrete cosine transform of length eight.

The list s(x) can be recovered from its transform S(u) by applying the inverse cosine transform (IDCT):

$$s(x) = \sqrt{2/n} \; \mathop{\varepsilon}_{u=0}^{n-1} C(u)S(u)\cos\frac{(2x+1)u\pi}{2n} \qquad x = 0,...,n$$

$$C(u) = 2^{-1/2} \quad \text{for } u = 0$$
$$= 1 \quad \text{otherwise}$$

This equation expresses s as a linear combination of the basis vectors. The coefficients are the elements of the transform S, which may be regarded as reflecting the amount of each frequency present in the input s.

We generate a list of random numbers to serve as a test input:

```
input1 = Table[Random[Real, {-1, 1}], {8}]
```

```
{0.203056,  0.980407,  0.35312,  -0.106651,  0.0399382,  0.871475,
-0.648355, 0.501067}
```

The DCT is computed by matrix multiplication:

```
output1 = DCTMatrix . input1
{0.775716, 0.3727, 0.185299, 0.0121461, -0.325, -0.993021,
0.559794,
-0.625127}
```

As noted above, the DCT is closely related to the discrete Fourier transform (DFT). In fact, it is possible to compute the DCT via the DFT: First create a new list by extracting the even elements, followed by the reversed odd elements. Then multiply the DFT of this re-ordered list by so-called "twiddle factors" and take the real part. We can carry out this process for n = 8 using Mathematica's DFT function.

```
DCTTwiddleFactors = N @ Join[{1},
 Table[Sqrt[2] Exp[-I Pi k /16], {k, 7}]]
{1., 1.38704 - 0.275899 I, 1.30656 - 0.541196 I, 1.17588
0.785695 I,
1. - 1. I, 0.785695 - 1.17588 I, 0.541196 - 1.30656 I,
0.275899 - 1.38704 I}
```

The function to compute the DCT of a list of length n = 8 is then:

```
DCT[list_] := Re[ DCTTwiddleFactors *
 InverseFourier[N[list[[{1, 3, 5, 7, 8, 6, 4, 2}]]]]]
```

Note that we use the function InverseFourier to implement what is usually in engineering called the forward DFT. Likewise, we use Fourier to implement what is usually called the inverse DFT. The function N is used to convert integers to reals because (in Version 2.2) Fourier and Inverse Fourier are not evaluated numerically when their arguments are all integers. The special case of a list of zeros needs to be handled separately by overloading the functions, since N of the integer 0 is an integer and not real.

```
Unprotect[Fourier, InverseFourier];
Fourier[x:{0 ..}]:= x;
InverseFourier[x:{0 ..}]:= x;
Protect[Fourier, InverseFourier];
```

We apply DCT to our test input and compare it to the earlier result computed by matrix multiplication. To compare the results, we subtract them and apply the Chop function to suppress values very close to zero:

```
DCT[input1]
```

```
{0.775716, 0.3727, 0.185299, 0.0121461, -0.325, -0.993021,
0.559794,
   -0.625127}
% - output1 // Chop
{0, 0, 0, 0, 0, 0, 0, 0}
```

The inverse DCT can be computed by multiplication with the inverse of the DCT matrix. We illustrate this with our previous example:

```
Inverse[DCTMatrix] . output1
{0.203056, 0.980407, 0.35312, -0.106651, 0.0399382, 0.871475,
-0.648355, 0.501067}
% - input1 // Chop
{0, 0, 0, 0, 0, 0, 0, 0}
```

As you might expect, the IDCT can also be computed via the inverse DFT. The "twiddle factors" are the complex conjugates of the DCT factors and the reordering is applied at the end rather than the beginning:

```
IDCTTwiddleFactors = Conjugate[DCTTwiddleFactors]
{1., 1.38704 + 0.275899 I, 1.30656 + 0.541196 I, 1.17588 +
0.785695 I,
   1. + 1. I, 0.785695 + 1.17588 I, 0.541196 + 1.30656 I,
   0.275899 + 1.38704 I}
IDCT[list_] := Re[Fourier[
   IDCTTwiddleFactors list] ][[{1, 8, 2, 7, 3, 6, 4, 5}]]
```

For example:

```
IDCT[DCT[input1]] - input1 // Chop
{0, 0, 0, 0, 0, 0,
   0, 0}
```

The Two-dimensional DCT

The one-dimensional DCT is useful in processing one-dimensional signals such as speech waveforms. For analysis of two-dimensional (2D) signals such as images, we need a 2D version of the DCT. For an n x m matrix s, the 2D DCT is computed in a simple way: The 1D DCT is applied to each row of s and then to each column of the result.

Thus, the transform of s is given by:

$$S(u,v) = \frac{2}{\sqrt{nm}} C(u)C(v) \sum_{y=0}^{m-1}\sum_{x=0}^{n-1} s(x,y)\cos\frac{(2x+1)u\pi}{2n}\cos\frac{(2y+1)u\pi}{2n}$$

$$u = 0,...,n \quad v = 0,...,m$$

$$C(u) = 2^{-1/2} \quad \text{for } u = 0$$
$$= 1 \quad\quad \text{otherwise}$$

Since the 2D DCT can be computed by applying 1D transforms separately to the rows and columns, we say that the 2D DCT is separable in the two dimensions.

As in the one-dimensional case, each element S(u, v) of the transform is the inner product of the input and a basis function, but in this case, the basis functions are n x m matrices. Each two-dimensional basis matrix is the outer product of two of the one-dimensional basis vectors. For n = m = 8, the following expression creates an 8 x 8 array of the 8 x 8 basis matrices, a tensor with dimensions {8, 8, 8, 8}:

```
DCTTensor = Array[

    Outer[Times, DCTMatrix[[#1]], DCTMatrix[[#2]]]&,

      {8, 8}];
```

Each basis matrix can be thought of as an image. The 64 basis images in the array are shown in figure.

The package GraphicsImage.m, included in the electronic supplement, contains the functions GraphicsImage and ShowImage to create and display a graphics object from a given matrix. GraphicsImage uses the built-in function Raster to translate a matrix into an array of gray cells. The matrix elements are scaled so that the image spans the full range of graylevels. An optional second argument specifies a range of values to occupy the full grayscale; values outside the range are clipped. The function ShowImage displays the graphics object using Show.

```
<< GraphicsImage.m

Show[GraphicsArray[

Map[GraphicsImage[#, {-.25, .25}]&,

Reverse[DCTTensor],

{2}] ]];
```

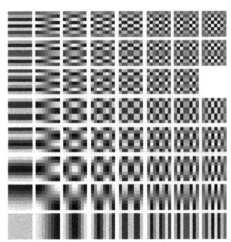

The 8 x 8 array of basis images for the two-dimensional discrete cosine transform. Each basis matrix is characterized by a horizontal and a vertical spatial frequency. The matrices shown here are arranged left to right and bottom to top in order of increasing frequencies.

To illustrate the 2D transform, we apply it to an 8 x 8 image of the letter A:

```
ShowImage[ input2 =

      {{0, 1, 0, 0, 0, 1, 0, 0}, {0, 1, 0, 0, 0, 1, 0, 0}

       {0, 1, 1, 1, 1, 1, 0, 0}, {0, 1, 0, 0, 0, 1, 0, 0},

       {0, 0, 1, 0, 1, 0, 0, 0}, {0, 0, 1, 0, 1, 0, 0, 0},

       {0, 0, 1, 0, 1, 0, 0, 0}, {0, 0, 0, 1, 0, 0, 0, 0}}]
```

```
-Graphics-
```

As in the 1D case, it is possible to express the 2D DCT as an array of inner products (a tensor contraction):

```
output2 = Array[

 (Plus @@ Flatten[DCTTensor[[#1, #2]] input2])&,

 {8, 8}];
```

```
ShowImage[output2]
```

```
-Graphics-
```

The pixels in this DCT image describe the proportion of each two-dimensional basis function present in the input image. The pixels are arranged as above, with horizontal and vertical frequency increasing from left to right and bottom to top, respectively. The brightest pixel in the lower left corner is known as the DC term, with frequency {0, 0}. It is the average of the pixels in the input, and is typically the largest coefficient in the DCT of "natural" images.

An inverse 2D IDCT can also be computed in terms of DCTTensor; we leave this as an exercise for the reader.

Since the two-dimensional DCT is separable, we can extend our function DCT to the case of two-dimensional input as follows:

```
DCT[array_?MatrixQ] :=

  Transpose[DCT /@ Transpose[DCT /@ array] ]
```

This function assumes that its input is an 8 x 8 matrix. It takes the 1D DCT of each row, transposes the result, takes the DCT of each new row, and transposes again. This function is more efficient than computing the tensor contraction shown above, since it exploits the built-in function InverseFourier.

We compare the result of this function to that obtained using contraction of tensors :

```
DCT[input2] - output2 // Chop // Abs // Max

0
```

The definition of the inverse 2D DCT is straightforward:

```
IDCT[array_?MatrixQ] :=

 Transpose[IDCT /@ Transpose[IDCT /@ array] ]
```

As an example, we invert the transform of the letter A:

```
ShowImage[Chop[IDCT[output2]]];
```

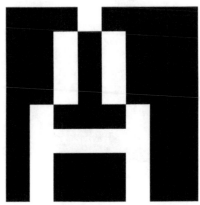

As noted earlier, the components of the DCT output indicate the magnitude of image components at various 2D spatial frequencies. To illustrate, we can set the last row and column of the DCT of the letter A equal to zero.

```
output2[[8]] = Table[0, {8}];
```

```
Do[output2[[i, 8]] = 0, {i, 8}];
```

Now take the inverse transform:

```
ShowImage[Chop[IDCT[output2]]];
```

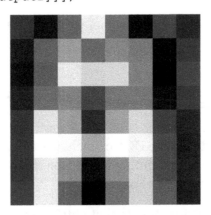

The result is a blurred letter A: The highest horizontal and vertical frequencies have been removed. This is easiest to see when the image is reduced in size so that individual pixels are not as visible.

2D Blocked DCT

To this point, we have defined functions to compute the DCT of a list of length n = 8 and the 2D DCT of an 8 x 8 array. We have restricted our attention to this case partly for simplicity of exposition, and partly because when it is used for image compression, the DCT is typically restricted to this size. Rather than taking the transformation of the image as a whole, the DCT is applied separately to 8 x 8 blocks of the image. We call this a blocked DCT.

To compute a blocked DCT, we do not actually have to divide the image into blocks. Since the 2D DCT is separable, we can partition each row into lists of length 8, apply the DCT to them, rejoin the resulting lists, and then transpose the whole image and repeat the process:

```
DCT[list_?(Length[#]>8&)] :=

  Join @@ (DCT /@ Partition[list, 8])
```

It may be worth tracing the progress of this deceptively simple piece of code as it works upon a 16 x 16 image. First, we observe the order in which Mathematica stores the three rules we have given for DCT:

```
?DCT

Global`DCT

DCT[(array_)?MatrixQ] := Transpose[DCT /@ Transpose[DCT /@ array]]

  DCT[(list_)?(Length[#1] > 8 & )] :=

  Apply[Join, DCT /@ Partition[list, 8]]

DCT[list_] := Re[DCTTwiddleFactors*

  InverseFourier[N[list[[{1, 3, 5, 7, 8, 6, 4, 2}]]]]]
```

When evaluating DCT of a 16 x 16 image, Mathematica begins by checking the first rule. It recognizes that the input is a matrix, and thus invokes the rule and applies DCT to each row.

When DCT is applied to a row of length 16, the second rule comes into play. The row is partitioned into two lists of length 8, and DCT is applied to each. These applications invoke the last rule, which simply computes the 1D DCT of the lists of length 8. The two sub-rows are then rejoined by the second rule. After each row has been transformed in this way, the entire matrix is transposed by the first rule. The process of partitioning, transforming, and rejoining each row is then repeated, and the resulting matrix is transposed again.

For a test image, we provide a small 64 x 64 picture of a space shuttle launch. We use the utility function ReadImageRaw, defined in the package GraphicsImage.m to read a matrix of graylevels from a file:

```
shuttle = ReadImageRaw["shuttle", {64, 64}];

ShowImage[shuttle]
```

-Graphics-

Applying the DCT to this image gives an image consisting of 8 × 8 blocks, each block a DCT of 8 × 8 pixels:

```
ShowImage[DCT[shuttle], {-300, 300}]
```

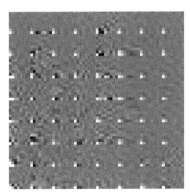

-Graphics-

The lattice of bright dots is formed by the DC coefficients from each of the DCT blocks. To reduce the dominance of these terms, we display the image with a clipped graylevel range. Note also the greater activity in the lower left compared to the upper right, which corresponds mainly to uniform sky.

The inverse DCT of a list of length greater than 8 is defined in the same way as the forward transform:

```
IDCT[list_?(Length[#]>8&)] :=

 Join @@ (IDCT /@ Partition[list, 8])
```

Here is a simple test:

```
shuttle - IDCT[DCT[shuttle]] // Chop // Abs // Max
```

0

Quantization

DCT-based image compression relies on two techniques to reduce the data required to represent the image. The first is quantization of the image's DCT coefficients; the second is entropy coding of the quantized coefficients. Quantization is the process of reducing the number of possible values of a quantity, thereby reducing the number of bits needed to represent it. Entropy coding is a technique for representing the quantized data as compactly as possible. We will develop functions to quantize images and to calculate the level of compression provided by different degrees of quantization. We will not implement the entropy coding required to create a compressed image file.

A simple example of quantization is the rounding of reals into integers. To represent a real number between 0 and 7 to some specified precision takes many bits. Rounding the number to the nearest integer gives a quantity that can be represented by just three bits.

```
x = Random[Real, {0, 7}]
```

```
2.78452
```

```
Round[x]
```

```
3
```

In this process, we reduce the number of possible values of the quantity (and thus the number of bits needed to represent it) at the cost of losing information. A "finer" quantization, that allows more values and loses less information, can be obtained by dividing the number by a weight factor before rounding:

```
w = 1/4;
```

```
Round[x/w]
```

```
11
```

Taking a larger value for the weight gives a "coarser" quantization.

Dequantization, which maps the quantized value back into its original range (but not its original precision) is acheived by multiplying the value by the weight:

```
w * % // N
```

```
2.75
```

The quantization error is the change in a quantity after quantization and dequantization. The largest possible quantization error is half the value of the quantization weight.

In the JPEG image compression standard, each DCT coefficient is quantized using a weight that depends on the frequencies for that coefficient. The coefficients in each 8 x 8 block are divided by a corresponding entry of an 8 x 8 quantization matrix, and the result is rounded to the nearest integer.

In general, higher spatial frequencies are less visible to the human eye than low frequencies. Therefore, the quantization factors are usually chosen to be larger for the higher frequencies. The following quantization matrix is widely used for monochrome images and for the luminance component of a color image. It is given in the JPEG standards documents, yet is not part of the standard, so we call it the "de facto" matrix:

```
qLum =

{{16,  11,  10,  16,  24,  40,  51,  61},

 {12,  12,  14,  19,  26,  58,  60,  55},

 {14,  13,  16,  24,  40,  57,  69,  56},

 {14,  17,  22,  29,  51,  87,  80,  62},

 {18,  22,  37,  56,  68,109,103,  77},

 {24,  35,  55,  64,  81,104,113,  92},

 {49,  64,  78,  87,103,121,120,101},

 {72,  92,  95,  98,112,100,103,  99}};
```

Displaying the matrix as a grayscale image shows the dependence of the quantization factors on the frequencies:

```
ShowImage[qLum];
```

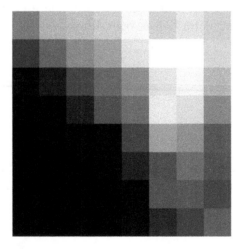

To implement the quantization process, we must partition the transformed image into 8 x 8 blocks:

```
        BlockImage[image_, blocksize_:{8, 8}] :=

          Partition[image, blocksize] /;

          And @@ IntegerQ /@ (Dimensions[image]/blocksize)
```

The function UnBlockImage reassembles the blocks into a single image:

```
UnBlockImage[blocks_] :=

 Partition[

 Flatten[Transpose[blocks, {1, 3, 2}]],

 {Times @@ Dimensions[blocks][[{2, 4}]]}]
```

For example:

```
     Table[i + 8(j-1), {j, 4}, {i, 6}] // MatrixForm

     1 2 3 4 5 6

     9 10 11 12 13 14

     17 18 19 20 21 22

     25 26 27 28 29 30

     BlockImage[%, {2, 3}] // MatrixForm

     1 2 3 4 5 6

     9 10 11 12 13 14


     17 18 19 20 21 22

     25 26 27 28 29 30

     UnBlockImage[%] // MatrixForm

     1 2 3 4 5 6

     9 10 11 12 13 14

     17 18 19 20 21 22

     25 26 27 28 29 30
```

Our quantization function blocks the image, divides each block (element-by-element) by the quantization matrix, reassembles the blocks, and then rounds the entries to the nearest integer:

```
DCTQ[image_, qMatrix_] :=

 Map[(#/qMatrix)&,

  BlockImage[image, Dimensions[qMatrix]],

  {2}] // UnBlockImage // Round
```

The dequantization function blocks the matrix, multiplies each block by the quantization factors, and reassembles the matrix:

```
IDCTQ[image_, qMatrix_] :=
 Map[(# qMatrix)&,
  BlockImage[image, Dimensions[qMatrix]],
  {2}] // UnBlockImage
```

To show the effect of quantization, we will transform, quantize, and reconstruct our image of the shuttle using the quantization matrix introduced above:

```
qshuttle = shuttle //
DCT // DCTQ[#, qLum]& // IDCTQ[#, qLum]& // IDCT;
```

For comparison, we show the original image together with the quantized version:

```
Show[GraphicsArray[
GraphicsImage[#, {0, 255}]& /@ {shuttle, qshuttle}]];
```

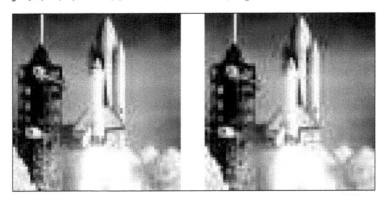

Note that some artifacts are visible, particularly around high-contrast edges.

Entropy

To measure how much compression is obtained from a quantization matrix, we use a famous theorem of Claude Shannon. The theorem states that for a sequence of symbols with no correlations beyond first order, no code can be devised to represent the sequence that uses fewer bits per symbol than the first-order entropy, which is given by:

$$h = -\varepsilon_i p_i \log_2(p_i)$$

where p_i is the relative frequency of the ith symbol.

To compute the first-order entropy of a list of numbers, we use the function Frequencies, from the standard package Statistics`DataManipulation`. This function computes the relative frequencies of elements in a list:

```
Frequencies[list_List] :=

  Map[{Count[list, #], #}&, Union[list]]


Characters["mississippi"]

{m, i, s, s, i, s, s, i, p, p, i}

Frequencies[%]

{{4, i}, {1, m}, {2, p}, {4, s}}
```

Calculating the first-order entropy is straightforward:

```
Entropy[list_] :=

  - Plus @@ N[# Log[2, #]]& @

  (First[Transpose[Frequencies[list]]]/Length[list])
```

For example, the entropy of a list of four distinct symbols is 2, so 2 bits are required to code each symbol:

```
Entropy[{"a", "b", "c", "d"}]

2.
```

Similarly, 1.82307 bits are required for this longer list with four symbols:

```
Entropy[Characters["mississippi"]]

1.82307
```

A list with more symbols and fewer repetitions requires more bits per symbol:

```
Entropy[Characters["california"]]

2.92193
```

The appearance of fractional bits may be puzzling to some readers, since we think of a bit as a minimal, indivisible unit of information. Fractional bits are a natural outcome of the use of what are called "variable word-length" codes. Consider an image containing 63 pixels with a greylevel of 255, and one pixel with a graylevel of 0. If we employed a code which used a symbol of length 1 bit to represent 255, and a symbol of length 2 bits to represent 0, then we would need 65 bits to represent the image, or in terms of the average bit-rate, $65/64 = 1..0156$ bits/pixel. The entropy as calculated above is a lower bound on this average bit-rate.

The compression ratio is another frequently used measure of how effectively an image has been compressed. It is simply the ratio of the size of the image file before and after compression. It is equal to the ratio of bit-rates, in bits/pixel, before and after compression. Since the initial bit-rate is usually 8 bits/pixel, and the entropy is our estimate of the compressed bit-rate, the compression ratio is estimated by 8/entropy.

We will use the following function to examine the effects of quantization:

```
f[image_, qMatrix_] :=

{Entropy[Flatten[#]], IDCT[IDCTQ[#, qMatrix]]}& @

  DCTQ[DCT[image], qMatrix]
```

This function transforms and quantizes an image, computes the entropy, and dequantizes and reconstructs the image. It returns the entropy and the resulting image. A simple way to experiment with different degrees of quantization is to divide the "de facto" matrix qLum by a scalar and look at the results for various values of this parameter:

```
test = f[shuttle, qLum/#]& /@ {1/4, 1/2, 1, 4};
```

Here are the reconstructed images and the corresponding entropies:

```
Show[GraphicsArray[

  Partition[

   Apply[

     ShowImage[#2, {0, 255}, PlotLabel -> #1,

       DisplayFunction -> Identity]&,

     test, 1],

   2] ] ]
```

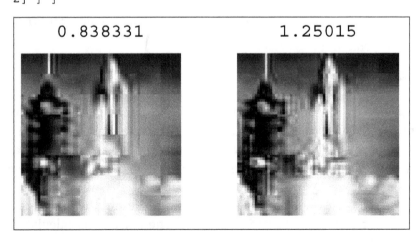

0.838331   1.25015

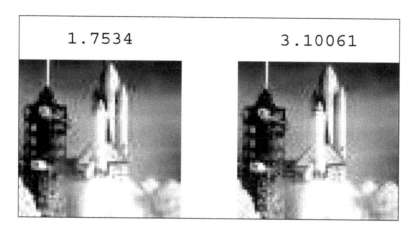

1.7534   3.10061

-graphicsArray-

Timing

Most of the computation time required to transform, quantize, dequantize, and re-construct an image is spent on forward and inverse DCT calculations. Because these transforms are applied to blocks, the time required is proportional to the size of the image. On a SUN Sparcstation 2, the timings increase (at a rate of 0.005 second/pixel) from about 20 seconds for a 64^2 pixel image to about 320 seconds for 256^2 pixels.

These times are much longer than for comparable functions written in a low-level lan-gauge such as C. For example, a C program performed the same computations in under 2 seconds for an image of 256^2 pixels, more than 100 times faster than our Mathematica functions. However, for the purposes for which our code was developed, namely education, algorithm development, and prototyping other applications, the timings are acceptable.

Discrete Wavelet Transform

Wavelet Transform has become an important method for image compression.Wavelet based coding provides substantial improvement in picture quality at high compression ratios mainly due to better energy compaction property of wavelet transforms.

Wavelet transform partitions a signal into a set of functions called wavelets. Wavelets are obtained from a single prototype wavelet called mother wavelet by dilations and shifting. The wavelet transform is computed separately for different segments of the time-domain signal at different frequencies.

Subband Coding

A signal is passed through a series of filters to calculate DWT.Procedure starts by passing this signal sequence through a half band digital low pass filter with impulse response h(n).Filtering of a signal is numerically equal to convolution of the tile signal with impulse response of the filter.

$$x[n]*h[n] = \sum_{k=-\infty}^{\infty} x[k].h[n-k]$$

A half band low pass filter removes all frequencies that are above half of the highest frequency in the tile signal. Then the signal is passed through high pass filter.The two filters are related to each other as:

$$h[L-1-n] = (-1)^n\, g(n)$$

Filters satisfying this condition are known as quadrature mirror filters.After filtering half of the samples can be eliminated since the signal now has the highest frequency as half of the original frequency.The signal can therefore be subsampled by 2,simply by discarding every other sample.This consitutes 1 level of decomposition and can mathmatically be expressed as:

$$Y1[n] = \sum_{k=-\infty}^{\infty} x[k]h[2n-k]$$

$$Y2[n] = \sum_{k=-\infty}^{\infty} x[k]g[2n+1-k]$$

where y1[n] and y2[n] are the outputs of low pass and high pass filters, respectively after subsampling by 2.

This decomposition halves the time resolution since only half the number of sample now characterizes the whole signal. Frequency resolution has doubled because each output has half the frequency band of the input. This process is called as sub band coding. It can be repeated further to increase the frequency resolution as shown by the filter bank.

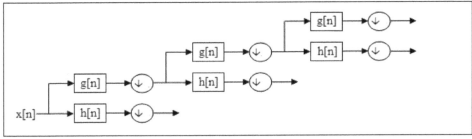

Filter bank.

Compression steps:

- Digitize the source image into a signal s, which is a string of numbers.

- Decompose the signal into a sequence of wavelet coefficients w.

- Use threshold to modify the wavelet coefficients from w to w'.

- Use quantization to convert w' to a sequence q.

- Entropy encoding is applied to convert q into a sequence e.

Digitation

Digitation The image is digitized first. The digitized image can be characterized by its intensity levels, or scales of gray which range from 0(black) to 255(white), and its resolution, or how many pixels per square inch.

Thresholding

In certain signals, many of the wavelet coefficients are close or equal to zero. Through threshold these coefficients are modified so that the sequence of wavelet coefficients contains long strings of zeros.

In hard threshold, a threshold is selected. Any wavelet whose absolute value falls below the tolerance is set to zero with the goal to introduce many zeros without losing a great amount of detail.

Quantization

Quantization converts a sequence of floating numbers w' to a sequence of integers q. The simplest form is to round to the nearest integer. Another method is to multiply each number in w' by a constant k, and then round to the nearest integer. Quantization is called lossy because it introduces error into the process, since the conversion of w' to q is not one to one function.

Entropy Encoding

With this method, a integer sequence q is changed into a shorter sequence e, with the numbers in e being 8 bit integers The conversion is made by an entropy encoding table. Strings of zeros are coded by numbers 1 through 100,105 and 106,while the non-zero integers in q are coded by 101 through 104 and 107 through 254.

DWT Results

Results obtained with the matlab code are shown below. Figure shows original Lena image. Figures show compressed images for various threshold values. As threshold value increases blurring of image continues to increase.

| Original Lena image | Compressed Image for threshold value 1 |
| Compressed Image for threshold value 2 | Compressed Image for threshold value 5 |

Lossless Compression

Lossless compression techniques, as their name implies, involve no loss of information. If data have been losslessly compressed, the original data can be recovered exactly from the compressed data. Lossless compression is generally used for applications that cannot tolerate any difference between the original and reconstructed data.

Text compression is an important area for lossless compression. It is very important that the reconstruction is identical to the original text, as very small differences can result in statements with very different meanings. Consider the sentences "Do not send money" and "Do now send money." A similar argument holds for computer files and for certain types of data such as bank records.

If data of any kind are to be processed or "enhanced" later to yield more information, it is important that the integrity be preserved. For example, suppose we compressed a radiological image in a lossy fashion, and the difference between the reconstruction Y and the original X was visually undetectable. If this image was later enhanced, the previously undetectable differences may cause the appearance of artifacts that could seriously mislead the radiologist. Because the price for this kind of mishap may be a human life, it makes sense to be very careful about using a compression schemethat generates a reconstruction that is different from the original.

Data obtained from satellites often are processed later to obtain different numerical indicators of vegetation, deforestation, and so on. If the reconstructed data are not identical to the original data, processing may result in "enhancement" of the differences. It may not be possible to go back and obtain the same data over again. Therefore, it is not advisable to allow for any differences to appear in the compression process.

There are many situations that require compression where we want the reconstruction to be identical to the original. There are also a number of situations in which it is possible to relax this requirement in order to get more compression. In these situations, we look to lossy compression techniques.

Run-length Encoding

Run-length encoding is a data compression algorithm that is supported by most bitmap file formats, such as TIFF, BMP, and PCX. RLE is suited for compressing any type of data regardless of its information content, but the content of the data will affect the compression ratio achieved by RLE. Although most RLE algorithms cannot achieve the high compression ratios of the more advanced compression methods, RLE is both easy to implement and quick to execute, making it a good alternative to either using a complex compression algorithm or leaving your image data uncompressed.

RLE works by reducing the physical size of a repeating string of characters. This repeating string, called a run, is typically encoded into two bytes. The first byte represents the number of characters in the run and is called the run count. In practice, an encoded run may contain 1 to 128 or 256 characters; the run count usually contains as the number of characters minus one (a value in the range of 0 to 127 or 255). The second byte is the value of the character in the run, which is in the range of 0 to 255, and is called the run value.

Uncompressed, a character run of 15 A characters would normally require 15 bytes to store:

AAAAAAAAAAAAAAA

The same string after RLE encoding would require only two bytes:

15A

The 15A code generated to represent the character string is called an RLE packet. Here, the first byte, 15, is the run count and contains the number of repetitions. The second byte, A, is the run value and contains the actual repeated value in the run.

A new packet is generated each time the run character changes, or each time the number of characters in the run exceeds the maximum count. Assume that our 15-character string now contains four different character runs:

AAAAAAbbbXXXXXt

Using run-length encoding this could be compressed into four 2-byte packets:

6A3b5X1t

Thus, after run-length encoding, the 15-byte string would require only eight bytes of data to represent the string, as opposed to the original 15 bytes. In this case, run-length encoding yielded a compression ratio of almost 2 to 1.

Long runs are rare in certain types of data. For example, ASCII plaintext seldom contains long runs. In the previous example, the last run (containing the character t) was only a single character in length; a 1-character run is still a run. Both a run count and a run value must be written for every 2-character run. To encode a run in RLE requires a minimum of two characters worth of information; therefore, a run of single characters actually takes more space. For the same reasons, data consisting entirely of 2-character runs remains the same size after RLE encoding.

In our example, encoding the single character at the end as two bytes did not noticeably hurt our compression ratio because there were so many long character runs in the rest of the data. But observe how RLE encoding doubles the size of the following 14-character string:

Xtmprsqzntwlfb

After RLE encoding, this string becomes:

1X1t1m1p1r1s1q1z1n1t1w1l1f1b

RLE schemes are simple and fast, but their compression efficiency depends on the type of image data being encoded. A black-and-white image that is mostly white, such as the page of a book, will encode very well, due to the large amount of contiguous data that is all the same color. An image with many colors that is very busy in appearance, however, such as a photograph, will not encode very well. This is because the complexity of the image is expressed as a large number of different colors. And because of this complexity there will be relatively few runs of the same color.

Variants on Run-length Encoding

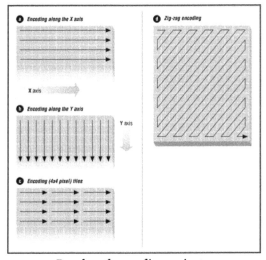

Run-length encoding variants.

There are a number of variants of run-length encoding. Image data is normally run-length encoded in a sequential process that treats the image data as a 1D stream, rather than as a 2D map of data. In sequential processing, a bitmap is encoded starting at the upper left corner and proceeding from left to right across each scan line (the X axis) to the bottom right corner of the bitmap. But alternative RLE schemes can also be written to encode data down the length of a bitmap (the Y axis) along the columns, to encode a bitmap into 2D tiles, or even to encode pixels on a diagonal in a zig-zag fashion. Odd RLE variants such as this last one might be used in highly specialized applications but are usually quite rare.

Another seldom-encountered RLE variant is a lossy run-length encoding algorithm. RLE algorithms are normally lossless in their operation. However, discarding data during the encoding process, usually by zeroing out one or two least significant bits in each pixel, can increase compression ratios without adversely affecting the appearance of very complex images. This RLE variant works well only with real-world images that contain many subtle variations in pixel values.

Make sure that your RLE encoder always stops at the end of each scan line of bitmap data that is being encoded. There are several benefits to doing so. Encoding only a simple scan line at a time means that only a minimal buffer size is required. Encoding only a simple line at a time also prevents a problem known as cross-coding.

Cross-coding is the merging of scan lines that occurs when the encoded process loses the distinction between the original scan lines. If the data of the individual scan lines is merged by the RLE algorithm, the point where one scan line stopped and another began is lost or, at least, is very hard to detect quickly.

Cross-coding is sometimes done, although we advise against it. It may buy a few extra bytes of data compression, but it complicates the decoding process, adding time cost. For bitmap file formats, this technique defeats the purpose of organizing a bitmap image by scan lines in the first place. Although many file format specifications explicitly state that scan lines should be individually encoded, many applications encode image data as a continuous stream, ignoring scan-line boundaries.

Have you ever encountered an RLE-encoded image file that could be displayed using one application but not using another? Cross-coding is often the the reason. To be safe, decoding and display applications must take cross-coding into account and not assume that an encoded run will always stop at the end of a scan line.

When an encoder is encoding an image, an end-of-scan-line marker is placed in the encoded data to inform the decoding software that the end of the scan line has been reached. This marker is usually a unique packet, explicitly defined in the RLE specification, which cannot be confused with any other data packets. End-of-scan-line markers are usually only one byte in length, so they don't adversely contribute to the size of the encoded data.

Encoding scan lines individually has advantages when an application needs to use only part of an image. Let's say that an image contains 512 scan lines, and we need to display only lines 100 to 110. If we did not know where the scan lines started and ended in the encoded image data, our application would have to decode lines 1 through 100 of the image before finding the ten lines it needed. Of course, if the transitions between scan lines were marked with some sort of easily recognizable delimiting marker, the application could simply read through the encoded data, counting markers until it came to the lines it needed. But this approach would be a rather inefficient one.

Another option for locating the starting point of any particular scan line in a block of encoded data is to construct a scan-line table. A scan-line table usually contains one element for every scan line in the image, and each element holds the offset value of its corresponding scan line. To find the first RLE packet of scan line 10, all a decoder needs to do is seek to the offset position value stored in the tenth element of the scan-line lookup table. A scan-line table could also hold the number of bytes used to encode each scan line. Using this method, to find the first RLE packet of scan line 10, your decoder would add together the values of the first nine elements of the scan-line table. The first packet for scan line 10 would start at this byte offset from the beginning of the RLE-encoded image data.

Bit-, Byte- and Pixel-Level RLE Schemes

The basic flow of all RLE algorithms is the same, as illustrated in figure.

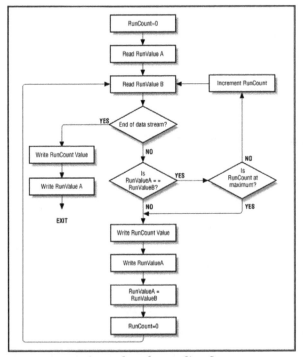

Basic run-length encoding flow.

The parts of run-length encoding algorithms that differ are the decisions that are made based on the type of data being decoded (such as the length of data runs). RLE schemes used to encode bitmap graphics are usually divided into classes by the type of atomic (that is, most fundamental) elements that they encode. The three classes used by most graphics file formats are bit-, byte- and pixel-level RLE.

Bit-level RLE schemes encode runs of multiple bits in a scan line and ignore byte and word boundaries. Only monochrome (black and white), 1-bit images contain a sufficient number of bit runs to make this class of RLE encoding efficient. A typical bit-level RLE scheme encodes runs of one to 128 bits in length in a single-byte packet. The seven least significant bits contain the run count minus one, and the most significant bit contains the value of the bit run, either 0 or 1. A run longer than 128 pixels is split across several RLE-encoded packets.

Byte-level RLE schemes encode runs of identical byte values, ignoring individual bits and word boundaries within a scan line. The most common byte-level RLE scheme encodes runs of bytes into 2-byte packets. The first byte contains the run count of 0 to 255, and the second byte contains the value of the byte run. It is also common to supplement the 2-byte encoding scheme with the ability to store literal, unencoded runs of bytes within the encoded data stream as well.

In such a scheme, the seven least significant bits of the first byte hold the run count minus one, and the most significant bit of the first byte is the indicator of the type of run that follows the run count byte. If the most significant bit is set to 1, it denotes an encoded run. Encoded runs are decoded by reading the run value and repeating it the number of times indicated by the run count. If the most significant bit is set to 0, a literal run is indicated, meaning that the next run count bytes are read literally from the encoded image data. The run count byte then holds a value in the range of 0 to 127 (the run count minus one). Byte-level RLE schemes are good for image data that is stored as one byte per pixel.

Pixel-level RLE schemes are used when two or more consecutive bytes of image data are used to store single pixel values. At the pixel level, bits are ignored, and bytes are counted only to identify each pixel value. Encoded packet sizes vary depending upon the size of the pixel values being encoded. The number of bits or bytes per pixel is stored in the image file header. A run of image data stored as 3-byte pixel values encodes to a 4-byte packet, with one run-count byte followed by three run-value bytes. The encoding method remains the same as with the byte-oriented RLE.

It is also possible to employ a literal pixel run encoding by using the most significant bit of the run count as in the byte-level RLE scheme. Remember that the run count in pixel-level RLE schemes is the number of pixels and not the number of bytes in the run.

Normally, an RLE method must somehow analyze the uncompressed data stream to determine whether to use a literal pixel run. A stream of data would need to contain many 1- and 2-pixel runs to make using a literal run efficient by encoding all the runs into a single packet. However, there is another method that allows literal runs of pixels to be added to an encoded data stream without being encapsulated into packets.

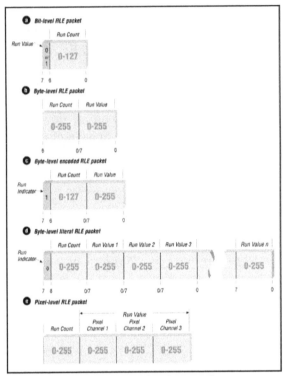

Bit-, byte- and pixel-level RLE schemes.

Consider an RLE scheme that uses three bytes, rather than two, to represent a run. The first byte is a flag value indicating that the following two bytes are part of an encoded packet. The second byte is the count value, and the third byte is the run value. When encoding, if a 1-, 2-, or 3-byte character run is encountered, the character values are written directly to the compressed data stream. Because no additional characters are written, no overhead is incurred.

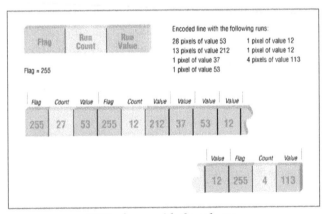

RLE scheme with three bytes.

When decoding, a character is read; if the character is a flag value, the run count and run values are read, expanded, and the resulting run written to the data stream. If the character read is not a flag value, it is written directly to the uncompressed data stream.

There are two potential drawbacks to this method:

- The minimum useful run-length size is increased from three characters to four. This could affect compression efficiency with some types of data.

- If the unencoded data stream contains a character value equal to the flag value, it must be compressed into a 3-byte encoded packet as a run length of one. This prevents erroneous flag values from occurring in the compressed data stream. If many of these flag value characters are present, poor compression will result. The RLE algorithm must therefore use a flag value that rarely occurs in the uncompressed data stream.

Vertical Replication Packets

Some RLE schemes use other types of encoding packets to increase compression efficiency. One of the most useful of these packets is the repeat scan line packet, also known as the vertical replication packet. This packet does not store any real scan-line data; instead, it just indicates a repeat of the previous scan line. Here's an example of how this works.

Assume that you have an image containing a scan line 640 bytes wide and that all the pixels in the scan line are the same color. It will require 10 bytes to run-length encode it, assuming that up to 128 bytes can be encoded per packet and that each packet is two bytes in size. Let's also assume that the first 100 scan lines of this image are all the same color. At 10 bytes per scan line, that would produce 1000 bytes of run-length encoded data. If we instead used a vertical replication packet that was only one byte in size (possibly a run-length packet with a run count of 0) we would simply run-length encode the first scan line (10 bytes) and follow it with 99 vertical replication packets (99 bytes). The resulting run-length encoded data would then only be 109 bytes in size.

If the vertical replication packet contains a count byte of the number of scan lines to repeat, we would need only one packet with a count value of 99. The resulting 10 bytes of scan-line data packets and two bytes of vertical replication packets would encode the first 100 scan lines of the image, containing 64,000 bytes, as only 12 bytes--a considerable savings.

Figure illustrates 1- and 2-byte vertical replication packets.

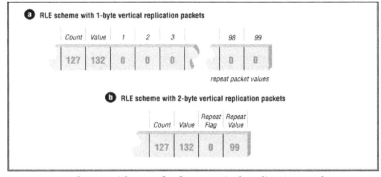

RLE scheme with 1- and 2-byte vertical replication packets.

Unfortunately, definitions of vertical replication packets are application dependent. At least two common formats, WordPerfect Graphics Metafile (WPG) and GEM Raster (IMG), employ the use of repeat scan line packets to enhance data compression performance. WPG uses a simple 2-byte packet scheme, as previously described. If the first byte of an RLE packet is zero, then this is a vertical replication packet. The next byte that follows indicates the number of times to repeat the previous scan line.

The GEM Raster format is more complicated. The byte sequence, 00h 00h FFh, must appear at the beginning of an encoded scan line to indicate a vertical replication packet. The byte that follows this sequence is the number of times to repeat the previous scan line minus one.

Lempel-Ziv-Welch

The Lempel-Ziv-Welch (LZW) algorithm is a very common compression technique. This algorithm is typically used in GIF and optionally in PDF and TIFF. Unix's 'compress' command, among other uses. It is lossless, meaning no data is lost when compressing. The algorithm is simple to implement and has the potential for very high throughput in hardware implementations. It is the algorithm of the widely used Unix file compression utility compress, and is used in the GIF image format.

The Idea relies on reoccurring patterns to save data space. LZW is the foremost technique for general purpose data compression due to its simplicity and versatility. It is the basis of many PC utilities that claim to "double the capacity of your hard drive".

Working of Lempel-Ziv-Welch

LZW compression works by reading a sequence of symbols, grouping the symbols into strings, and converting the strings into codes. Because the codes take up less space than the strings they replace, we get compression. Characteristic features of LZW include,

- LZW compression uses a code table, with 4096 as a common choice for the number of table entries. Codes 0-255 in the code table are always assigned to represent single bytes from the input file.

- When encoding begins the code table contains only the first 256 entries, with the remainder of the table being blanks. Compression is achieved by using codes 256 through 4095 to represent sequences of bytes.

- As the encoding continues, LZW identifies repeated sequences in the data, and adds them to the code table.

- Decoding is achieved by taking each code from the compressed file and translating it through the code table to find what character or characters it represents.

Example: ASCII code. Typically, every character is stored with 8 binary bits, allowing up to 256 unique symbols for the data. This algorithm tries to extend the library to 9 to 12 bits per character. The new unique symbols are made up of combinations of symbols that occurred previously in the string. It does not always compress well, especially with short, diverse strings. But is good for compressing redundant data, and does not have to save the new dictionary with the data: This method can both compress and uncompress data. There are excellent article's written up already, you can look more indepth here and also Mark Nelson's article is commendable.

Implementation

The idea of the compression algorithm is the following: as the input data is being processed, a dictionary keeps a correspondence between the longest encountered words and a list of code values. The words are replaced by their corresponding codes and so the input file is compressed. Therefore, the efficiency of the algorithm increases as the number of long, repetitive words in the input data increases.

LZW ENCODING

```
*   PSEUDOCODE

1   Initialize table with single character strings

2   P = first input character

3   WHILE not end of input stream

4     C = next input character

5     IF P + C is in the string table

6       P = P + C

7     ELSE

8       output the code for P

9       add P + C to the string table

10      P = C

11    END WHILE

12 output code for P
```

Testing the code below:

lzw.c   lzw.exe   test.lzw   test.out   testIMG.png

Output:

Compression using LZW

Example: Use the LZW algorithm to compress the string: BABAABAAA The steps involved are systematically shown in the diagram below.

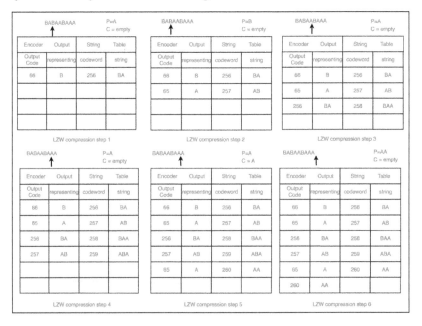

LZW Decompression

The LZW decompressor creates the same string table during decompression. It starts with the first 256 table entries initialized to single characters. The string table is updated for each character in the input stream, except the first one. Decoding achieved by reading codes and translating them through the code table being built.

LZW Decompression Algorithm

```
*  PSEUDOCODE

1 Initialize table with single character strings

2 OLD = first input code
```

```
3 output translation of OLD

4 WHILE not end of input stream

5  NEW = next input code

6  IF NEW is not in the string table

7    S = translation of OLD

8    S = S + C

9  ELSE

10    S = translation of NEW

11   output S

12   C = first character of S

13   OLD + C to the string table

14   OLD = NEW

15 END WHILE
```

Example: LZW Decompression: Use LZW to decompress the output sequence of: <66><65><256><257><65><260>

The steps involved are systematically shown in the diagram below.

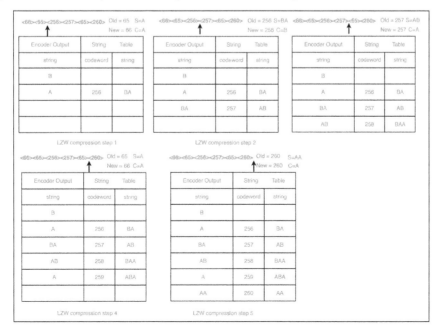

Huffman Coding

Huffman codes developed by D.A. Huffman in 1952 are optimal codes that map one sym-bol to one code word. Huffman coding is one of the well-liked technique to eliminate coding redundancy. It is a variable length coding and is used in lossless compression. Huffman encoding assigns smaller codes for more frequently used symbols and larger codes for less frequently used symbols. Variable-length coding table can be constructed based on the probability of occurrence of each source symbol. Its outcome is a prefix code that expresses most common source symbols with shorter sequence of bits. The more probable of occurrence of any symbol the shorter is its bit representation.

Huffman coding generate the smallest probable number of code symbols for any one source symbol. The source symbol is likely to be either intensities of an image or intensity mapping operation output. In the first step of huffman procedure, a chain of source re-ductions by arranging the probabilities in descending order and merging the two lowest probable symbols to create a single compound symbol that replaces in the successive source reduction. This procedure is repeated continuously upto two probabilities of two compound symbols are only left. This process with an example is illustrated in table.

Huffman Source Reduction

Original Source		Source Reduction			
Source	Probability	1	2	3	4
a2	0.4	0.4	0.4	0.4	0.6
a6	0.3	0.3	0.3	0.3	0.4
a1	0.1	0.1	0.2	0.3	
a4	0.1	0.1	0.1		
a3	0.06	0.1			
a5	0.04				

In table the list of symbols and their corresponding probabilities are placed in descend-ing order. A compound symbol with probability '0.1' is obtained by merging the least probabilities '0.06' and '0.04'. This is located in source reduction column '1' . Once again the probabilities of source symbols are arranged in descending order and the procedure is continued until only two probabilities are recognized. These probabilities observed at far right are ' 0.6' and '0.4' shown in the table.

Huffman Assignment Procedure

Original Source			Source Reduction								
Source	Probability	Code	1	Code	2	Code	3	Code	4	Code
a2	0.4	1	0.4	1	0.4	1	0.4	1	0.6	0

a6	0.3	00	0.3	00	0.3	00	0.3	00	0.4	1
a1	0.1	011	0.1	011	0.2	010	0.3	01		
a4	0.1	0100	0.1	0100	0.1	011				
a3	0.06	01010	0.1	0101						
a5	0.04	01011								

In the second step, huffman procedure is to prepare a code for each compact source starting with smallest basis and operating back to its original source. As shown in the table, the code symbols 0 and 1 are assigned to the two symbols of probabilities '0.6' and '0.4' on the right. The source symbol with probability 0.6 is generated by merging two symbols of probabilities ' 0.3' and '0.3' in the reduced source. So to code both of these symbols the code symbol 0 is appended along with 0 and 1 to make a distinction from one another. This procedure is repeated for each reduced source symbol till the original source code is attained. The final code become visible at the far-left in table. The average code length is defined as the product of probability of the symbol and number of bits utilized to represent the same symbol.

$$L_{average} = (0.4)(1)+(0.3)(2)+(0.1)(3)+(0.1)(4)+(0.06)(5)+(0.04)(5)$$
$$= 2.2 \text{ bits per symbol}.$$

The source entropy calculated is

$$\ddot{u}\ddot{u}\ddot{u}\ddot{u}\ddot{u}\sum_{k=0}^{L} \left(\ \right)\log_2\left[\ \left(\ \right)\right] = 2.14 \quad /$$

Then the efficiency of Huffman code $2.14/2.2 = 0.973$.

Huffman Decoding

In huffman coding the optimal code is produced for a set of symbols. A unique error less decoding scheme is achieved in a simple look-up-table approach. Sequence of huffman encoded symbols can be deciphered by inspecting the individual symbols of the sequence from left-to-right. Using the binary code present in Table, a left-to-right inspection of the encoded string '1010100111100' unveils the decoded message as "a2 a3 a1 a2 a2 a6". Hence with huffman decoding process the compressed data of the image can be decompressed.

Audio Compression

Audio compression is typically known as dynamic range or dynamic audio compression. It's a type of amplifier used in all professional recordings today and most of those from the last 40 years. Compression evens out the dynamic range, or the span between the loudest and softest parts of a recording. Compression is useful to smooth out a vocal track that pitches from very loud to incomprehensibly soft. Think of it as heightening the soft signals and reducing the loud signals to average out the overall volume.

Compression also keeps an instrument range within the range of your recording equipment, enabling you to record a more clear, clean sound. Technically speaking, if instruments become too loud or too soft during a recording, the sound levels can pitch too high or too low within the range your equipment can capture. In recordings without compression, the resulting high or low becomes muddied or distorted because the level is either too strong or too weak and doesn't fall within the equipment's range. It's similar to how human ears have a smaller range of high and low sounds than many animals.

Working of Compression

A big part of what makes working in audio recording so fun is all the tools available today to produce the sound you want.

But with so many effects, people often confuse them; audio compressors and limiters are one example. Though they have similar functionality, they're two separate types of amplifiers that have two different jobs. Limiters are a type of compression, but they only serve to limit, or cut out, a level that's too high. Compressors, meanwhile, average out both the high and low end of a sound within a designated range.

How you apply compression can vary according to the sound you want. Compression is triggered when a signal reaches your equipment's threshold. What's known as "the knee" in compression is how a signal transitions from uncompressed to compressed. You can control that by how fast the signal moves from uncompressed to compressed and back again — or by what's known as the "attack" and "release." You can experiment with these two effects depending on how you want your recording to sound.

The popular music you hear today is heavily compressed, meaning the sound is sleek, and once compressed, the overall level is raised higher. Try listening to a record from the 1960s or earlier and then flip to a pop music station on the radio. You will easily hear the difference.

Video Compression

Video compression is the art of throwing as much data away as possible without it showing. Video compression methods tend to be lossy – that is, what comes out after decoding isn't identical to what was originally encoded. By cutting video's resolution, colour depth and frame rate, PCs managed postage stamp-size windows at first, but then ways were devised to represent images more efficiently and reduce data without affecting physical dimensions. The technology by which video compression is achieved is known as a codec, an abbreviation of compression/decompression. Various types of codec have been developed – implementable in either software and hardware, and sometimes utilising both – allowing video to be readily translated to and from its compressed state.

Lossy techniques reduce data – both through complex mathematical encryption and through selective intentional shedding of visual information that our eyes and brain usually ignore – and can lead to perceptible loss of picture quality. Lossless compression, by contrast, discards only redundant information. Codecs can be implemented in hardware or software, or a combination of both. They have compression ratios ranging from a gentle 2:1 to an aggressive 100:1, making it feasible to deal with huge amounts of video data. The higher the compression ratio, the worse the resulting image. Colour fidelity fades, artefacts and noise appear in the picture, the edges of objects become over-apparent, until eventually the result is unwatchable.

By the end of the 1990s, the dominant techniques were based on a three-stage algorithm known as DCT (Discrete Cosine Transform). DCT uses the fact that adjacent pixels in a picture – either physically close in the image (spatial) or in successive images (temporal) – may be the same value. A mathematical transform – a relative of the Fourier transform – is performed on grids of 8×8 pixels (hence the blocks of visual artefacts at high compression levels). It doesn't reduce data but the resulting coefficient frequency values are no longer equal in their information-carrying roles. Specifically, it's been shown that for visual systems, the lower frequency components are more important than high frequency ones. A quantisation process weights these accordingly and ejects those contributing least visual information, depending on the compression level required. For instance, losing 50 per cent of the transformed data may only result in a loss of five per cent of the visual information. Then entropy encoding – a lossless technique – jettisons any truly unnecessary bits.

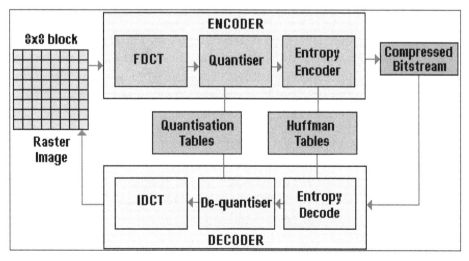

Initially, compression was performed by software. Limited CPU power constrained how clever an algorithm could be to perform its task in a 25th of a second – the time needed to draw a frame of full-motion video. Nevertheless, Avid Technology and other pioneers of NLE (non-linear editing) introduced PC-based editing systems at the end of the 1980s using software compression. Although the video was a quarter of the resolution of broadcast TV, with washed-out colour and thick with blocky artefacts, NLE signalled a revolution in production techniques. At first it was used for off-line editing, when material is trimmed down for a programme. Up to 30 hours of video may be shot for a one-hour documentary, so it's best to prepare it on cheap, non-broadcast equipment to save time in an on-line edit suite.

Although the quality of video offered by the first PC-based NLE systems was worse than the VHS VCRs used for off-line editing, there were some advantages. Like a word processor for video, they offered a faster and more creative way of working. A user could quickly cut and paste sections of video, trim them and make the many fine-tuning edits typical of the production process. What's more, importing an accurate EDL (edit decision list) generated by an NLE system into the on-line computer on a floppy disk was far better than having to type in a list of time-codes. Not only was NLE a better way to edit but, by delivering an off-line product closer to the final programme, less time was needed in the on-line edit suite.

NLE systems really took off in 1991, however, when hardware-assisted compression brought VHS-quality video. The first hardware-assisted video compression is known as M-JPEG (motion JPEG). It's a derivation of the DCT standard developed for still images known as JPEG. It was never intended for video compression, but when C-Cube introduced a codec chip in the early 1990s that could JPEG as many as 30 still images a second, NLE pioneers couldn't resist. By squeezing data as much as 50 times, VHS-quality digital video could be handled by PCs.

In time, PCs got faster and storage got cheaper, meaning less compression had to be used so that better video could be edited. By compressing video by as little as 10:1 a new breed of non-linear solutions emerged in the mid-1990s. These systems were declared ready for on-line editing; that is, finished programmes could essentially be played out of the back of the box. Their video was at least considered to be of broadcast quality for the sort of time and cost-critical applications that most benefited from NLE, such as news, current affairs and low-budget productions.

The introduction of this technology proved controversial. Most images compressed cleanly at 10:1, but certain material – such as that with a lot of detail and areas of high contrast – were degraded. Few viewers would ever notice, but broadcast engineers quickly learnt to spot the so-called ringing and blocky artefacts DCT compression produced. Also, in order to change the contents of the video images, to add an effect or graphic, material must first be decompressed and then recompressed. This process, though digital, is akin to an analogue generation. Artefacts are added like noise with each cycle in a process referred to as concatenation. Sensibly designed systems render every effect in a single pass, but if several compressed systems are used in a production and broadcast environment, concatenation presents a problem.

Compression technology arrived just as proprietary uncompressed digital video equipment had filtered into all areas of broadcasters and video facilities. Though the cost savings of the former were significant, the associated degradation in quality meant that acceptance by the engineering community was slow at first. However, as compression levels dropped – to under 5:1 – objections began to evaporate and even the most exacting engineer conceded that such video was comparable to the widely used BetaSP analogue tape. Mild compression enabled Sony to build its successful Digital Betacam format video recorder, which is now considered a gold standard. With compression a little over 2:1, so few artefacts (if any) are introduced that video goes in and out for dozens of generations apparently untouched.

The cost of M-JPEG hardware has fallen steeply in the past few years and reasonably priced PCI cards capable of a 3:1 compression ratio and bundled with NLE software are now readily available. Useful as M-JPEG is, it wasn't designed for moving pictures. When it comes to digital distribution, where bandwidth is at a premium, the MPEG family of standards – specifically designed for video – offer significant advantages.

References

- Lossy-compression-algorithm, computer-science: sciencedirect.com, Retrieved 25 August, 2019

- Xfrmcode, mpeghtml: bretl.com, Retrieved 04 July, 2019

- Lossless-compression, computer-science: sciencedirect.com, Retrieved 09 May, 2019

- Lzw-lempel-ziv-welch-compression-technique: geeksforgeeks.org, Retrieved 27 April, 2019

- What-Is-Audio-Compression: sanfordbrown.edu, Retrieved 18 February, 2019

4
Multimedia Software

Multimedia software is used to edit digital data such as images, audios and videos. Audio and video software perform operations such as cut, copy, paste, play, record, etc. on media files. Some of the multimedia software includes DAZ3D, MakeHuman, RawTherapee, Baudline, Djay, Final Scratch, Astra, etc. These diverse multimedia software have been thoroughly analyzed in this chapter.

As its name implies, multimedia software always involves several types of media that are interlinked with each other. The term media is understood to include music, videos and animated images that have been created and optimized using multimedia software. Multimedia software is often used in multimedia presentations, which integrate and connect all of the above-mentioned elements. This helps to liven up what has been said and makes it easier to present ideas more effectively.

Adding background music is recommended as a first step, as it does not take much time, yet can have a remarkable effect on any presentation. It's important to find a music software package that lets you make music that fits the purpose. Multimedia software is also relevant for animated images. A distinction is made here between videos and animated sequences of images, so-called slideshows. Creating slideshows usually involves photo editing; raw images are edited digitally and enriched by adding different filters and effects. Subsequently applying the appropriate multimedia software can make your photos come alive. The result is a digital slideshow that presents the images in the desired sequence, adds artistic fades and, if desired, music. This procedure is reminiscent of digital video editing that uses the same approach. After the video editing by using a multimedia software the edited raw footage is enriched by adding different elements and effects, allowing you to wrap up your video with style.

There is a large selection of multimedia software available. Multimedia subjects include children's learning, the arts, reference works, health and medicine, science, history, geography, hobbies and sports, games, and much more. Because of the large storage requirements of this type of media, most multimedia software comes on a compact disk (CD-ROM) format.

To use multimedia software, your system must meet certain minimum requirements set forth by the Multimedia Personal Computer (MPC) Marketing Council. These requirements include a CD-ROM drive, hard disk drive with ample storage capacity, a `486 or better central processing unit (CPU), at least 4 to 8 megabytes of RAM (memory), a 256 color or better video adapter, and a sound card with speakers or headphones. Most new computers far exceed these specifications. A microphone is optional if you want to record your own sounds. While these are suggested minimum requirements, many multimedia programs would run better on computer equipped with a Pentium 4 or AMD Athlon CPU and 512 or more megabytes of RAM.

Since much of the software purchased today contains multimedia content, we are now referring to multimedia software as the software used to *create* multimedia content. Examples incluse *authoring* software, which is used to create interactive multimedia courseware which is distributed on CD or available over the Internet. A teacher could use such a program to create interesting interactive lessons for the students which are viewed on the computer. A business could create programs to teach job skills or orient new employees.

Another category of multimedia involves the recreational use of music. Songs can be copied from CDs or downloaded from the Internet and stored on the hard drive. The music can then be *burned* onto a CD or transfered to a walkman-like device called a MP3 player or a "julebox."

There is also software for the creation, arranging, performance and recording of music and video. Through the use of a MIDI (Music Instrument Digital Interface) connector installed in the computer, the computer can be connected to musical instruments such as electronic keyboards. A music student or musician could then create a multiple track recording, arrange it, play it back, change the key or tempo, and print out the sheet music. Another type of software which is recently gaining popularity is digital audio recording software, which allows the computer to be connected to a digital audio mixer, usually through USB or "Firewire" connectors, and record live music onto the hard drive. The "tracks" can then be mixed, effects added, and music CDs can then be made from the master recording.

Image Software

DAZ 3D

Daz Productions, Inc., commonly known as Daz 3D, is a 3D content and software company specializing in providing rigged 3D human models, associated accessory content and software to the hobbyist as well as the prosumer market. Originally a part of Zygote Media Group, a general purpose, application-agnostic 3D content broker, Daz 3D split off as "Digital Art Zone" in 2000 to focus on supplying content for the Poser market.

Daz 3D continue to focus on 3D content development, but also began to expand their own 3D software offerings as well, with purchases of several notable 3D applications:

- Bryce, a fractal-based landscape modeler and renderer acquired from Corel by DAZ in 2004.

- Hexagon, a 3D mesh modeler originally developed by eovia, acquired by DAZ in 2006.

- Carrara, a general purpose 3D modeler/animation package also acquired from eovia in 2006.

Additionally, Daz 3D developed their own scene creator software, Daz Studio, as an alternative to Poser.

In 2016 Daz 3D spun off Tafi, a 3D content company intended to focus more on the game developer space.

Free 3D Software

In 2012 Daz 3D shifted their strategy from selling 3D software and content to one of giving the 3D software away for free and focusing more on the selling of the content. This began with offering Daz Studio for free in 2012, which gave customers the ability to render images and video and expanded in 2017 when Daz 3D added Hexagon to the list of their free software products and added the ability to do 3D modeling to that mix.

Figure Technology

Daz 3D has had many versions of its human figures and characters, but in 2011 they launched a significant change in the underlying technology. Instead of each figure being designed individually, Daz 3D moved to their Genesis platform, in which figures were derived as morphs from the base mesh. Two of the key differences that this technology created were: The ability for characters to be blended into a huge variety of shapes, and since these shapes were all derived from a common base, add-on content like clothing, hair, and additional morphs would not only work on all characters, but could actually change with the characters.

The Genesis platform has gone through several versions since the launch in 2011:

- Genesis 2: One of the shortcomings of the Genesis platform was that although it allowed extremely flexibility in the shape of characters and clothing, it also toned down some of the elements of what made a male or female figure unique. Genesis 2, released in 2013, changed this by splitting the Genesis base figure into two separate base figures: Genesis 2 Male and Genesis 2 Female.

- Genesis 3: Up until Genesis 3 the Genesis figures had been using TriAx Weight Maps, where many other industry platforms were using Dual Quaternion. This changed in Genesis 3, released in 2015, to allow Daz 3D figures to be more compatible with other 3D software platforms as well as Game Development platforms.

- Genesis 8: The jump in version naming from Genesis 3 to Genesis 8 was in order to address confusion in naming conventions. Although Genesis had reached its fourth version, most of the Daz 3D flagship characters were now on their eight versions. In order to avoid the confusion of Victoria 8 or Michael 8 being Genesis 4 characters, Daz 3D shifted the versioning of Genesis to match with the character versions. Genesis 8 also includes significant changes in the figure's backward compatibility with previous generations and their content as well as Joint and muscle bends and flexing and facial expressions.

MakeHuman

MakeHuman is free and open source 3D computer graphics middleware designed for the prototyping of photorealistic humanoids. It is developed by a community of programmers, artists, and academics interested in 3D character modeling.

Technology

MakeHuman is developed using 3D morphing technology. Starting from a standard (unique) androgynous human base mesh, it can be transformed into a great variety of characters (male and female), mixing them with linear interpolation. For example, given the four main morphing *targets* (baby, teen, young, old), it is possible to obtain all the intermediate shapes.

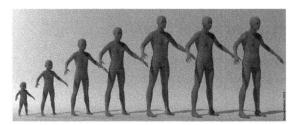

Interpolation of MakeHuman characters: the 1st, 3rd, 5th, and 7th are *targets*, while the others are intermediate shapes.

Using this technology, with a large database of morphing targets, it's virtually possible to reproduce any character. It uses a very simple GUI in order to access and easily handle hundreds of morphings. The MakeHuman approach is to use sliders with common parameters like height, weight, gender, ethnicity and muscularity. In order to make it available on all major operating systems, beginning from 1.0 alpha 8 it's developed in Python using OpenGL and Qt, with an architecture fully realized with plugins.

The tool is specifically designed for the modeling of virtual 3D human models, with a simple and complete pose system that includes the simulation of muscular movement. The interface is easy to use, with fast and intuitive access to the numerous parameters required in modeling the human form.

The development of MakeHuman is derived from a detailed technical and artistic study of the morphological characteristics of the human body. The work deals with *morphing*, using linear interpolation of both translation and rotation. With these two methods, together with a simple calculation of a form factor and an algorithm of mesh relaxing, it is possible to achieve results such as the simulation of muscular movement that accompanies the rotation of the limbs.

The ancestor of MakeHuman was *MakeHead*, a python script for Blender, written by Manuel Bastioni, artist and coder, in 1999. A year later, a team of developers had formed, and they released the first version of *MakeHuman* for Blender. The project evolved and, in 2003, it was officially recognized by the Blender Foundation and hosted on http://projects. blender.org. In 2004, the development stopped because it was difficult to write a Python script so big using only Blender API. In 2005, MH was moved outside Blender, hosted on SourceForge and rewritten from scratch in C. At this point, version counting restarted from zero. During successive years, the software gradually transitioned from C to C++.

While performant, it was too complex to develop and maintain. Hence, in 2009, the team decided to go back to the Python language (with a small C core) and to release MakeHuman as version 1.0 pre-alpha. Development continued at a pace of 2 releases per year. The stable version 1.0.0 was officially released March 14, 2014. MakeHuman 1.1.0 has been released May 14, 2016, around two years later. The most recent intermediate version is 1.1.1, as of March 5, 2017.

A community website was established June 2015 featuring a forum section, a wiki, and a repository for user contributed content for the program.

Evolution towards a Universal Model Topology

The aim of the project is to develop an application capable of modeling a wide variety of human forms in the full range of natural poses from a single, universal mesh. For this purpose, the design of a 3D humanoid mesh that can readily be parametrically manipulated to represent anatomical characteristics has been pursued, the mesh includes a common skeleton structure that permits character posing. MakeHuman Team developed a model that combines different anatomical parameters to transition smoothly from the infant to the elderly, from man to woman and from fat to slim.

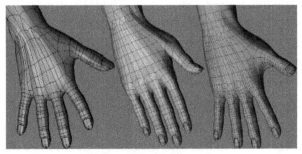

Evolution of the hand topology.

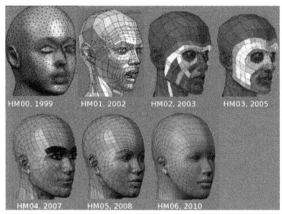
Evolution of the head topology.

The initial mesh occupies a middle ground, being neither pronounced masculine, nor pronounced feminine, neither young nor old and having a medium muscular definition. Goal was to depict a fair-built androgynous form, named the *HoMunculus*. The current MakeHuman mesh has evolved through successive steps of MakeHuman project, incorporating lessons learned, community feedback and the results of considerable amounts of studies and experimentation.

Evolution of the mesh for the human model:

- A first universal mesh prototype (head only), done in 1999 using makeHead script, was adapted for the early MakeHuman in 2000.

- The first professional mesh (HM01) for a human model was realized by Enrico Valenza in 2002.

- A second remarkable mesh (K-Mesh or HM02) was modelled by Kaushik Pal in 2003.

- The third model was created by Manuel Bastioni upon the Z-Mesh or HM03 in 2005.

- With experience from preceding versions, a fourth mesh (Y-Mesh or HM04) was done by Gianluca Miragoli (aka Yashugan) in 2007.

- The fifth mesh (HM05) was built on the previous one by Gianluca Miragoli and Manuel Bastioni in 2008.

- A sixth mesh (HM06) was also created by Gianluca Miragoli in 2010.

- Another mesh version was released in 2010 by Waldemar Perez Jr., André Richard, Manuel Bastioni.

- The latest and state-of-the-art mesh, released in 2013, was modeled by Manuel Bastioni.

Since the first release of makeHead (1999) and MakeHuman (2000), a challenge had been to construct a universal topology that retained all of the capabilities but added ability to interactively adjust the mesh to accommodate anatomical variety found in the human population. This could have been addressed by dramatically increasing the number of vertices for the mesh, but the resultant, dense mesh would have limited performance on processing computers. Technically, the model developed for MakeHuman is:

- Light and optimized for subdivision surfaces modelling (15,128 vertices).

- Quads only. The human mesh itself is *triangles free*, using Catmull-Clark subdivision for extra resolution to base meshes.

- Only E(5) Pole and the N(3) Pole, without holes and without 6-edge poles.

Research Usage

Because of the freedom of the license, MakeHuman software is widely used by researchers for scientific purposes:

- MakeHuman mesh is used in industrial design, to verify the anthropometry of a project, and in virtual reality research, to quickly produce avatars from measures or camera views.

- MakeHuman characters are used in biomechanics and biomedical engineering, to simulate the behaviour of the human body under certain conditions or treatments. The human character model for a project of the construction of artificial mirror neuron systems was also generated by MakeHuman.

- The software was used for visuo-haptic surgical training system development. These simulations combine tactile sense with visual information and provide realistic training scenarios to gain, improve, and assess resident and expert surgeons' skills and knowledge.

- Full-body 3D virtual reconstructions have been performed using MakeHuman, and 3D analysis of early Christian burials (archaeothanatology).

- The tool has also been used to create characters to perform Sign Language movements.

3D Movie Maker

3D Movie Maker (commonly shortened to 3DMM) is a children's computer program developed by Microsoft Home's Microsoft Kids subsidiary in 1995. Using the program, users can make films by placing 3D characters and props into pre-rendered environments, as well as adding actions, sound effects, music, text, speech and special effects. Movies are then saved in the .3mm file format.

The program features two helper characters to guide users through the various features of the program: The character McZee (voiced by Michael Shapiro) provides help throughout the studio while his assistant Melanie provides other various tutorials. In Nickelodeon 3D Movie Maker, the user is instead guided by Stick Stickly.

3D Movie Maker is built on BRender, a 3D graphics engine created by Argonaut Software. The models and backgrounds were done by Illumin8 Digital Pictures (a now-defunct graphics studio) using Softimage modeling software, while the cinematic introduction and help sequences were done by Productions Jarnigoine, a now-inactive production company founded by Jean-Jacques Tremblay. In 1998, a user named Space Goat created the website 3dmm.com that allows users to upload movies and mods for 3DMM. 3dmm.com is still used today by many 3DMM enthusiasts.

Filmmaking in 3D Movie Maker is a straightforward process, allowing users to create various kinds of movies with ease. By default, 40 actors/actresses are available (each with 4 different costumes and a number of actions), as well as 20 different props. Twelve different scenes are available to the user, each containing several different camera angles. Many sample voice and MIDI music clips are included, but original voices can be recorded using a microphone while external .wav and .MIDI files can be imported.

The way movies are made in 3DMM is not like that of a movie camera. In 3DMM, a movie camera works by recording frames in quick succession. 3DMM stores the positions of the characters and objects for each frame; it moves at about 6 to 8 frames per second, which makes the movies choppier than expected. The finished movie can only be viewed inside 3DMM using the virtual auditorium or the studio, unless converted to a video file format with a third-party utility. The application's user interface is centered upon a theater building consisting of several rooms: the ticket booth, where the user is greeted by McZee and then asked to play or create a movie; the lobby and concession stand; the theater for watching movies; and other rooms for tutorials and tools.

The infamous Comic Sans font also made its first appearance in 3D Movie Maker.

Versions

- A Japanese expansion pack for 3DMM was released with characters from the popular children's manga and anime series *Doraemon*. It consists of 11 new scenes, 5 new characters and 96 new voice lines.

- Nickelodeon 3D Movie Maker is a Nickelodeon-themed version of 3D Movie Maker. This version includes 12 unique actors and 11 unique scenes from classic Nicktoons such as Rocko's Modern Life, Ren & Stimpy and Aaahh!!! Real Monsters. An unofficial expansion pack was later created, which allowed Nickelodeon actors, props, scenes, music and sounds to be used in the original 3D Movie Maker.

- Demo versions: These only feature the studio, don't allow the opening/saving of movies and only feature two actors and one prop. They are Bongo, Nakita and a red car for 3D Movie Maker, while for Nickelodeon 3D Movie Maker they are Ren, Stimpy and a spaceship.

Third-party

Several user-made expansion packs and animation tools exist, such as:

- 3DMM Animation Pro (2002): Binds mouse movements to the keyboard, which allows directors to create more fluid movements on the screen.

- Doraemon Expansion Pack: This pack was only released in Japan.

- 3DMM Expansion Pack (2003): A user-made expansion pack known as "Frankie's Expansion" after its creator Frank Weindel, who introduced the first new textures, actors and objects to the software since release.

- Virtual 3D Movie Maker An expansion management program that allows users to include their own customized expansions in their movies and allow them to be freely distributed.

- 7gen (2005): A GUI for creating V3DMM expansions.

- 3DMM Pencil++ 2: A program for editing 3D Movie Maker datafiles that allows users to edit expansions.

- Nickelodeon Expansion Pack: An unofficial expansion pack that adds all the actors, props, textures, scenes and sounds from Nickelodeon 3D Movie Maker.

Moviestorm

Moviestorm is a real-time 3D animation app published by Moviestorm Ltd. The software is available to and used by people of all age groups and appeals to those with a diverse range of backgrounds and interests, from amateur and professional film makers, through to businesses and education, as well as people just looking to simply tell stories or create messages to share using video. Moviestorm enables the user to create animated movies, using machinima technology. It takes the user from initial concept to finished, distributed movies. Sets and characters can be created and customised, and scenes can be filmed using multiple cameras.

Moviestorm is being used predominantly in education by students of film and media studies as a means to develop their skills and expand their portfolio, as well as a collaborative cross-curricular creative tool in education sectors from elementary to high school.

The software's website features a Web 2.0 social media service, which includes a video hosting service, and an online community where movie-makers can talk about their movies, find collaborators, and organise online events. Moviestorm also makes use of Twitter, YouTube and Facebook to release the latest news on the software and to interact with both current and potential users.

Business Model

Users new to the program can try it for 14 days for free by registering at the website. Thereafter users can purchase the application outright with different content bundling options. Moviestorm Points can also be bought to acquire additional content from the online marketplace, or gifted to other users in return for advice or assistance or in payment for a user-created modification. Subscribers have access to the *Modders Workshop* a tool which allows them to create their own 'props' and a wizard allows the direct import of models from Google SketchUp version 6. As of 2011, users can create their own custom "gestures" with the release of the Moviestorm skeletons.

Subscribers can also increase their points at any time by buying more points from the online marketplace. A subscription can be discontinued at any time, and resumed later with no penalty.

Examples of use

Screenshot from a movie made with Moviestorm.

Children's Animation

Blockhouse TV, based in Norwich, UK, utilised Moviestorm in their animated series for children, *Jack and Holly*. The first season, *Jack and Holly's Christmas Countdown*, was released in 2010. The second season, *Jack and Holly's Cosmic Stories*, was released in 2011.

Film and Media Teaching

Moviestorm has been used in film schools and media courses in many countries. Wan Smolbag Theatre in Vanuatu was one of the first to adopt it in 2008, under tutor John Herd. Students trained on Moviestorm have gone on to successful careers with the island's TV network. It is in use at many different educational sectors, from elementary schools to sixth form colleges and universities.

In addition to film teaching, Moviestorm has been used in educational contexts for a variety of other media, including computer games and music.

Other Education

Some teachers have found Moviestorm useful as a cross-curricular tool for collaborative creative expression. Paul Carr at Sakuragaoka Junior and Senior High School, Japan uses it to help teach English to Japanese students. One of his techniques is to create silent videos for which the students then have to compose dialog. Other teachers have found it useful for helping autistic students to make presentations, since they can prepare their presentation as a video instead of having to stand up in front of a class.

Business

Commercial companies including Oracle Corporation and Fujitsu have used Moviestorm to create low-cost training videos. Other companies have used it to create cheap advertising content that can be produced in-house. Think Industries in Eastern England is an advertising and marketing company that uses Moviestorm to pitch its ideas to prospective clients. "Pitching is key, and you have to stand out," said owner Philip Morley in an interview in 2011. "Video is just so much more powerful than text. People will watch even if they don't read documents. It's now cost-effective to create custom videos for every pitch.

Music Video

Moviestorm has been used as a low-cost alternative for bands wanting to create animated videos. The first commercial band to do so was Vice Romania in November 2008. Their video to *This Is It* was created by Lucinda McNary of Two Moon Graphics in Kansas. Moviestorm footage was combined with a character filmed in DAZ3D and composited using greenscreen.

In 2009, Priscilla Angelique started using Moviestorm to create videos for several tracks on her London-based label A Priscilla Thing. "Music videos are a very expensive and time consuming process but Moviestorm allows me to achieve shots and effects that even with a modest budget would still be very out of reach," she said in an interview in late 2010.

In November 2011, Chicago chiptune band I Fight Dragons ran a contest challenging

Moviestorm users to make the official video for their single, *Working*. (Moviestorm user and then-film student Kera "162" Hildebrandt would win the contest with her entry.)

Previsualization and Film Pitching

Moviestorm's rapid production has led to it being used by live action filmmakers and scriptwriters for pre-production. Since the footage used in previsualization is not intended to be included in the final product, the quality of the graphics is not a critical consideration. Independent filmmaker D.L. Watson in Oregon used it to create a complete animated storyboard on his short film *The Letter* (2009). London-based scriptwriter Dean P. Wells uses it to test out movie ideas and then creates trailers based on his scripts.

Seamless3d

Seamless3d is an open-source 3D modeling software available under the MIT license.

The models for the virtual reality world Techuelife Island were created using Seamless3d technology. Techuelife Island is showcased by Blaxxun as an example of what is possible when using the interactive multi-user Blaxxun platform.

Build Node Technology

Seamless3d can be used as a mesh editor and an animator, however its key feature is its build node technology.

Build nodes allow the user to perform a sequence of complex operations in real time whenever a control point in the 3d window is dragged.

NURBS Surface Poly Editing (NSPE)

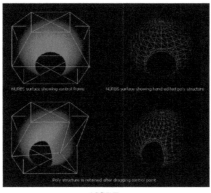

NSPE.

NSPE allows the user to hand edit the polygons on NURBS surfaces. This includes being able to drag the vertices anywhere along the NURBS surface as well as join the vertices together, break the vertices apart and color them. NSPE has a significant advantage over simply converting a NURBS surface to a polygon mesh for editing because NSPE lets the user be able continue to modify the NURBS surface for the hand edited polygon structure.

Because NSPE ensures that when a polygon's vertex is dragged it will always be on the NURBS surface, NSPE greatly helps the user to avoid unintentionally changing the shape of the model when optimizing for real time animation.

Fusing NURBS Surfaces

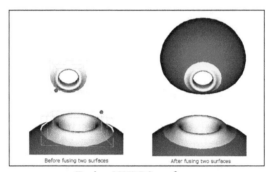

Fusing NURBS surfaces

By including a FuseSurface feature designed for fusing 2 NURBS surfaces together, Seamless3d allows for the creation of smooth continuous curvy models made from multiple NURBS surfaces.

SeamlessScript

Seamless3d has its own built in script compiler which compiles SeamlessScript (a very fast light weight scripting language) into native machine code. SeamlessScript is designed to look and feel a lot like JavaScript while being able to be compiled by a standard C++ compiler. This allows the user to develop complex animation sequences using a C++ IDE which gives the user access to professional debugging aids such as single step execution.

Seamless3d Format

Seamless3d format (smls) is a text-based human readable format with some aspects common to VRML.

The following example shows the code (containing SeamlessScript) for an animated spinning box:

#SMLS V2.127 utf8

```
Seamless{
```

```
    effect ColorEffect{}

    skeleton DEF part Part{}

    build BoxBuild{

      part USE part

    }

}

Anim{

  play TRUE

  pause FALSE

  loop TRUE

  period 4

  void onFrame(float v){

    part.rotation = Rotation(0, 1, 0, PI * 2 * v);

  }

}
```

Seamless3d Chat

The Multi-User Seamless3d chat server designed for 3D World Wide Web browsing is open source under the MIT license and can be compiled for both Linux and Windows. Currently the Seamless3d modeller is used as the 3D chat client. An online Seamless3d chat server has been in continuous service since April 2009. The general public can freely use it for their own custom made worlds and avatars.

Features

- Exports to VRML, X3D (including H-Anim), OBJ and POV-Ray formats.

- Imports VRML and X3D VRML Classic formats.

- Imports Canal/Blaxxun Avatar Studio avatars·

- Imports H-Anim.

- Imports and Exports Biovision Hierarchy Motion Capture (BVH) files.

- Support for FFmpeg which allows for the creation of AVI, MPG, MP4 and FLV movie formats.

- Transform hierarchies.

- Morphing.

- Skinned animation.

- Texture mapping.

- JPEG and PNG texture formats (and BMP when using DirectX).

- Béziers & NURBS lathes and NURBS patches.

- Tangent matched NURBS Surface Fusion.

- Nurbs Surface Poly Modeling (NSPE).

- Software robot demonstration help.

- Scripting.

- Key-frame based and Script based animation.

- Sound synthesis using NURBS.

- Seamless3d files are a compact human readable text format.

- Multi-User 3D chat web browsing.

Neuroimaging Software

Amira

Amira is a software platform for 3D and 4D data visualization, processing, and analysis. It is being actively developed by Thermo Fisher Scientific in collaboration with the Zuse Institute Berlin (ZIB), and commercially distributed by Thermo Fisher Scientific.

Amira is an extendable software system for scientific visualization, data analysis, and presentation of 3D and 4D data. It is used by thousands of researchers and engineers in academia and industry around the world. Its flexible user interface and modular architecture make it a universal tool for processing and analysis of data from various modalities; e.g. micro-CT, PET, Ultrasound. Its ever-expanding functionality has made it a versatile data analysis and visualization solution, applicable to and being used in many fields, such as microscopy in biology and materials science, molecular biology, quantum physics, astrophysics, computational fluid dynamics (CFD), finite element modeling (FEM), non-destructive testing (NDT), and many more. One of the key features, besides data visualization, is Amira's set of tools for image segmentation and geometry reconstruction. This allows the user to mark (or segment) structures and regions of interest in 3D image volumes using automatic, semi-automatic, and manual tools. The segmentation can then be used for a variety of subsequent tasks, such as volumetric analysis, density analysis, shape analysis, or the generation of 3D computer models for visualization, numerical simulations, or rapid prototyping or 3D printing, to name a few. Other key Amira features are multi-planar and volume visualization, image registration, filament tracing, cell separation and analysis, tetrahedral mesh generation, fiber-tracking from diffusion tensor imaging (DTI) data, skeletonization, spatial graph analysis, and stereoscopic rendering of 3D data over multiple displays and immersive virtual reality environments, including CAVEs. As a commercial product Amira requires the purchase of a license or an academic subscription. A time-limited, but full-featured evaluation version is available for download free of charge.

Amira Options

Microscopy Option

- Specific readers for microscopy data.

- Image deconvolution.

- Exploration of 3D imagery obtained from virtually any microscope.

- Extraction and editing of filament networks from microscopy images.

DICOM Reader

- Import of clinical and preclinical data in DICOM format.

Mesh Option

- Generation of 3D finite element (FE) meshes from segmented image data.

- Support for many state-of-the-art FE solver formats.

- High-quality visualization of simulation mesh-based results, using scalar, vector, and tensor field display modules.

Skeletonization Option

- Reconstruction and analysis of neural and vascular networks.

- Visualization of skeletonized networks.

- Length and diameter quantification of network segments.

- Ordering of segments in a tree graph.

- Skeletonization of very large image stacks.

Molecular Option

- Advanced tools for the visualization of molecule models.
- Hardware-accelerated volume rendering.
- Powerful molecule editor.
- Specific tools for complex molecular visualization.

Developer Option

- Creation of new custom components for visualizing or data processing.
- Implementation of new file readers or writers.
- C++ programming language.
- Development wizard for getting started quickly.

Neuro Option

- Medical image analysis for DTI and brain perfusion.
- Fiber tracking supporting several stream-line based algorithms.
- Fiber separation into fiber bundles based on user defined source and destination regions.
- Computation of tensor fields, diffusion weighted maps.
- Eigenvalue decomposition of tensor fields.
- Computation of mean transit time, cerebral blood flow, and cerebral blood volume.

VR Option

- Visualization of data on large tiled displays or in immersive Virtual Reality (VR) environments.
- Support of 3D navigation devices.
- Fast multi-threaded and distributed rendering.

Very Large Data Option

- Support for visualization of image data exceeding the available main memory, using efficient out-of-core data management.
- Extensions of many standard modules, such as orthogonal and oblique slicing, volume rendering, and isosurface rendering, to work on out-of-core data.

Dextroscope

The Dextroscope is a Virtual Reality (VR) environment designed to provide medical professionals with deeper understanding of a patient's complex 3D anatomical relationships and pathology. Although its main intended purpose is to enable surgeons to plan a surgical procedure (in particular, neurosurgery), it has also proven useful in research in cardiology, radiology and medical education. The Dextroscope was designed to be a practical variation of Virtual Reality which introduced an alternative to the prevalent trend of full immersion of the 1990s. Instead of immersing the whole user into a virtual reality, it just immersed the hands of the neurosurgeon into the patient data.

The Dextroscope allows its user to interact intuitively with a Virtual Patient. The Virtual Patient is composed of computer-generated 3D multi-modal images obtained from any DICOM tomographic data including CT, MRI, MRA, MRV, functional MRI and CTA, PET, SPECT and Tractography. It can work with any multi-modality combination, supporting polygonal meshes as well.

The user sits at the Dextroscope 3D interaction console and manipulates the Virtual Patient using both hands in a similar manner to how one would manipulate a real object. Using stereoscopic visualisations displayed via a mirror, the Dextroscope user sees the Virtual Patient floating behind the mirror but within easy reach of the hands and uses flexible 3D hand movements to rotate and manipulate the object of interest. The Dextroscope allows virtual segmentation of organs and structures, making accurate 3D measurements, etc.

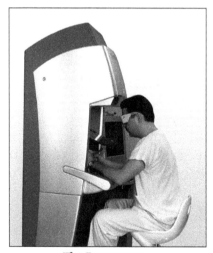
The Dextroscope.

In one hand the user holds an ergonomically shaped handle with a switch that, when pressed, allows the 3D image to be moved freely as if it were an object held in real space. The other hand holds a pencil shaped stylus that is used to select tools from a virtual control panel and perform detailed manipulations and operations on the 3D image. The user does not see the stylus, handle or his/her hands directly, as they are hidden behind the surface of the mirror. Instead he/she sees a virtual handle and stylus calibrated to appear in exactly the same position as the real handle and stylus. The business end of the virtual handle can be selected to be anything that the software can create - drill tool, measurement tool, cutter, etc. Experience has shown that it is unnecessary to model the user's hands, provided that he/she can see and feel the real tools and that these perceptions match the virtual scene. This is highly advantageous since the hands would otherwise clutter the workspace and obscure the view of the object of interest.

One of the uses of the Dextroscope is to allow surgeons to interact with and manipulate the Virtual Patient and plan the ideal surgical trajectory – for example, by simulating inter-operative viewpoints or the removal of bone and soft tissue. Apart from being much faster to work this way than using a mouse and keyboard, this approach also provides the medical professional, typically a surgeon, with a greater degree of control over the 3D image – with the hands literally being able to reach inside to manipulate the image interior.

Manipulating the Virtual Patient – Virtual Reality Toolsets

The Dextroscope provides an extensive set of virtual tools that can be used to manipulate the 3D image. For example, there are dedicated tools to perform data segmentation to extract surgically relevant structures like the cortex or a tumor, extract blood vessels, adjust the color and transparency of displayed structures to see deep inside the patient and even simulate some surgical procedures – such as the removal of bone using a simulated skull drilling tool.

Typical structures that can be segmented are tumors, blood vessels, aneurysms, parts of the skull base, and organs. Segmentation is done either automatically (when the structures are demarcated clearly by their outstanding image intensity – such as the cortex) or through user interaction (using for example an outlining tool to define the extent of the structure manually). A virtual 'pick' tool allows the user to pick a segmented object and uncouple it from its surroundings for closer inspection. A measurement tool provides accurate measurement of straight and curving 3D structures such as the scalp, and measure angles, such as those between vessels or bony structures (for example, when planning the insertion of a screw into the spine).

Raw Image Processing Software

Adobe Lightroom

Adobe Lightroom (officially Adobe Photoshop Lightroom) is a family of image organization and image manipulation software developed by Adobe Systems for Windows, macOS, iOS, Android, and tvOS (Apple TV). It allows importing/saving, viewing, organizing, tagging, editing, and sharing large numbers of digital images. Unlike Photoshop, Lightroom's edits are always non-destructive by keeping the original image and the edits applied to it saved separately. Despite sharing its name with Adobe Photoshop, it cannot perform many Photoshop functions such as doctoring (adding, removing or altering the appearance of individual image items), rendering text or 3D objects on images, or modifying individual video frames. Lightroom is not a file manager like Adobe Bridge. It cannot operate on files unless they are imported into its database first, and only in recognized image formats.

Initially, Adobe Lightroom was one product only. But as of 2017, it has become a family of products consisting of Lightroom CC and Lightroom Classic CC. While similar, these two products have significant differences, mainly in how they store images and interact with Adobe's cloud storage offering, and in feature parity.

Lightroom Classic CC is focused on the following workflow steps:

- Library: Similar in concept to the 'Organizer' in Adobe Photoshop Elements and other image organizers, this module imports and exports images, creates image collections, organizes images by their metadata, and adds ratings to them. Library is the gateway into Lightroom.

- Develop: Supports non-destructive editing of images *en masse*. This module is more for retouching, i.e., enhancing and improving digital photographs, including changing color balance, improving tone, removing red-eye effect, sharpening, reducing noise, cropping, straightening or converting to black-and-white. It cannot create or edit non-photographic images (such as drawings, symbols, line arts or diagrams or maps), or render text or 3D objects. It has very limited photo doctoring features. TIFF, JPEG, PSD (Photoshop), PNG, CMYK (edited in RGB color space) and raw image formats are supported . It has several standard presets for color correction or effects, and supports sharing custom presets online. Another often used feature in the Develop module is the ability to synchronize edits from one selected photo to the whole selection.

- Map: Added in Lightroom 4, it facilitates geographically organizing photos based on embedded or manually added geolocation data (since end of 2018 this is no longer supported for up to Lightroom CC 2015.x/Lightroom 6.x).

- Book: Added in Lightroom 4, it allows creating photobooks.

- Slideshow: Allows creating slideshows from any number of photos, to which music or a background can be added.

- Print: Prints images. Printing parameters such as layout and orientation can be adjusted.

- Web: Creates a web gallery for website owners. Several templates to influence layout are available.

RawTherapee

RawTherapee is computer software for processing photographs. It comprises a subset of image editing operations specifically aimed at non-destructive post-production of raw photos and is primarily focused on improving a photographer's workflow by facilitating the handling of large numbers of images. It is notable for the advanced control it gives the user over the demosaicing and developing process. It is cross-platform, with versions for Windows, macOS and Linux.

RawTherapee was originally written by Gábor Horváth of Budapest, Hungary, and was re-licensed as free and open-source software under the GNU General Public License Version 3 in January 2010. It is written in C++, using a GTK+ front-end and a patched version of dcraw for reading raw files. The name used to stand for "The Experimental Raw Photo Editor"; however that acronym has been dropped, and RawTherapee is now a full name in itself.

Features

RawTherapee involves the concept of non-destructive editing, similar to that of some other raw conversion software. Adjustments made by the user are immediately reflected in the preview image, though they are not physically applied to the opened image but the parameters are saved to a separate sidecar file. These adjustments are then applied during the export process.

All the internal processing is done in a high precision 32-bit floating point engine.

Input File Formats

RawTherapee supports most raw formats, including Pentax Pixel Shift, Canon Dual-Pixel, and those from Foveon and X-Trans sensors. It also supports common non-raw image formats like JPEG, PNG and TIFF. It also supports high dynamic range, 16/24/32-bit raw DNG images.

RawTherapee uses a patched version of dcraw code to read and parse raw formats, with additional tweaks and constraints to parameters such as white levels and the raw crop area based on in-house measurements. Thus, RawTherapee supports all the formats supported by dcraw.

User Interface

RawTherapee provides the user with a file browser, a queue, a panel for batch image adjustments, a 1:1 preview of the embedded JPEG image in the case of raw files, and an image editing tab.

The file browser shows photo thumbnails along with a caption of the shooting information metadata. The browser includes 5-star rating, flagging, and an Exif-based filter. It can be used to apply a profile, or parts of a profile, to a whole selection of photos in one operation.

A toolbox alongside the file browser allows for batch image adjustments.

The queue tab allows one to put exporting photos on hold until done adjusting them in the Editor, so that the CPU is fully available to the user while tweaking a photo, instead of processing photos while the user is trying to tweak new ones which could result in a sluggish interface. Alternatively, it can be used to process photos alongside tweaking new ones, if one has a CPU capable of handling the workload.

The Editor tab is where the user tweaks photos. While the image is opened for editing, the user is provided with a preview window with pan and zoom capabilities. A color histogram is also present offering linear and logarithmic scales, and separate R, G, B and L channels. All adjustments are reflected in the history queue and the user can revert any of the changes at any time. There is also the possibility of taking multiple snapshots of the history queue, allowing for various versions of the image being shown. These snapshots are not written to the sidecar file and are subsequently lost once the photo has been closed, however work is underway on migrating the PP3 sidecar system to XMP which already supports storing snapshots.

Adjustment Tools and Processing

- The following Bayer demosaicing algorithms are available: AMaZE, IGV, LMMSE, EAHD, HPHD, VNG4, DCB, AHD, fast or mono, as well as none. Raw files from X-Trans sensors have the 3-pass, 1-pass and fast demosaicing methods at their disposal.

- Processing profiles support via sidecar files with the ability to fully and partially load, save and copy profiles between images.

- Processing parameters can be generated dynamically based on image metadata using the Dynamic Profile Builder.

- Exposure control and curves in the L*a*b* and RGB color spaces.

- CIECAM02 mode.

- Advanced highlight reconstruction algorithms and shadow/highlight controls.

- Tone mapping using edge-preserving decomposition.

- Pre-crop vignetting correction and post-crop vignetting for artistic effect.

- Graduated filter.

- Various methods of sharpening.

- Various methods of noise reduction.

- Detail recovery.

- Removal of purple fringing.

- Manual and automatic pre- and post-demosaic chromatic aberration correction.

- Advanced wavelet processing.

- Retinex processing.

- White balance (presets, color temperature, spot white balance and auto white balance).

- Channel mixer.

- Black-and-white conversion.

- Color boost and vibrance (saturation control with the option of preserving natural skin tones).

- Hue, saturation and value adjustments using curves.

- Various methods of color toning.

- Lockable color picker.

- Wide gamut preview support on Windows and Linux, while the macOS preview is limited to sRGB.

- Soft-proofing support.

- Color-managed workflow.

- ICC color profiles (input, working and output).

- DCP color profiles (input).

- Support for Adobe Lens Correction Profiles (LCP).

- Cropping, resizing, post-resize sharpening.

- Rotation with visual straightening tool.

- Distortion correction.

- Perspective adjustment.

- Dark frame subtraction.

- Flat field removal (hue shifts, dust removal, vignetting correction).

- Hot and dead pixel filters.

- Metadata (Exif and IPTC) editor.

- A processing queue to free up the CPU during editing where instant feedback is important and to make maximal use of it afterwards.

Output Formats

The output format can be selected from:

- TIFF (8-bit and 16-bit).

- JPEG (8-bit).

- PNG (8-bit and 16-bit).

Audio Software

Baudline

The baudline time-frequency browser is a signal analysis tool designed for scientific visualization. It runs on several Unix-like operating systems under the X Window System. Baudline is useful for real-time spectral monitoring, collected signals analysis, generating test signals, making distortion measurements, and playing back audio files.

Applications

- Acoustic cryptanalysis.

- Audio codec lossy compression analysis.

- Audio signal processing.

- Bioacoustics research.

- Data acquisition (DAQ).

- Infrasound monitoring.

- Musical acoustics.

- Seismic data processing.

- SETI.

- Signal analysis.

- Software Defined Radio.

- Spectral analysis.

- Very low frequency (VLF) reception.

- WWV frequency measurement.

Features

- Spectrogram, Spectrum, Waveform, and Histogram displays.

- Fourier, Correlation, and Raster transforms.

- SNR, THD, SINAD, ENOB, SFDR distortion measurements.

- Channel equalization.

- Function generator.

- Digital down converter.

- Audio playing with real-time DSP effects like speed control, pitch scaling, frequency shifting, matrix surround panning, filtering, and digital gain boost.

- Audio recording of multiple channels.

- JACK Audio Connection Kit sound server support.

- Import AIFF, AU, WAV, FLAC, MP3, Ogg Vorbis, AVI, MOV, and other file formats.

Sonic Visualiser

Sonic Visualiser is an application for viewing and analysing the contents of music audio files. It is free software distributed under the GNU General Public License that people use to visualise, analyse, and annotate sound files. The program is useful in musical as well as scientific work, and is notable for its ability to use highly specialised third-party plugins in the vamp plugin format. It was developed at the Queen Mary University of London's Centre for Digital Music and is compatible with Linux, OS X, and Windows operating systems.

Logic Pro (MacOS)

Logic Pro is a digital audio workstation (DAW) and MIDI sequencer software application for the macOS platform. It was originally created in the early 1990s as Notator Logic, or Logic, by German software developer C-Lab, later Emagic. It became an Apple product, eventually known as Logic Pro, after Apple bought Emagic in 2002. It is the 2nd most popular DAW – after only Ableton Live – according to a survey conducted in 2015.

A consumer-level version based on the same interface and audio engine but with reduced features, called Logic Express, was also available at a reduced cost. Apple's GarageBand, another application using Logic's audio engine, is bundled in iLife, a suite of software which comes included on any new Macintosh computer. On December 8, 2011, the boxed version of Logic Pro was discontinued, along with Logic Express, and Logic Pro is now only available through the Mac App Store.

Features

Logic Pro provides software instruments, audio effects and recording facilities for music synthesis. It also supports Apple Loops – royalty-free, professionally recorded instrument loops. Logic Pro and Express share many functions and the same interface. Logic Express is limited to two-channel stereo mixdown, while Logic Pro can handle multichannel surround sound. Both can handle up to 255 audio tracks, depending on system performance (CPU and hard disk throughput and seek time). Logic Pro can work with MIDI keyboards and control surfaces for input and processing, and for MIDI output. It features real-time scoring in musical notation, supporting guitar tablature, chord abbreviations and drum notation. Advanced MIDI editing is possible though Logic Pro's MIDI Transform Window, where velocity, pitch, pitch-bends, humanize and precise note positioning are effected.

Software Instruments

The software instruments included in Logic Pro X include: Drum Kit Designer, Drum Machine Designer, ES, ES2, EFM1, ES E, ES M, ES P, EVOC 20 PolySynth, EXS24 mkII, Klopfgeist, Retro Synth, Sculpture, Ultrabeat, Vintage B3, Vintage Clav, Vintage Electric Piano. These instruments produce sound in various ways, through subtractive synthesis (ES, ES2, ES E, ES M, ES P, Retro Synth), frequency modulation synthesis (EFM1), wavetable synthesis (ES2, Retro Synth), vocoding (EVOC 20 PolySynth), sampling (EXS24 mikII, Drum Kit Designer), and component modeling techniques (Ultrabeat, Vintage B3, Vintage Clav, and Vintage Electric Piano, Sculpture). As of version 10.2, Logic Pro X also includes Alchemy, a sample-manipulation synthesizer that was previously developed by Camel Audio. The software instruments are activated by MIDI information that can be input via a MIDI instrument or drawn into the MIDI editor.

The Space Designer plugin attempts to emulate the characteristic echo and reverberation of a physical environment, using a method called convolution.

Audio Effects

Audio effects include amp and guitar pedal emulators, delay effects, distortion effects, dynamics processors, equalization filters, filter effects, imaging processors, metering tools, modulation effects, pitch effects, and reverb effects. Among Logic's reverb plugins is Space Designer, which uses convolution reverb to simulate the acoustics of audio played in different environments, such as rooms of varying size, or emulate the echoes that might be heard on high mountains.

Distributed Processing

The application features distributed processing abilities (in 32-bit mode), which can function across an Ethernet LAN. One machine runs the Logic Pro app, while the other machines on the network run the Logic node app. Logic will then offload the effects and synth processing to the other machines on the network. If the network is fast enough (i.e. gigabit Ethernet) this can work in near real-time, depending on buffer settings and CPU loads. This allows users to combine the power of several Macintosh computers to process Logic Pro's built-in software instruments and plug-ins, and 3rd party processing plug-ins. As of version 10.0.7, Logic can access 24 processing threads, which is inline with Apple's flagship 12-core Mac Pro.

Versions

Early Versions

Logic 5 featured significant improvements in user interface, and increased compatibility with more types of computers, operating systems, and a wide range of audio interfaces. Logic 5.5.1 was the last version to be released for Windows. From Logic 6 onwards, the software would only be available on Mac OS.

With *Logic 6*, Emagic added the availability of separately packaged software products that were closely integrated add-ons developed specifically for use with Logic, including software instruments, the EXS sampler and audio processing plug-ins. The Logic 6 package also included the stand-alone program Waveburner, for burning redbook audio CD standard-compliant CDR masters for replication, however, that application was considered a free bonus feature; it was not advertised as part of the package and did not include printed documentation. PDF documentation was included on the installer disc.

In March 2004 Apple released *Logic Pro 6*, which consolidated over 20 different Emagic products, including all instrument and effect plug-ins, Waveburner Pro (CD Authoring application), and Pro Tools TDM support, into a single product package. Apple also released a scaled down version of Logic called Logic Express, replacing two previous versions that filled that position called Logic Silver and Logic Gold. Apple began promoting Logic Pro as one of its flagship software 'Pro' applications for the Macintosh platform.

Logic Pro 7

Logic Pro 7 was released September 29, 2004. Most notably, Apple modified the interface of Logic 7 to look more like a product that was developed by Apple.

Additions to Logic Pro 7 included: the integration of Apple Loops, Distributed Audio Processing (a technology for combining the power of multiple computers on a network), 3 new instruments including Sculpture (a sound modeling synth) and Ultrabeat (a drum synth and sequencer), and 9 new effect plug-ins including Guitar Amp Pro (guitar amp simulator), and a linear phase corrected version of their 6 channel parametric equalizer. In total, Logic Pro 7 now included 70 effect plug-ins and 34 instrument plug-ins.

Pro-Tools TDM compatibility, which had been a feature of Logic since version 3.5, was not supported by Logic 7.2 on Intel-based Mac computers; TDM support returned with the release of Logic 8.

Logic Pro 8

On September 12, 2007, Apple released the Logic Studio suite that included *Logic Pro 8*. Logic Pro was no longer a separate product, although a limited version Logic Express 8 was released on the same day, and remained a separate product.

Significant changes were made for Logic 8. Logic Pro 8 was now mainly Cocoa code, but still included some Carbon Libraries. Alongside changes such as the new processing plug-in (Delay Designer), Apple included features such as Quick Swipe Comping, similar to Soundtrack Pro 2, and multi-take management.

Apple also made changes to ease of use. These include the discontinuation of the XSKey dongle, and a streamlined interface. Each plug-in used in the channel strip opens in a new window when double-clicked. Many of the features found in Logic 7 have been consolidated into one screen. Other additions to the new interface included consolidated arrange windows, dual channel strips, built in browsers (like that in GarageBand) and production templates.

Logic Pro 9

On July 23, 2009, *Logic Pro 9* was announced. A major new feature included "Flex Time", Apple's take on "elastic" audio, which allows audio to be quantized. A version of the pedalboard from GarageBand was included, together with a new virtual guitar amplifier where the modeled components could be combined in different ways. There were also a number of improvements to audio editing, fulfilled user requests such as "bounce in place" and selective track and channel strip import, as well as an expanded content library including one more Jam Pack. Some of the bundled software, including MainStage 2 and Soundtrack Pro 3, was also improved.

Logic Pro 9 is Universal Binary, although not officially supported for use on Power-PC computers. SoundDiver, which had been quietly bundled with previous versions, was dropped, eliminating support for arguably the world's most popular synthesizer editor/librarian. As Apple has bundled so many software instruments with Logic, it is not likely that we'll see the return of integration with external synthesizer hardware to the Logic platform.

On January 12, 2010, Apple released Logic Pro 9.1, an Intel only release, thereby officially discontinuing Logic for the PowerPC platform. Logic Pro 9.1 has the option of running in 64-bit mode, which allows the application to address more memory than in the past. Says Apple "With 64-bit mode, the application memory is not limited to 4GB as with 32-bit applications, so there is essentially no practical limit by today's standards." Third party plug-ins that are 32-bit are still compatible, but will run from a 'wrapper' inside Logic Pro itself.

On December 9, 2011, Apple announced that Logic Pro Studio 9 would no longer be available on DVD, and would only be sold via the Mac App Store. The price was reduced from $499 to $199.99 for the Logic Pro app, and $29.99 for MainStage. The download was just over 400MB, and 19GB of optional loops were available as in-app downloads.

This version of Logic Pro Studio 9 no longer allows users to access any microtunings in Scala format other than those provided with the software by Apple.

Logic Pro X

Released as successor to Logic Pro 9 on July 16, 2013, *Logic Pro X* (10.0.0) included a new, single-window customizable interface, with a design in line with Final Cut Pro X, as well as new features. New tools in this release are *Drummer*, a virtual session player that automatically plays along with your song in a wide variety of drumming styles and techniques, and *Flex Pitch*, a Flex Time equivalent for pitch editing in audio recordings. Also, a new "Smart Controls" feature allows users to map parameters from an array of plugins to a single, convenient control interface. Redesigned keyboards and synths were included, together with new stomp boxes, bass amp and drum kit designers, and a chord arpeggiator. A completely rebuilt sound and loop library was introduced, along with a new Patch architecture. Logic Pro X has also improved track organization by allowing users to group multiple tracks into 'folder' like categories (e.g., acoustics, synthesizers, vocals, percussion, etc.). In addition to this organization, Logic Pro X allows individuals to trigger 'solo,' 'mute,' and 'volume' controls for each group. Further improvements were made to score editing, exporting (now compatible with MusicXML format), and introduces MIDI plug-in compatibility. Coinciding with the release of Logic Pro X was the release of a companion iPad app called Logic Remote, which allows wireless control of Logic Pro X, including *Touch Instruments* for playing and recording software instruments as well as tools for navigating, making basic edits and mixing.

Since this release, Logic Pro X runs in 64-bit mode only and no longer works with 32-bit plug-ins. Logic Pro X is capable of transferring most data from previous projects saved in Logic Pro 5 and later, though the transfer to 64-bit only means older 32-bit plugins will no longer work.

The current version is Logic 10.4.7, where 10.4 introduced a new reverb called Chromaverb, and new functionality like Smart Tempo, as well as the option to undo mixer actions. In addition, version 10.4 introduced support for version 2 of the ARA (Audio Random Access) standard.

Audacity (Audio Editor)

Audacity is a free and open-source digital audio editor and recording application software, available for Windows, macOS, Linux, and other Unix-like operating systems. Audacity was started in the fall of 1999 by Dominic Mazzoni and Roger Dannenberg at Carnegie Mellon University and was released on May 28, 2000 as version 0.8.

As of November 20, 2019, it is the most popular download from FossHub, with over 80 million downloads since March 2015. Previously, downloads were served from Google Code and SourceForge, with a combined total in excess of 100 million downloads. Audacity won the SourceForge 2007 and 2009 Community Choice Award for Best Project for Multimedia.

Features and Usage

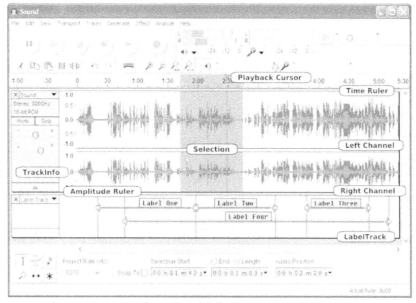

Audacity's main panel annotated. All the components that have been labelled are custom for Audacity.

In addition to recording audio from multiple sources, Audacity can be used for post-processing of all types of audio, including podcasts by adding effects such as normalization, trimming, and fading in and out. Audacity has also been used to record and mix entire albums, such as by Tune-Yards. It is also currently used in the UK OCR National Level 2 ICT course for the sound creation unit.

Audacity's features include:

- Four user-selectable themes enable the user to choose their preferred look and feel for the application (version 2.2.0 and later).

  - Four user-selectable colorways for waveform display in audio tracks (version 2.2.1 and later).

- Recording and playing back sounds.

  - Scrubbing (Version 2.1.1 and later).

  - Timer Record enables the user to schedule when a recording begins and ends to make an unattended recording.

  - MIDI playback is available (from version 2.2.0 onwards).

  - Punch and Roll recording - for editing on-the-fly (from version 2.3.0 onwards).

- Editing.

  - Via cut, copy, and paste, with unlimited levels of undo.

  - Features of modern multitrack audio software including navigation controls, zoom and single track edit, project pane and XY project navigation, non-destructive and destructive effect processing, audio file manipulation (cut, copy, paste).

  - Amplitude envelope editing.

  - Precise adjustments to the audio speed (tempo) while maintaining pitch in order to synchronize it with video or run for a predetermined length of time.

  - Conversion of cassette tapes or records into digital tracks by splitting the audio source into multiple tracks based on silences in the source material.

- Cross-platform operation — Audacity works on Windows, macOS, and other Unix-like systems (including Linux and BSD).

  - Audacity uses the wxWidgets software library to provide a similar graphical user interface on several different operating systems.

- A large array of digital effects and plug-ins. Additional effects can be written with Nyquist, a Lisp dialect.

  - Built-in LADSPA, VST(32-bit) and Nyquist plug-in support.

  - Noise Reduction based on sampling the noise to be minimized.

  - Vocal Reduction and Isolation for the creation of karaoke tracks and isolated vocal tracks.

  - Adjusting audio pitch while maintaining speed and adjusting audio speed while maintaining pitch.

  - LADSPA, VST (32-bit) and Audio Unit (macOS) effects now support real-time preview (from version 2.1.0 onwards). Note: Real-time preview does not yet support latency compensation.

  - Saving and loading of user presets for effect settings across sessions (from 2.1.0 onwards).

- Multitrack mixing:

  - Support for multi-channel modes with sampling rates up to 96 kHz with 32 bits per sample.

- Audio spectrum analysis using the Fourier transform algorithm.

- Importing and exporting of WAV, AIFF, MP3 (via the LAME encoder, now integrated as part of Audacity), Ogg Vorbis, and all file formats supported by libsndfile library. Versions 1.3.2 and later supported Free Lossless Audio Codec (FLAC). Version 1.3.6 and later also supported additional formats such as WMA, AAC, AMR and AC3 via the optional FFmpeg library.

- Detection of dropout errors while recording with an overburdened CPU

- From 2.3.2 onwards, mod-script-pipe for driving Audacity from Python now comes with Audacity and it can be enabled via preferences.

- A full downloadable Manual *(or available online without downloading).*

Audacity supports the LV2 open standard for plugins and can therefore load software like Calf Studio Gear.

Limitations

Audacity supports only 32-bit or 64-bit VST audio effect plug-ins, depending on which architecture it was built for, but not both at the same time. It does not support instrument VST (VSTi) plugins.

Audacity lacks dynamic equalizer controls and real time effects while recording.

Audacity does not natively import or export WMA, AAC, AC3 or most other proprietary or restricted file formats; rather, an optional FFmpeg library is required.

Language Support

In addition to English language, the Graphical User Interface of the Audacity software program is translated into Afrikaans, Arabic, Basque, Bulgarian, Catalan, Chinese (simplified), Chinese (traditional), Czech, Danish, Dutch, Finnish, French, Galician, German, Greek, Hungarian, Irish, Italian, Japanese, Lithuanian, Macedonian, Norwegian (Bokmål), Polish, Portuguese, Romanian, Russian, Slovak, Slovenian, Spanish, Swedish, Turkish, Ukrainian, and Welsh.

The documentation, the Audacity Manual, is available only in English. The Audacity Forum offers technical support in: Spanish, French, Russian and German.

Audacity Architecture

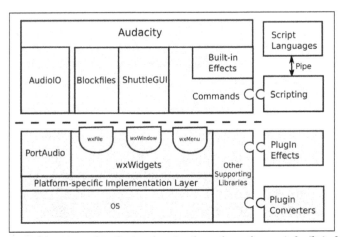

Software architecture of Audacity showing how the software is built in layers.

The diagram illustrates the layers and modules in Audacity. Note the three important classes within wxWidgets, each of which has a reflection in Audacity. Higher-level abstractions result from related lower-level ones.

For example, the BlockFile system is a reflection of and is built on wxWidgets' wxFiles. Lower down in the diagram is a narrow strip for "Platform Specific Implementation Layers."

Both wxWidgets and PortAudio are OS abstraction layers. Both contain conditional code that chooses between different implementations depending on the target platform.

Reception

The free and open nature of Audacity has allowed it to become very popular in education, encouraging its developers to make the user interface easier for students and teachers.

CNET rated Audacity 5/5 stars and called it "feature rich and flexible". Preston Gralla of *PC World* said, "If you're interested in creating, editing, and mixing you'll want Audacity." Jack Wallen of *Tech Republic* highlighted its features and ease-of-use. Michael Muchmore of *PC Magazine* rated it 3.5/5 stars and said, "Though not as slick or powerful as programs from the likes of Adobe, Sony, and M-Audio, Audacity is surprisingly feature-full for free software."

In *The Art of Unix Programming*, Eric S. Raymond says of Audacity "The central virtue of this program is that it has a superbly transparent and natural user interface, one that erects as few barriers between the user and the sound file as possible."

Djay

Djay is a digital music mixing software program for Mac OS X, Microsoft Windows, iPad, iPhone, and iPod touch created by the German company algoriddim. It allows playback and mixing of digital audio files with a user interface that tries to simulate the concept of "two turntables and a microphone" on a computer. Before the commercial release in November 2007, Djay had initially been released as freeware in June 2006. In December 2010 the software was also released for the iPad, and subsequently for iPhone and iPod touch in March 2011.

Its interface consists of two turntables, a mixer and a music library showing songs and playlists from iTunes. It also supports Spotify integration.

Djay for iPad received an Apple Design Award in 2011.

Features

iTunes Integration

Djay's iTunes integration allows the user to mix songs directly from the iTunes library. It provides the option of browsing the library, for example by Playlist, Artist, Album, Genre, Key or History. Dragging songs onto the turntables in Djay, transforms them into virtual records complete with album art.

Automix

Automix mode enables Djay to automatically mix songs from the iTunes library, and play them instantaneously with DJ-style transitions. Using the Automix Queue the user can step in any time and immediately queue up tracks.

Transitions

Djay's instantaneous beat and tempo detection allows the user to match the BPM of two songs for a transition. On pressing the SYNC button the software automatically syncs the BPM of the two songs so that both are smoothly aligned.

Record Live Performance

Djay allows the user record live mixes and save them in high-quality sound files. It also contains a built-in organizer arranges, previews or exports the recordings.

Multi-touch Trackpad Control

Mac has a tool called the Multi-Touch trackpad. Djay can dynamically utilize this track-pad to fully control the software with versatile Multi-Touch gestures. For example, a rotating gestures can adjust the EQ, while two finger swipe gesture can scratch the record and operate the crossfader.

Live Sampler

There is a built-in sample pack featuring 20 high-quality sounds made by ueberschal, a company in the sampling industry. In addition, Djay allows the user to create custom samples from the turntables or the microphone.

Mixer and EQ controls

Djay consists of a 3-band equalizers, gain, line faders, and a crossfader that provide the user with the necessary tools needed for a DJ setup to seamlessly blend one song into another.

Harmonic Match

The software can automatically detect a song's key and matches it to songs of the same key within the iTunes music library. It also allows the user to transpose songs into different keys, and even sort the entire music library by key.

High-quality Audio FX

Djay includes three FX control panes for different mixing styles: a one-touch panel for instant FX, a custom pane, and a 2D touch interface. Effects include Flanger, Phaser, Echo, Gate, Bit Crusher, Filter (High Pass, Low Pass), as well as six preconfigured instant effects: Absorb, Drift, Sway, Crush, Punch, Twist are bundled in with Djay.

Beat-matched Looping and Cue Points

Djay has a range of different looping styles: Auto, Manual and Bounce. The use can manually set loop in and out points, use Auto-Loop to continuously loop part of a song, or remix live using Bounce-Loop to mash up the song, all in perfect sync with the beat.

iCloud Integration

The program can work with iCloud (and iTunes Match), meaning the user can sync it with the iTunes library in the cloud. In other words, tunes are synced between every iOS device connected on the cloud. All of these devices can run Djay, and cues and BPM information edited or added in will appear immediately in all of the others. There is a remote control available for iOS to control the Djay app on the MacBook over WiFi.

Pre-cueing

Djay allows the user to preview and prepare the next song through headphones before playing it on the main speakers by simply connecting a USB audio interface or splitter cable. The software offers different audio hardware configurations.

Live Microphone

Djay allows the user to add live microphone input into the mix. Using Echo or Pitch-Changer effects once can transform vocals for an appropriate MC performance.

MIDI Controllers

Djay supports controllers such as Vestax, Numark and other manufacturers. In addition, Djay features a MIDI learn system allowing users to configure and map any controller to their preference.

Final Scratch

Final Scratch is a DJ tool created by the Dutch company N2IT with input from Richie Hawtin (aka Plastikman) and John Acquaviva that allows manipulation and playback of digital audio sources using traditional vinyl and turntables. It seeks to cross the divide between the versatility of digital audio and the tactile control of vinyl turntablism.

Concept

Special vinyl records pressed with a digital timecode are played on normal turntables. The timecode signal is interpreted by a computer, connected to the turntables through an interface called the ScratchAmp. The signal represents where the stylus is on the record, in which direction it is traveling, and at what speed. This information is interpreted by the computer and used to play back a digital audio file which has been 'mapped' to the turntable. In practical terms, this means that any audio file can be manipulated as though it was pressed on vinyl.

Advantages/Disadvantages

Advantages:

- Ability to play audio tracks unavailable on vinyl e.g. pre-arranged loops, unreleased music or rare tracks.

- The use of CD deck features (software permitting) such as keylock, pitch shift, looping, instant cue locating and visual indicators of audio features such as loud or quiet parts.

- The ability to prevent needle skips on the vinyl being reflected in the playback of the audio track being played/controlled (software permitting).

Disadvantages:

- Reliability; depending on the hardware/software configuration used, vinyl emulation systems may use more system resources than some laptops or PCs offer, making them unsuitable for this use.

Internal Workings

The internal workings of Final Scratch are quite simple to understand. Multiple open source software libraries have been created to decode the Final Scratch time code. The information here comes from those libraries.

A basic Final Scratch setup consists of five pieces of equipment.

- A computer running a compatible software, usually Native Instrument's Traktor.

- The ScratchAmp.

- Two turntables or two CD decks made for DJing.

- Two time coded vinyl records or time coded CDs.

- An audio DJ mixer.

ScratchAmp

The ScratchAmp is a firewire (FS 2, FS Open) or USB (FS 1) audio device. It has two phono/line stereo level inputs to read the timecode from the record or the CD, and two line level stereo outputs to feed into the audio DJ mixer line channels. It also has two phono stereo outputs for pass-through of the actual phono audio signal. This is useful for DJs who wish to play both digital audio tracks AND traditional vinyl; allowing them to switch between the two sources without disconnecting or re-connecting audio jacks in the middle of a DJ set.

The ScratchAmp does not store any audio on its own, it is simply a purpose built external Soundcard. It communicates with a PC—usually a laptop—over the firewire or USB connection. The laptop uses Final Scratch compatible software (typically Traktor DJ Studio) to interpret the timecode signal from the supplied special vinyl/CD, then play back a digital audio file based on that signal, allowing traditional DJ vinyl control of MP3, WAV and Apple AAC audio files. The Laptop software then sends audio data back, over the same firewire/USB connection to the scratch amp, which then sends an audio signal out through the line level output, for playing through a DJ Mixer or Amp.

Audio/Data Routing

A step by step series of events detailing how Final Scratch operates;

- Timecoded audio signal pressed onto vinyl/CD picked up by vinyl/CD turntable.

- Signal routed into ScratchAmp via phono connection, then into the PC via USB or Firewire.

- DJ software decodes timecode signal and determines position, speed and direction the Vinyl/CD is being played or manipulated.

- DJ software plays the selected "mapped" digital audio file synchronous to the vinyl/CD playback.

- Digital audio file audio signal is sent to the Scratchamp phono connectors for connection to a DJ mixer or amp.

Vinyl/CD Time Code

The most complex piece of the Final Scratch setup is the code pressed onto the vinyl. A 1200 hertz amplitude modulated sine wave is pressed into the left and right channels with a phase difference of 90 degrees. Each channel holds one of the two bit streams required for the time code. In one cycle of either wave form, two bits are stored: one on the positive voltage peak and one on the negative voltage valley. The relative amplitudes of these peaks represent either a binary one or zero. A relatively high amplitude on either peak represents a one, a relatively low amplitude represents a zero. In each channel is a separate bitstream, the left channel is not identical to the right (disregarding the phase difference).

Finding Position

The time codes themselves consist of 40 individual bits, or 20 cycles on each channel's waveform. On the right channel the bit sequence of 0, 0, 0, 1 represents the start sequence for a single time code. Those four bits along with the four corresponding bits on the left channel and the next 16 bits on each channel can be decoded as an integer position value which represents where the needle is on the record.

Finding Speed

The speed at which the record is spinning can be found by comparing the frequency of the waveform being read from the record to the true frequency of the wave form on the record at normal speed. This difference represents the change from the normal speed at which the record turns.

Finding Direction

The direction which the record is spinning at any given time can be found using the phase difference between the waves on the two channels. This procedure is the same as that used to determine the direction in which a ball mouse is moving.

Issues Regarding Time Code Errors

Because a single time code is made up of 40 consecutive bits, read errors can cause a timecode to be unreadable even if a single bit is misread. A bit that has become unreadable due to a scratch can make an entire 40 bit long time code permanently unreadable. Dust can have a similar effect on the time code. The time code implements very little error checking, an attribute strong in a number of other vinyl control systems.

Video Software

Any Video Converter

Any Video Converter is a video converter developed by Anvsoft Inc. for Microsoft Windows and macOS. It is available in both a free and paid version. Any Video Converter Windows version has won the CNET Downloads 5 star award.

Features

The software converts most video files including AVI, FLV, MOV, MP4, MPG, M2TS, MTS, RMVB, AVCHD, MKV, WebM (V8), QT, WMV, VOB, 3GP, 3GPP2, DivX, and more into other formats such as AVI, MOV, MP4, FLV, WMV, MP3, etc. The resulting output files can be transferred to an iPod, iPhone, iPad, Apple TV, PSP, Samsung, HTC, Android, BlackBerry, Nokia, Xbox, Smartphones, etc.

This freeware also performs functions such as downloading videos from online video-sharing sites such as YouTube, Niconico, MetaCafe, etc. Users can edit videos as they like such as cutting, rotating, flipping, adding video effects, combining multiple videos into one file. Moreover, It also allows users to create HTML5 videos with embedding code ready to use for websites, burn videos to DVD or AVCHD DVD disc, boost video conversion speed up to 6X faster with CUDA acceleration. It can also use AMD APP Encoder for X264/H264 video encoding.

Reception

The software has been reviewed as being "ridiculously easy to use" and "interface is easy to manipulate".

AVC was featured as Lifehacker's Download of the Day on November 30, 2006.

Windows Vista Magazine had a tutorial on converting video files with the software for viewing on a PSP in its April 2007 issue. The software was also reviewed in 2008 by MacLife for its capability to convert files for viewing on an iPod.

The free version of AVC is ad-supported. While it does not appear to contain malware, the Windows installer does default to include potentially unwanted programs (PUPs) such as virus scanners and/or toolbars. However, the user can avoid installing these PUPs by selecting the Customize Install option and not accepting installation of the optional, recommended software.

Freemake Video Converter

Freemake Video Converter is a freemium entry-level video editing app (in spite of its name) developed by Ellora Assets Corporation. The program can be used to convert between video formats, rip video DVDs, create photo slideshows and music visualizations. It can also burn compatible video streams to DVD or Blu-ray Discs or upload them directly to YouTube.

Features

In spite of its name, Freemake Video Converter is an entry-level video editing app. It can perform simple non-linear video editing tasks, such as cutting, rotating, flipping, and combining multiple videos into one file with transition effects. It can also create photo slideshows with background music. Users are then able to upload these videos to YouTube.

Freemake Video Converter can read the majority of video, audio, and image formats, and outputs to AVI, MP4, WMV, Matroska, FLV, SWF, 3GP, DVD, Blu-ray, MPEG and MP3. The program also prepares videos supported by various multimedia devices, including Apple devices (iPod, iPhone, iPad), Xbox, Sony PlayStation, and Samsung, Nokia, BlackBerry, and Android mobile devices. The software is able to perform DVD burning and is able to convert videos, photographs, and music into DVD video.

The user interface is based on Windows Presentation Foundation technology. Freemake Video Converter supports NVIDIA CUDA technology for H.264 video encoding (starting with version 1.2.0).

Important Updates

Freemake Video Converter 2.0 was a major update which integrated two new functions: ripping video from online portals and Blu-ray Disc creation and burning. Version 2.1 implemented suggestions from users, including support for subtitles, ISO image creation, and DVD to DVD/Blu-ray conversion. With version 2.3 (earlier 2.2

Beta), support for DXVA has been added to accelerate conversion (up to 50% for HD content).

Version 3.0 added HTML5 video creation support and new presets for smartphones.

Version 4.0 (introduced in April 2013) added a freemium "Gold Pack" of extra features that can be added if a "donation" is paid. Starting with version 4.0.4, released on 27 August 2013, the program adds a promotional watermark at the end of every video longer than 5 minutes unless Gold Pack is activated. Version 4.1.9, released on 25 November 2015 added support to Drag & Drop functions which was not available on prior versions.

Since at least version 4.1.9.44 (May 1, 2017), the Freemake Welcome Screen is added in the beginning of video and the big Freemake Logo is watermarked in the center of the whole video. This makes the free outputs useless and users are forced to pay money or stop using it. Version 4.1.9.31 (August 11, 2016) does not have this restriction.

Freemake video converter loading screen.

Licensing Issues

FFmpeg has added Freemake Video Converter v1.3 to its *Hall of Shame*. An issue tracker entry for this product, opened on 16 December 2010, says it is in violation of GNU General Public License as it is distributing components of FFmpeg project without including due credit. Ellora Assets Corporation has not responded yet.

Bundled Software from Sponsors

Since version 4.0, Freemake Video Converter's installer includes a potentially unwanted search toolbar from Conduit as well as SweetPacks malware. Although users can decline the software during install, the opt-out option is rendered in gray which could mistakenly give the impression that it's disabled.

Digital Video Broadcasting Software

Astra

Astra is a professional software to organize Digital Broadcasting Service for TV operators and broadcasters, internet service providers, hotels, etc. Astra is an acronym for "Advanced Streaming Application".

Astra supports many protocols and standards to receive channels from different sources. Received channels prepares and transmits into the IP network. Built-in scripting language (Lua) allow to customize business logic of the application.

Features

- Data format: MPEG-TS.

- Receiving formats and standards:

    ◦ DVB-S, DVB-T, DVB-C, ATSC, ASI.

    ◦ RTSP.

    ◦ HTTP.

    ◦ HLS.

    ◦ UDP, RTP.

    ◦ MPEG-TS Files.

- Transmitting formats and standards:

    ◦ HTTP.

    ◦ HLS.

    ◦ UDP, RTP.

    ◦ MPEG-TS Files.

    ◦ DVB.

- Data processing:

    ◦ Descrambling: DVB-CI.

    ◦ MPEG-TS Demultiplexing – extract single channel from the Multi Program Transport Stream.

    ◦ MPEG-TS Multiplexing – combine several channels into single Multi Program Transport Stream.

    ◦ DVB-T2 MI Decapsulation.

    ◦ Analyzing MPEG-TS Streams.

- ○ Redundancy for incoming streams.

- ○ MPEG-TS PID Remapping and Filtering.

- • Other:

  - ○ Scripting language: Lua.

  - ○ Web-Interface.

  - ○ REST API for management.

  - ○ HbbTV.

  - ○ Telemetry and monitoring.

  - ○ Access Authorization.

  - ○ EPG Export (XMLTV or JSON).

DVB Dream

DVB Dream is a proprietary software for watching & recording of digital TV & radio with help of a digital TV tuner card (Internal PCI/PCI-Express cards or external USB devices). It supports the standards DVB-S (satellite), DVB-C (cable), DVB-T (terrestrial), ISDB-T, ISDB-S and ATSC.

It has STB-like features including PIP (Picture-in-picture), record, Timeshift, EPG, Scheduler, Unicable support, Positioner support (including GotoX.X/USALS), UH-D(4K)/HD/HEVC/H264 support, child lock, remote control support.

There are also features that cannot be seen on STBs but provided with help of flexible Windows GUI environment. These are: Multi PIP(watching more than 1 channel at the same time)), Multi record (recording more than 1 channel at the same time), LAN Streaming, VLC or MPC Integration, Auto-zap, Unique channel list system by grouping/ordering/filtering by several flexible options, Render-less mode, Multi monitor support, Command line support, Plugins support.

Being a Windows application, user interface can be customized with help of themes and foldable GUI elements. It can be localized in most of the languages (29 languages are supported, as in 2015).

ProgDVB

The ProgDVB is universal and powerful tool for receive, watching and listening analog both digital a TV and broadcastings from any sources (satellite, cable and on-the-air TV, Internet etc), and also review of media files with transmission possibility all of this via various types of networks.

By means of ProgDVB you can watch HD telecast, do output the picture on several monitors (including on TV set), viewing by means of CI scrambled channels, record the yours liked programs, use YouTube and Internet TV, Radio. You can use one program for several types a TV and broadcastings irrespective of an amount of devices and type of received content (DVB-S, DVB-S2, DVB-C, DVB-T, ATSC, ISDB-T, IPTV).

Also in ProgDVB following functions are implemented:

- Picture in Picture (to eight channels simultaneously),

- support of the basic types of remote control and possibility of bind keys,

- Operation simultaneously with several cards,

- Record in all main formats, including *.ts,

- Support 3D television,

- Original videorenderer,

- Convenient scheduler, compatible with MS,

- Preview of all channels of the list (Mosaic),

- Support a TV program guide with different extension,

- Multilingual interface,

- Adjustment of language preferences of audio streams and subtitles,

- Support ?64 OS versions,

- Possibility of a choice and editing of the interface (Skin Editor),

- Provision able transparent OSD with adaptation for a different ratio of broadcasting format,

- Equalizer,

- Automatic gain control,

- Built-in PrintScreen,

- Adjusted Time shift buffer,

- Numeration, sorting and grouping of channels,

- Quick search of channels,

- TV program guide and logos in the channel list,

- Parental controls,

- Possibility of a choice of a demultiplexer,

- Color correction of the picture with a profile choice,

- Choice of display ratio with cropping possibility,

- Automatic update of the program, channel bases, transponders.

References

- Multimedia-software: magix.com, Retrieved 08 June, 2019

- James Crook (March 15, 2012). "Chapter 2. Audacity". The Architecture of Open Source Applications. Amy Brown, Greg Wilson. ISBN 978-1257638017

- Stalling, D.; Westerhoff, M.; Hege, H.-C. (2005). C.D. Hansen and C.R. Johnson (ed.). "Amira: A Highly Interactive System for Visual Data Analysis". The Visualization Handbook: 749–767. CiteSeerX 10.1.1.129.6785. doi:10.1016/B978-012387582-2/50040-X. ISBN 9780123875822

- Aworski, Nick; Thibeault, Matthew D. (2011). "Technology for Teaching: Audacity. Free and open-source software". Music Educators Journal. 98 (2): 39–40. doi:10.1177/0027432111428745. ISSN 0027-4321

5
Applications

There are a wide-range of applications of multimedia in the fields of teaching and language learning, digital libraries, video conferencing, webcasting, interactive gaming, etc. This chapter delves into these varied applications of multimedia to provide an in-depth understanding of the subject.

Multimedia in Teaching and Language Learning

Information Technology in the School

Computers have become ubiquitous. They are applied in business, as home entertainment devices and as a teaching/learning aid. This fact cannot be disregarded in the education of the youth. The ability to operate personal computers and related IT devices is an indispensible skill in modern information society. For the young generation to develop the skill, they are to be regularly and permanently exposed to the latest achievements in technology. That is why it is vital to popularize the idea of information technology in the school in various forms and at various levels of education, from kindergarten to university.

It has to be noted that the education programmes and curricula, although developed by outstanding specialists, may become outdated before they actually reach the classroom. The publishing of textbooks may take even years so that teachers are often rightly concerned about the validity and currency of the textbook content.

Sometimes, in the pursuit of their individual interests, students get updated about the latest scientific and technological findings by surfing the Internet. On the one hand, it is a positive phenomenon, on the other hand it makes educators think how to keep teaching curricula updated. This, in turn, implies further questions: How to pass on the knowledge by means of modern and more attractive teaching aids? In the light of the financial situation of the school system in Poland, it is not easy to find an answer to either of the questions. Fortunately, due to the unbelievable pace of the IT development, what is currently the most modern and expensive, will soon become cheaper and more available when new solutions appear. The dynamic character of the changes provides an opportunity for schools, most of which are equipped with IT labs, multimedia software and access to the Internet. It has to be kept in mind that some five or ten years ago the situation was different and few schools could pride themselves on having a modern IT lab.

As the time passes, the requirements that educational services have to meet evolve. Social changes following the economic ones created the demand for up-to date educated staff. Finding such employees may be a real challenge for an employer. Owing to that, it is essential to offer education in the fields in which specialists are sought. Besides, in the long-term perspective it turns out that the skills acquired at school are insufficient and education must therefore be continued in the form of lifelong learning. Both state and private educational institutions respond to this need, offering many courses financed by resources coming from EU projects. The development of the lifelong learning provides a unique opportunity to enhance, or to change qualifications.

Modern Information Technology helps develop students' abilities by boosting the following:

- Learning: It enhances ways of gaining knowledge and skills, it facilitates problem-solving and decision-making, it integrates experiences and various elements of knowledge,

- Thinking: It facilitates understanding phenomena in their full complexity and enables their holistic perception, it also boosts creativity,

- Searching abilities: It helps to search, classify, and make use of information coming from various sources,

- Ability to act: It improves the organization of work and facilitates the use of various techniques and tools, it develops a flexible attitude to one's qualification and a constant need to improve them,

- Communication skills: It provides means for individual and group presentations and for effective communication thereby promoting unlimited contact among humans,

- Co-operation: It helps working in a local or global group and reaching agreement, it can be used for making and sustaining contact and developing relationships.

Teaching Aids in Lifelong Learning

Lifelong learning makes use of the same teaching aids as regular school learning. Because of the character of lifelong learning, however, the most valuable teaching aids are those that enable access to the source of knowledge without the necessity to participate in group meetings. It is also important that the pace of learning can be individually adjusted to suit one's needs, abilities, and the amount of time available. Thus, lifelong learning very often takes the form of e-learning, which is characterized by an unconstrained choice of the educational institution, learning time and speed. The basic condition that has to be met for e-learning to take place is access to a computer and to the internet. It goes without saying that when we mention a computer, we mean a complete IT infrastructure including a video camera, sound transmission devices, multimedia projectors, etc. All the devices employed in e-learning are based on digital technology.

Interactive Whiteboard

The device is a relatively recent invention, which explains why there are few interactive whiteboards in schools: The price is too high. An interactive whiteboard is a valuable part of laboratory equipment and it can take a central place in an instructor's work, next to the traditional board, or, as has been occasionally claimed, it can even replace the traditional board. In e-learning, however, the interactive whiteboard has a lot of advantages, which should be fully exploited. An interactive whiteboard can be seen in figure. A number of similar boards can be obtained on the market from various producers and sellers. Next to a multimedia projector and a computer, the board operates with electronic tablets enabling a student to observe what is being presented on the board, and what is more, to actively participate in the visual presentation of the topic discussed.

The tablet usually comes in two versions: For the teacher and for the student. A teacher's tablet makes it possible for the teacher to view test results on a colour LCD, and a student's tablet is equipped with a black-and-white display showing the battery charge level. The wireless technology enables connecting up to 30 tablets to one computer and working with 9 tablets at a time. In this way, a multi-user system is created which is intended to support and increase students' motivation for group learning. Both the teacher and students can work on the same document at the same time. It is an ideal solution for activating the group, making simulations, or surveys.

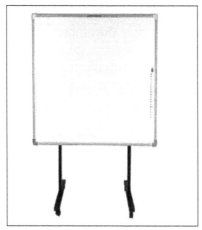

An interactive whiteboard - Interwrite DualBoard.

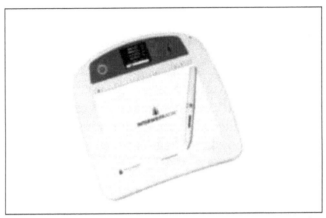

Wireless tablet Interwite Mobi produced by Interwrite Learning.

The teacher's tablet provides a full, though discreet control over students' work. Due to the fact that the teacher can see answers entered by students on the display, s/he can assess the results immediately upon completing the task and discuss errors with particular students.

The wireless connection between the tablet and the board makes it possible for the teacher to add or alter information on the board from any place in the classroom. The same can be done in classrooms without an interactive whiteboard, as long as there is a computer, a projector, and any screen.

The interactive whiteboard operates as a touch screen, on which teachers and students can display the contents of computer files, or take notes. They can use it as an ordinary board, and subsequently save and print a text, pictures, etc. There are so many possibilities offered by the interactive whiteboard that they cannot be enumerated here. The most effective use of the device involves the use of a multimedia projector and a computer. Then, writing on the board with a pen is purely virtual and what is written is displayed by means of a projector.

At present a number of companies compete against one another on the IT market, which provides an incentive for further development and enhancing the possibilities of interactive whiteboards. Some models are more technologically advanced than others but all of them have the same basic functions of an interactive whiteboard. Thus, selecting a particular model for educational purposes should be based on assessing its individual properties.

Interactive whiteboards have become an indispensable tool to be used in training courses, in teaching, and all sorts of presentations. The interactive whiteboards of the latest generation employ a wireless technology. They are characterized by an excellent quality of display and highly functional software.

In schools nowadays, the most often used devices are computers and multimedia projectors.

Classes are conducted according to the schema below:

- Before the class teachers prepare didactic materials in the electronic form. Such materials can also be used for round-up lessons, exercises and tests. The materials can be printed out or displayed by means of a projector.

- Using a projector makes it possible to display text files with data or video files. It is also possible to present multimedia materials.

Using an interactive whiteboard opens a number of new possibilities:

- On the surface of an interactive whiteboard one can write with erasable markers or attach magnets to it. An interactive whiteboard can be mounted on the wall, next to, or instead of a traditional board, it can also be moved around the classroom on a floor stand.

- The computer in which the text or graphic files are stored can be connected to a projector. The files will be displayed on the board. Then, by means of an electronic pen one can write comments and notes directly on the board, which is not possible with the usual projector screen. When the whole surface available is covered with notes, it is moved upwards as in an ordinary text document. Thus, the writing surface on the board is unlimited.

- The interactive whiteboard has a function of saving the notes and comments written on it by means of an electronic pen. They are subsequently available at the computer disc. Teachers can use such applications as PowerPoint, Word and Excel, which do not require the Internet connection. Students can solve tasks and do exercises on the board, which makes their class participation more active.

All the boards which are currently produced can work in a number of modes. There are usually three modes, which, combined with additional external devices, offer several possibilities to the teacher.

- The CLASS mode i.e., interactive mode: It enables interactive work with the board and additional devices, such as tablets (see section 3). Each element of the interaction is displayed on the board or on some other surface so that every person participating in the interaction can observe the ongoing changes.

- The OFFICE mode: The user can work on such applications as PowerPoint, Microsoft Word and Excel. In this mode it is possible to add notes directly to the slide, document, or sheet. The notes are saved and stored as part of the original file.

- The WHITEBOARD mode is the simplest, since it requires only the board and a computer. When working in this mode, one makes notes, drawings and calculations by means of an electronic pen with a built-in marker on the board. All such notes, drawings, etc. will be saved as computer files so that a complete account of a meeting, lecture, or training session can be stored. No projectors are used, so data input to the computer are not to be retrieved and displayed on the board again. Whatever is written on the board with the marker will be displayed on the computer screen in the same colour as on the board. Also when using a marker with a protected tip for writing on the board, whatever is written will be displayed on the computer screen (though not on the board) in the colour in which the pen normally writes.

As the characteristic above shows, the board offers possibilities which are not available for traditional classroom boards. Next to the obvious advantages, however, there are also drawbacks. This can be explained by several factors, such as:

- Being able to use the potential of the device requires knowledge about its operation as well as skills and practice in applying it. Training the staff in order to provide such knowledge and skills is highly advisable. Instructors teaching technical subjects do not show greater difficulties with operating the device but instructors teaching humanities generally do.

- The devices require careful servicing and maintenance. As electronic devices they also require frequent recharging of batteries for pens. Besides, the board itself has to be systematically calibrated by technicians.

- Although the devices are portable, an unforeseen change in the class timetable, or necessity to move classrooms is, in fact, troublesome and takes up the time which should be spent on teaching.

- Electricity breakdowns or other emergency situations may render the board unusable.

Working with an interactive whiteboard with educational software.

Obviously, the difficulties mentioned above are not inherent properties of the device but they may happen due to external organizational problems or some other situations in the school. Such factors hinder the educational process, yet, it is impossible to avoid them in a teacher's everyday practice.

Digital Libraries

Traditional library and information centers maintain the conventional media like books, video, films, audio, tapes, gramophone records, micro films and microfiche which store the information material. It was not possible to many readers to view different media at a time till recently. Now it is possible to the readers of the library to view different media at a time with the invention of multimedia technology, which store vast amount of data/information in electronic media and retrieve and present in more than one media to satisfy.

- Widen the horizon of information: Multimedia technology widens the horizon of information. The world of graphics, sound, animation, video and hypertext is very quickly making its way into our lives, becoming accessible and affordable to an increasing number of people. The libraries are beginning the use the multimedia, letting the new technology help them expand their sphere of activities in the information horizon. It helps in basic functions of a library i.e. acquisition, organization and dissemination of the information.

- Information storage: Regardless of whether the information is in printed or electronic media, libraries store and maintain all kinds of information. Space is always the key problem to store the conventional form of information. A large amount of storage space is required to provide to the users of the library with immediate access to the exploring data/information. This problem is solved through the multimedia products, which store vast amount of data/information in different media using the authorware tools. Multimedia can be used in various library operations and services.

- Dissemination of information: One of the common uses of the Internet and Web Multimedia is to make available large amounts of information, in the easiest and most comprehensible way possible. Many Web sites, especially those that act as libraries of information, have turned to multimedia technology to guide the user through the maze of data. On-line electronic magazine (e-zine) is a good example to use multimedia technology to disseminate the information.

- Publishing: Many conventional paper magazine and newspaper published now have on-line versions, offering many features and services not available from the newsstand copy. Searching through article archives, listening to actual interviews, viewing descriptive animation, and interacting with the publication are among the many capabilities of an electronic format. These additional features are so appealing that many magazines now include CD-ROMS with the publication and many offer the entire magazine as a multimedia production in a cardboard magazine-shaped folder. The Internet version of the magazines offer publishes the capability to expand their publications readership and consequentially their advertising revenues. Multimedia converts the first line user into a regular visitor. Electronic multimedia magazines hosted and circulated on the web are revolutionizing the publishing industry, and are yet another pointer to the possibilities of multimedia on the net.

- Library networking: The phenomenal growth of Internet/ WWW is the most exciting development of multimedia. Global communication facilities make it possible to connect the libraries of various countries with one another. Future libraries around the world will be able to share information resources in a way that was never possible before and satisfy the readers with information in different media.

- User orientation, training, etc.: By developing multimedia systems proper and effective user orientation programmes can be organised for the users of the library to understand the services and facilities of the library. It also helps the library staff for understanding the latest techniques of library procedures and services in interactive mode by using multimedia CD's.

- Reference sources, services etc.: Several reference sources such as dictionaries, encyclopedias, directories, yearbooks, magazines and journals are now available in the market in multimedia format. Through these reference sources, the information services can be provided to the users of the library in very effective manner.

- Solve space problem: library is a growing organism and every library faces the space problem to accommodate all published information in print media. But now new technology, a single CDROM can store upto 650 MB of information, 2,40,000 of text, which solves the problems of space as storing in paper media format occupied huge space.

- Durable storage media: Information in CD-ROM disc is more durable in comparison to other media as it is free from dust, environment and other hazards.

- Maintenance and management: A large amount of information can be stored in a single digital disc, which can be easily maintained and managed then other printed formats.

Video Conferencing

Video conferencing is a technology by means of which two or more parties situated in different geographical locations can watch and converse with each other by means of two-way transmission of video and audio data in near real-time.

A representational image of video conferencing technology offering
two-way transmission of audio and video data.

From once being a high profile, owned by a famous few, this technology has made inroads to every middle class homestead that owns a healthy broadband connection. It can be a simple point to point conversation between two persons, or a multipoint conference between many at different locations. When video conferencing is offered on telephone networks, it is also called VVOIP (Video and Voice over Internet Protocol). Video Conferencing is almost a subset of Internet Multimedia Subsystems (IMS).

Components of a V. C. System

Components of a Generic Video Conferencing System:

- Video input: Webcams connected to computers or video cameras to capture the motion of participants.

- Audio input: Microphones to convert the voice of participants into an electrical signal which is then converted into a digital signal during processing.

- Processing unit: A data processing unit performs the function of converting the data into a packet stream for transmission on the transmitting end, and for receiving the network data and converting it into a presentable format on the receiving end.

- Transmission medium: The communication channel over which the data is transmitted from one place to another. It can be a telephone network or a digital internet broadband network. The network also might contain firewalls which are designed to block any kind of unwanted network traffic. Appropriate modules like Session Border Controllers are usually used on the network to detect various kinds of packets and to allow the videoconference packets to pass.

- Output unit: The output terminals are connected to the receiver unit to present the output in a suitable format. These are usually a monitor or screen for displaying the video and speakers to deliver the sound from the other end.

- Usually, all the components are present both in the transmission location and the receiving location as communication is bidirectional.

Classification

Classification of Video Conferencing Systems:

There can be two broad classifications of video conferencing equipment:

- Standalone dedicated systems.

- Desktop Systems.

Standalone Dedicated Systems: These are devices specially made for the sole purpose of video conferencing with every necessary component packaged into a single board or console which is connected to a high quality camera, wired or wireless. These cameras are often called PTZ cameras for their ability of Panning, Tilting and Zooming. Omni-directional microphones are used to gather sound from all directions. Traditionally, conference was believed to be between many people simultaneously. But, as the technology penetrated deeper into the market, variants offering different levels of conversations have cropped up. The consoles offering capabilities for large groups are usually non-portable and very expensive. They are suited for large rooms like auditoriums. Smaller variants of the same technology are also available for conference rooms. Small videoconferencing devices are usually portable and intended for use by individuals. The camera and audio equipment is fixed, like in the case of smart phones.

Desktop Systems: Web-cameras and microphones can be connected to desktop systems and software built for the purpose of videoconferencing installed on it to use a normal desktop system for video conferencing. The codec need to be installed as a part of the software to support the transmission and reception of the data.

Architecture

Various components like the camera, the microphone and the transmission medium are considered to be the nitty-gritty for supporting video conferencing. The core of the system lies inside the data processing unit. The handling of the video conferencing process happens in a layered form with each layer interacting with the layer immediately below and above it and performing a certain essential function. These layers can be termed as (from top to bottom) User Interface, Conference Control Layer, Signalling Plane and Media Plane. We can always draw a comparison of these layers with the seven layers of the OSI.

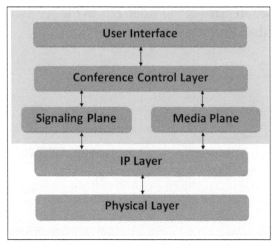

A diagram representing architecture of a video conferencing system.

User Interface: The end user is not concerned with all the jargon that takes place inside the data processing unit. The customer wants a user friendly interface which can be used by any literate person to setup and start a call. The instructions and the coding inside any system has to be presented as a black box to the user, and all the complexity of the system summed up in a few easy to use and understand buttons and switches. This simplification is done by the user interface. It acts as a bridge between the inner, complex world of bits and bytes and the external, world of the humans. These interfaces may be graphical, or voice interactive. We have all encountered both of these types of interfaces at some point in time. This layer is used for scheduling and setting up the call. Every configurable option of the system is presented to the user using this interface which ultimately affects the operation of the other lower layers of the console.

Conference Control Layer: The resource allocation, management and routing of the packets is performed at this layer. The creation, scheduling, session management, addition and removal of participants, and tear down of a conference take place at this layer.

Signalling Plane: This is a main part of the entire layered structure as the protocols responsible for having a successful video call run at this layer. The protocols are in the form of a code stack that signals the various endpoints to connect or tear down. The major protocols that have been used or are being used for video conferencing are the H.323 protocol and the Session Initiation Protocol (SIP). The session parameters and control of incoming and outgoing signals is done at this layer.

Media Plane: The mixing and streaming of audio and video streams takes place at this layer. It is analogous to the 4th layer of the OSI i.e. the Transport layer (or let us say, it is resident in the 4th layer itself). The protocols running at this layer are the User Datagram Protocol (UDP), Real-time Transport Protocol (RTP) and Real-Time Transport Control Protocol (RTCP). The RTP and UDP carry payload parameter information like the type of codec, frame rate, size of the video etc. to the receiving end, while the RTCP is more of a quality control Protocol for error detection.

Protocols

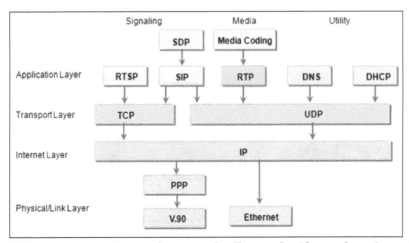

A block diagram representing popular protocols of layers of a video conferencing system.

Session Initiation Protocol: It is a widely used Application Layer protocol for communication sessions like voice and video calls over internet protocol capable of running over TCP, UDP and SCTP. It is a text based protocol which has many elements based on HTTP's request/response model along with most of its header fields and rules. Typical requests and responses are REGISTER, INVITE, ACK, CANCEL, BYE, Success, Redirection etc. The function of the requests can be easily inferred from the command itself. It helps in creating, modifying and tearing off sessions between calling parties. Though it has many features of SS7 signalling, SIP is a peer to peer protocol implemented at the end points of the network in contrast to the SS7 signalling which is implemented in the core systems. The reason for its popularity among the subset of VoIP protocols having many other protocols like MEGACO, H.323 etc is that it has its roots in IP network community (designed by IETF) thus being more native than others which have their roots in telecommunications industry (designed by ITU). The standard defines many network entities like the User Agent at the end point like the SIP phone, a Proxy server for routing requests, a registrar for registering URI(Universal Resource Indicators) for devices, a Session Border Controller for NAT Traversal and a Gateway to interface the SIP network with other networks.

H.323 Protocol: It is a widely deployed recommendation from ITU for voice and video conferencing by equipment manufacturers for internet real-time applications. It is a part of the ITU-T H.3X series protocols for multimedia communications over ISDN, PSTN and 3G networks. It has H.225.0 protocol for Registration, Admission and Status (RAS) signalling and call-signalling between the user equipment and a gatekeeper into the network, H.245 control protocol for multimedia communication and Real-Time Transport Protocol (RTP) for sending and receiving information between entities.

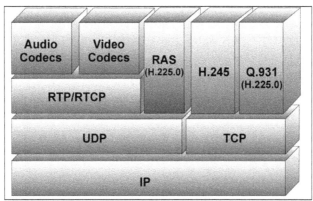

A figure demonstrating session border controller for nat traversal and a gateway to interface the sip networks to other network.

Network Topologies

It is possible that each participant (in case of more than two) is located in different locations. In such a scenario, the synchronization between all the participating units has to be done. There are two ways this may be done. First, each unit makes an individual direct link to every other link and maintains connection with them throughout the session. This method is particularly overburdening for any network equipment and incurs significant network bandwidth and costs. The apparent advantage of this method is the selectivity that can be provided to each user for provisioning ad-hoc connections. Also, there is no single point of failure; if a link between two participants, say A and B breaks, then the topology being like that of a mesh, would not disturb any other connections. The video relayed between points is of better quality because of the absence of any central manager throttling bandwidth. This decentralized multipoint architecture uses H.323 standards.

The other architecture that takes the load off the terminal equipment uses a Multipoint Control Unit (MCU). An MCU performs the function of a bridge, interconnecting the calls from different sources. The terminal equipment may call the MCU or the MCU may initiate the connection to all the parties. Thus, the topology now changes to that of a star. This MCU can purely be software, or a combination of hardware and software. It can be logically divided into two main modules: A Multipoint Controller and a Multipoint Processor. The controller works on the signalling plane and controls the conference creation, closing etc., negotiates with every unit in the conference and controls resources. The mixing and handling of media from each terminal is done by the Media Processor which resides in the Media Plane. It creates the data stream for each terminal and redirects it to the destination end point. The presence of a central manager can help shaping the bandwidth used up on each link.

When bandwidth is at a premium a technique called Voice activated Switch (VAS) can be used. So in a conference, when one party at a location is speaking, only that party is made visible to other participants. But, problems may arise if more than one person starts talking simultaneously. In that case, it becomes a contingency problem for the one with the loudest voice will be given preference. The other mode is Continuous Presence Mode, where the MCU combines the video streams from all the end points into a common stream and transmits it to all the end points. This way, every participant can see everyone else simultaneously. These unified images are often called 'layouts'. However in both the cases the voice is transmitted to every endpoint in a full duplex mode.

Codec (Coder-decoder):

Even with the best available networks and bandwidths, it would be impractical to send video in its uncompressed form. So, some kind of video compression has to be in place to compress the video to reduce the size of the bit stream to be transmitted. This is achieved with the use of codec (Coder-Decoder). Now, video compression can be done through two approaches. First, to find the information that is repetitive, and then, replace the repetitive information by a shortcut before transmission. This shortcut can then be replaced by original information at the receiving end restoring the video to its original form. (Just like a macro in programming) Other approach involves elimination of unimportant data from the frames, so that only the information perceptible to the human eyes is visible. This can drastically reduce the size of digital data to be transmitted, but can result in very poor quality video. Two major methods have been employed to achieve video compression to minimize losses and size at the same time:

- Block Based Compression: Each frame of the video, which is a single image, is divided into small blocks of information called pixels. The algorithm then keeps a track of how the values at each pixel varies with each frame and time.

- Object Based Compression: More advanced Codec algorithm classify the objects in the frames and keep track of movable and stationary objects. Thus less data may be used to store the information of stationary objects, and more detail of the moving objects be provided. Such techniques are more efficient that the simpler block based compression methods.

In order to standardize the compression methods, the Moving Picture Experts Group has come up with several standards like the MPEG-4 standard.

Standards

The ITU has three set of standards for video conferencing to bridge the divide of different methods:

- ITU H.320: A standard for video conferencing over PSTN and ISDN lines popular in Europe, it is a recommendation on protocol suites formerly named as Narrowband Visual Telephone Systems and Terminal Equipment. It contains different protocols like the H.221, H.230, audio codec like G.711 and video codec like

H.261 and H.263. Standards like H.323 have been used in videoconferencing systems. But, the new protocols like Session Initiation Protocol (SIP) are becoming more popular because they can work would between different forms of communication like voice, data, instant messaging etc.

- ITU H.264 Scalable Video Coding: The compression algorithm to achieve highly error resilient video streams over a normal IP network without the need of any QoS enabled lines. This standard has brought the technology of videoconferencing to the masses by enabling video conferencing from a simple desktop terminal.

- ITU V.80: A standard made compatible with the H.324 standard for video conferencing over POTS (Plain Old Telephone System).

Issues in Implementation

Acoustic Echo Cancellation: It is an algorithm to detect and suppress echoes that might enter the audio device after reflection from the surroundings after some delays. If left unchecked, echoes can cause problems like the speaker hearing his own voice. Increase the intensity of this echo, and one may hear reverberations and a much aggravated condition due to feedback may cause howling effect. Most professional Video Conferencing Systems employ AEC for best performance.

Security: Poorly configured video conferencing systems are honey pots for hackers to exploit and trespass the company's online premises. Sensitive information may be transacted over a video conferencing session which, if not secured properly might fall into wrong hands. Security and integrity of such data is so important that many countries have laws to enforce the same, like the Health Insurance Portability and Accountability Act (HIPPA) and the Sarbanes-Oxley Act (2002) of the United States. Common encryption methods are the 56-bit DES and the 128 bit AES encryption.

Besides, many people argue that the following three issues hinder video conferencing from becoming an everyday technology.

- Eye Contact: Eye contact is a prime essential of building a one to one conversation when video is available. However, the video conferencing systems may give an impression that the person is avoiding eye contact by looking elsewhere, while he had been looking in the screen all the time. This problem is partially resolved by having the camera in the screen itself. Much research is going on and image processing going on to achieve stereo reconstruction of the image to remove any such parallax effect.

- Camera Consciousness: Being aware of being on camera has a psychological effect on people and many a times, also impairs communication rather than making it clear.

- Latency: Apart from large bandwidth requirements, a small round trip time is required for reduced delays between frames. Any delay beyond 150-300ms becomes noticeable and distracting.

Other than these, mass adoption of videoconferencing is low because of the following probable causes:

- Complexity: Most users are not technical and look forward for a simple interface.

- Lack of interoperability: Many of the video conferencing systems cannot interconnect without an intervening gateway. The software solutions can seldom connect to hardware solutions. Different standards are being used by different people and hence additional configuration is required when connecting dissimilar systems.

- Bandwidth and quality of service: Most broadband connections being offered have dissimilar upload and download speeds. Upload speeds are often very less as compared to the download speeds and hence poses a bottleneck to the success of videoconferencing.

- Expense: Dedicated videoconferencing systems have special considerations regarding the architecture of the rooms in which they will be installed like the acoustics and reverberations, and hence are not the only thing which incurs initial cost for setting up a conferencing system.

Applications and Conclusion

Applications:

Deaf, hard of hearing and mute people find videoconferencing a particularly lucrative option as a means of communicating with each other in sign language thus eliminating the need of any 'in between' proxy.

Education seems to be the field which has benefited the most from videoconferencing. Videoconferencing has provided students with an opportunity to learn by participating in two-way communication forums. Through videoconferencing students are now able to visit other parts of the world to speak and interact with their peers and avail other educational facilities through virtual field trips.

It is a highly useful technology for real-time telemedicine and telenursing applications such as diagnosis, consulting and transmission of medical images. Rural areas in particular can benefit from videoconferencing as experts now would no longer need to visit a remote place. Instead the patients may contact the doctor over of videoconferencing interface.

Businesses with distributed locations have been using videoconferencing internally to conduct meetings between employees at various locations to achieve a closer synchronisation of operation throughout the company.

Since 2007 a new concept of press videoconferencing has evolved which allowed journalists to attend conferences in some other part of the world without leaving the office premises. IMF has many journalists on their registrations list for closed conferences of this type.

Videoconferencing has opened an option for the law and order enforcing agencies to allow witnesses to testify on a videoconference if they are reluctant to attend the physical legal setting due to any reason like psychological stress. The pros and cons are still debated as it might be a violation of certain laws.

Webcasting

A webcast is a specific type of media that allows a single content source, or video clip, to reach many viewers or listeners. This type of technology uses streaming media, and can be distributed over the Internet on demand or as a live broadcast. The best description is that a webcast is essentially broadcasting, but over the internet instead of TV or radio. Many radio and TV stations will also webcast through the internet, using their online radio or TV streaming, and may even have their own Internet station. Besides these traditional "casting" companies, E-learning organizations and investor relations tend to use webcasting to communicate with the commercial sector and as a form of communication. This type of media has flourished because the technology needed for webcasting is not expensive. This has allowed many independent shows and individuals to webcast online frequently.

Distribution of Webcasting

This form of media is distributed using streaming media technology. In simple terms, this means that the data can be displayed to the browser or plug-in application before the entire file has been transmitted. There are storage and bandwidth recommendations for webcasting that depend on the required storage space, number of clients viewing the cast and the length of the media. Several different types of data can be sent, each on their own stream. Audio and video data are sent on separate audio and video data streams and then assembled on a container bit stream. This bit stream is then sent from the server to the client using a specific transport protocol, which may vary as there are several to choose form. For webcasting, synchronized multimedia integration language or SMIL is very important. This is a type of XML language that describes the webcast or multimedia. This provides the information for visual transitions, timing, media embedding, animations and other things so that audio, images, video, text and links can all be presented at the same time. It is very similar to HTML.

Main Webcasters

The main webcasters are radio and TV stations, and many have their own streaming channels. The Digital Media Association represents some of the largest webcasting companies found on the web, including Live365, Pandora and Yahoo. In the United States, Brain Swell Media or BSM, is one of the largest webcasting companies. Reuters and Thomson is one of the largest webcasting service providers found around the world with webcasts from Broadcast One in Hong Kong, StreamX in Australia, NeTVision in Germany, RAW in the UK and CCBN in the US. More than 30% of their webcasts are videos and media clips. Of importance to all companies and independent webcasters is the International Webcasting Association, also known as the IWA, which works to promote efficient and effective streaming media and webcasting over the internet. It helps to form the future of the webcasting industry.

- DiMA – Digital Media Association.

Webcasting in the Commercial Sector

Webcasting is typically used within the commercial sector as a way of providing investor information. The company can provide information to many more people because they no longer have to travel to the company's headquarters. Individuals simply log onto their computer at home and watch the provided webcast. For example, companies will choose to have Annual general Meetings webcasted to all investors, many of whom would normally not be able to attend the meeting in person. The commercial sector may also use webcasting as a way to hold meetings, presentations or business from afar when travel may be problematic or when time is an issue.

The Rise of Independent Media

Webcasting has been of huge benefit to independent media as almost anyone with an internet connection and webcam can do webcasting. Almost anyone can do webcasting and there are many independent stations found on the internet, those that offer video and those that are dedicated to radio. These independent shows are produced by average individuals and can cover a large range of topics. The low cost of streaming media brought the internet and information sharing to everyone that owns the necessary, inexpensive equipment. Additionally, the success of social media sites has allowed for further development of independent media sharing.

Webcasting Origins

The concept of webcasting was unveiled in 1989 at InterTainment '89 from GTE laboratories. The first webcast was not made until October 1995 when Brian Raila and James Paschetto, both from GTE laboratories, showed the first streaming media prototype at the Voice Mail Association meeting in Switzerland. The first company to feature video webcasting was Onsteam Media by Alan Saperstein. HotelView contained thousands of two minute videos providing details on hotels around the world. The actual term, webcasting, was not developed until the mid-1990s. A group of streaming pioneers, Peggy Miles from InterVox Communications, Craig Schmeider from Applied Media resources, William Mutual from ITV.net, Howard Gordon from Xing Technologies and Mark Cuban from AudioNet, picked a term that best described this type of streaming media.

Examples of Webcasting

There are many different types of webcasting. Podcasts are those webcasts that were designed specifically to be watched on portable media devices. The name Podcast originated with the iPod as webcasts were designed to be watched on these devices. Many times, individuals will use the term netcast instead of podcasts, so as not to connect the webcast specifically with the iPod as these can be viewed on many other types of portable media devices. Media clips are normally short video or audio clips that tend to act as promotional material. For example, a movie clip is webcasted to help promote a new movie. Many times actors will promote the movie by using these short media clips.

Another type of webcasting is a Vlog, which is video blogging. Instead of providing written entries, the individual will combine video links and embedded videos within images, text and metadata. Entries can be given in one take or separated into different parts.

Many television webcasters will provide Webisodes for viewers. These webisodes are short episodes that can act as a preview or bonus to support the actual TV show. The webisode will not have been broadcast with the original show on the TV.

Wedcasts are a special type of webcast, as these offer wedding broadcasting across the internet. Many chapels, specifically wedding chapels, offer this as it provides the opportunity for many individuals to see the wedding live without actually attending.

Another form of webcast is a webinar which is a type of web conferencing or online seminar. Video chats, voice and text can be shared across the world to allow those that live far away to gain the provided information. This is very popular with universities and colleges that offer distance learning as well as other E-learning companies.

Many of the above mentioned webcasts use video data, but there are webcasts, known as Web radio, which offer only audio data. These web radio stations function just like regular radio stations, but they are streamed through the internet. Therefore, an individual in California can tune into a radio station that originates in Russia if they so desire.

Permissions

Index